P9-CKK-013

MARTINIQUE

3rd edition

Claude Morneau

ULYSSES
TRAVEL PUBLICATIONS
Travel better... enjoy more

Editorial *Series Director:* Claude Morneau; *Project Supervisor:* Pascale Couture; *Editor:* Claude Morneau.

Research and Composition *Author:* Claude Morneau.

Production *Design:* Patrick Farei (Atoll Direction); *Proofreading:* Tara Salman; *Cartography:* André Duchesne, Patrick Thivierge (Assistant), Isabelle Lalonde; *Layout:* Tara Salman, Christian Roy.

Illustrations *Cover Photo:* AEF - Éric Bouvet Image Bank; *Interior Photos:* Tibor Bognár, Claude Hervé-Bazin, Claude Morneau, Lorette Pierson, Office du tourisme de la Martinique au Canada; *Chapter Headings:* Jennifer McMorran; *Drawings:* Marie-Annick Viatour, Lorette Pierson; *Colors* Isabelle Lalonde.

Special Thanks Marie-Claude Bellance (Office du Tourisme de la Martinique in Canada); George Landy (Office Départemental du Tourisme de la Martinique); Danièle Frappier (Caribe Sol); Muriel Wiltord, Valérie Vulcain and Sylvie Régina (Martinique Promotion Bureau, New York City); Myron Clement (Clement-Petrocik); Richard Bizier (recipes). Also to Diane Harnois and Josée Dufresne.

Thanks to SODEC and the Department of Canadian Heritage for their financial Support.

Distributors

AUSTRALIA:
Little Hills Press
11/37-43 Alexander St.
Crows Nest NSW 2065
☎ (612) 437-6995
Fax: (612) 438-5762

BELGIUM AND LUXEMBOURG:
Vander
Vrijwilligerlaan 321
B-1150 Brussel
☎ (02) 762 98 04
Fax: (02) 762 06 62

CANADA:
Ulysses Books & Maps
4176 Saint-Denis
Montréal, Québec
H2W 2M5
☎ (514) 843-9882, ext.2232
or 1-800-748-9171
Fax: 514-843-9448
www.ulysses.ca

GERMANY AND AUSTRIA:
Brettschneider
Fernreisebedarf
Feldfirchner Strasse 2
D-85551 Heimstetten
München
☎ 89-99 02 03 30
Fax: 89-99 02 03 31

GREAT BRITAIN AND IRELAND:
World Leisure Marketing
9 Downing Road
West Meadows, Derby
UK DE21 6HA
☎ 1 332 34 33 32
Fax: 1 332 34 04 64

ITALY:
Centro Cartografico del Riccio
Via di Soffiano 164/A
50143 Firenze
☎ (055) 71 33 33
Fax: (055) 71 63 50

NETHERLANDS:
Nilsson & Lamm
Pampuslaan 212-214
1380 AD Weesp (NL)
☎ 0294-465044
Fax: 0294-415054
E-mail: nilam@euronet.nl

PORTUGAL:
Dinapress
Lg. Dr. Antonio de Sousa de Macedo, 2
Lisboa 1200
☎ (1) 395 52 70
Fax: (1) 395 03 90

SCANDINAVIA:
Scanvik
Esplanaden 8B
1263 Copenhagen K
DK
☎ (45) 33.12.77.66
Fax: (45) 33.91.28.82

SPAIN:
Altaïr
Balmes 69
E-08007 Barcelona
☎ 454 29 66
Fax: 451 25 59
E-mail: altair@globalcom.es

SWITZERLAND:
OLF
P.O. Box 1061
CH-1701 Fribourg
☎ (026) 467.51.11
Fax: (026) 467.54.66

U.S.A.:
The Globe Pequot Press
6 Business Park Road
P.O. Box 833
Old Saybrook, CT 06475
☎ 1-800-243-0495
Fax: 1-800-820-2329
E-mail: sales@globe-pequot.com

Other countries, contact Ulysses Books & Maps (Montréal), Fax: (514) 843-9448

No part of this publication may be reproduced in any form or by any means, including photocopying, without the written permission of the publisher.

Canadian Cataloguing in Publication Data

Morneau, Claude
    Martinique

    3rd ed.
    (Ulysses Travel Guides)
    Translation of: Martinique.
    Includes index.

    ISBN 2-89464-136-2

    1. Martinique-Guidebooks.   I. Title   II. Series.
F2081.2.M6713 1998   917.298'204   C98-940810-8

«J'évitais de passer sur le trottoir qui borde la bibliothèque Schœlcher car ce bâtiment étrange me faisait peur. Je l'observais parfois de loin, depuis mon banc habituel de La Savane, enviant les Lycéens qui, après leur parade amoureuse à l'Allée des Soupirs, leurs rigolades et leurs chahutages entre les bancs de marbre, se paraient soudain d'un masque de sérieuseté comme s'ils s'apprêtaient à pénétrer dans un temple.»

"I used to avoid walking by the Schœlcher Library, for this strange building frightened me. I sometimes observed it from afar, from my usual bench in La Savane, envious of the highschool students who, after parading amorously through the Allée des Soupirs, would fool around among the marble benches, then suddenly assume a serious air, as if they were about to enter a temple."

- Raphaël Confiant
L'Allée des Soupirs

TABLE OF CONTENTS

LIST OF MAPS

Help make Ulysses Travel Guides even better!

The information contained in this guide was correct at press time. However, mistakes can slip in, omissions are always possible, places can disappear, etc. The author and publisher hereby disclaim any liability for loss or damage resulting from omissions or errors.

We value your comments, corrections and suggestions, as they allow us to keep each guide up to date. The best contributions will be rewarded with a free book from Ulysses Travel Publications. All you have to do is write us at the following address and indicate which title you would be interested in receiving (see the list at end of guide).

Ulysses Travel Publications
4176 Rue Saint-Denis
Montréal, Québec
Canada H2W 2M5
www.ulysses.ca
guiduly@ulysse.ca

TABLE OF SYMBOLS

🚢	Ulysses' Favourite
☎	Telephone number
⇆	Fax number
≡	Air conditioning
⊗	Fan
≈	Pool
ℜ	Restaurant
⊛	Whirlpool
△	Sauna
⊘	Gym
ℝ	Refrigerator
K	Kitchenette
tv	Colour television
pb	Private bathroom
sb	Shared bathroom
‖	*Gîtes Ruraux* classification (see p 49)
½b	half-board (lodging + 2 meals)
fb	full-board (lodging + 3 meals)
bkfst	Breakfast included

ATTRACTION CLASSIFICATION

★	Interesting
★★	Worth a visit
★★★	Not to be missed

HOTEL CLASSIFICATION

The prices in the guide are for one room, double occupancy, not including taxes.

RESTAURANT CLASSIFICATION

The prices in the guide are for a meal for one person, including taxes and tip, but not drinks.

All prices in this guide are in French francs.

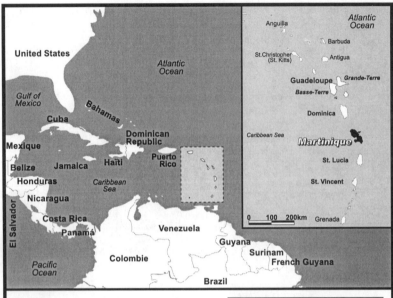

United States

Atlantic Ocean

Gulf of Mexico

Bahamas

Cuba

Mexique

Dominican Republic

Belize

Jamaica

Haïti

Puerto Rico

Honduras

Caribbean Sea

Nicaragua

El Salvador

Costa Rica

Panamá

Venezuela

Guyana

Pacific Ocean

Colombie

Surinam

French Guyana

Brazil

Anguilla

Atlantic Ocean

Barbuda

St.Christopher (St. Kitts)

Antigua

Guadeloupe

Grande-Terre

Basse-Terre

Dominica

Caribbean Sea

Martinique

St. Lucia

St. Vincent

0   100   200km

Grenada

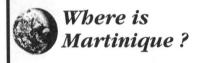

Where is Martinique ?

Martinique

Overseas French Department
Main City: Fort-de-France
Language: French, Creole
Population: 384,000 inhab.
Currency: French franc
Area: 1,100 km²

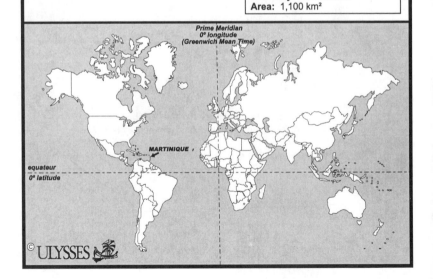

Prime Meridian
0° longitude
(Greenwich Mean Time)

MARTINIQUE

equateur
0° latitude

© ULYSSES

PORTRAIT

The island we know today as Martinique was known in the past by other beautiful names. According to legend, it was once called Matinino, or "Island of Women", while the Carib Indians referred to it as Madinina, or "Island of Flowers".

You'll understand the inspiration as you set foot on this tropical volcanic island, a little bit of France lost in the Antilles, a colourful Creole land, home of Aimé Césaire and Patrick Chamoiseau, birthplace of Empress Josephine, and inspiration to Gauguin. Indeed, this island, bathed in light, steeped in music, trimmed with superb beaches and where luxuriant vegetation abounds, will inspire anyone who takes the time to discover it.

The sun, the sea, the food, the turbulent history, the poetry, the people... Everything about Martinique makes it a beautiful, fascinating place to visit.

GEOGRAPHY

Martinique, which is part of the Lesser Antilles island chain, covers an area of 1,100 square kilometres. Its west coast looks out on the Caribbean, its east coast on the Atlantic. The island is separated from Dominica in the north by the Dominica Passage (also called the Martinique Passage) and from St. Lucia in the south by the St. Lucia Channel. It measures 70 kilometres at its longest point and about 30 kilometres at its widest with 350 kilometres of shoreline.

Martinique's highest peak is the notorious volcano, **Montagne Pelée** (1,397 m), which erupted in 1902, claiming the lives of 30,000 people and completely destroying the city of **Saint-Pierre**.

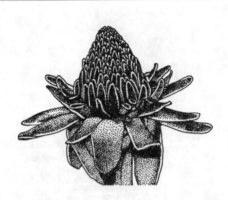

Torch lily

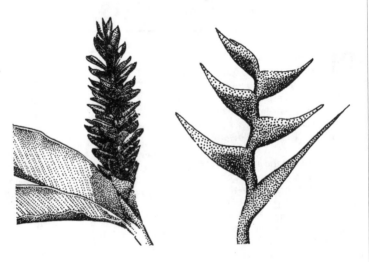

Alpinia   *Lobster claw*

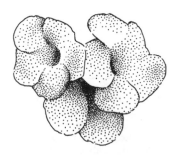

Golden trumpet

Hibiscus

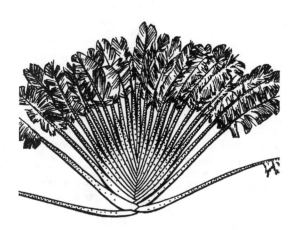

Traveller's joy

Montagne Pelée towers above the northernmost part of the island. From this point outwards, the terrain drops lower, the closer you get to the coast and the farther you head south, though the transition is not quite so smooth in the latter instance, due to the imposing **Pitons du Carbet**, a series of peaks just south of the volcano, including Piton Lacroix, or Morne Pavillon (1,196 m), Piton de l'Alma (1,105 m), Piton Dumauzé (1,109 m), Piton Boucher (1,070 m) and Morne Piquet (1,160 m).

Inland, the northern part of the island is covered with a dense tropical rain forest, something highly unusual in the Caribbean. In fact, this type of forest is more likely to be found in Central America than it is in the Antilles, which, other than Guadeloupe and Dominica, tend to have a drier landscape. The grey- and black-sand beaches lining the coast are reminders of the island's volcanic origin.

The **Plaine du Lamentin** covers the central part of the island, forming a transitional area between the north and the south. It stretches eastward, adjacent to the **Baie de Fort-de-France**. More than a third of the island's population is concentrated in this area.

The southernmost part of the island is sprinkled with small hills known as *mornes*, the highest of which is the **Montagne du Vauclin** (504 m). This entire region is trimmed with gorgeous white-sand beaches, making it a veritable paradise for even the most demanding beach-goers. The beach at **Grande Anse des Salines**, on the southernmost part of the coast, is known the world over.

As a general rule, the sea is calm on the Caribbean or "leeward" coast. The Atlantic or "windward" coast, especially in the south, has beaches tucked inside little bays which are often pounded by heavy surf. Fortunately, there are a few coral reefs which protect the shore from the waves and thus create calm swimming areas, like those off of **Le François** and **Le Robert**.

FLORA

One of Martinique's greatest assets is its rich and varied flora, which should come as no surprise to those familiar with the island's Carib name, Madinina ("Island of Flowers"). The unruly luxuriance of the tropical rain forest in the north and the thousands of multicoloured flowers found all over the island are the obvious cornerstones of Martinique's reputation. But you should also familiarize yourself with the island's mangrove swamps, a sort of flooded forest, and the unusual vegetation of the more arid south, where cacti have a thorny defense against prying hands.

The Tropical Rainforest

The plant species in the tropical rainforest in the northern part of the island may be divided into three overlapping categories. First, on the ground, there are the epiphytes – lianas, orchids, philodendrons, etc.

The second level of this dense forest is made up of a series of trees, all of which are about 20 metres high. These include tree ferns, cannas, bamboo, mahoganies and magnolias.

Finally, the last level is made up of trees measuring up to 40 metres, which shelter the lower layers with their leaves. This category includes the yellow mangrove, the chestnut and the white gum, out of which the Carib Indians built their boats.

The Mangrove Swamp

Mangrove swamps, which are common in the tropics, are found in muddy coastal areas. In Martinique, you will find an excellent example of this type of forest along the Baie de Fort-de-France, in the Génipa reserve. Another smaller one covers part of the Presqu'île de la Caravelle.

The mangroves stretch their long roots right into the sea, or, when too far inland to do so, into stagnant water. The area is swarming with mosquitoes, making it rather unpleasant to explore at great length.

The Southern Vegetation

The southern part of the island is more arid than the north and its flora is consequently quite different. Cacti are abundant, though many were planted by farmers to demarcate, and thereby protect, their land. You'll also find the opuntia, better known as the prickly pear or, in the Antilles, the *raquette* (snowshoe), which serves a similar purpose.

The other widespread plant species in the south is the manchineel tree, which grows along certain beaches. This tree produces a poisonous fruit, as well as thick sap that can cause serious burns. Most of the manchineel trees on the island are marked with a red paint stripe.

Along the Coasts

The beaches stretching along the edges of the island are usually hidden behind a curtain of trees, sometimes palms, bending toward the sea, other times, sea grapes, which are small trees with round, waxy leaves.

The *ti-baume*, a kind of bush belonging to the spurge family, can be found along the Caribbean coast.

Cultivated Land

In the areas that have been cleared for habitation, which are mostly on the Plaine du Lamentin and on hillsides, you can find various other imported plant species. Many large plots of land have been used to cultivate sugar cane, which is now gradually being replaced by bananas and pineapples.

Some of the trees scattered across the island were imported from Madagascar (flamboyant), India (mango and rose apple) and Tahiti (breadfruit). Some of the flowers that seem so characteristically Martinican aren't even indigenous to the island. This is true of the anthurium, hibiscus (tropical Asia), poinsettia, bougainvillea (Brazil), allamandes (South America), and red lavender (Indonesia), just to name a few. In fact, the only flower that is 100% Martinican is the canna, which thrives in the forest.

FAUNA

Having been separated from the American continent so long ago, Martinique, like the other islands of the Lesser Antilles, has little in the way of indigenous fauna.

There are, however, a few animals native to the island, including the *manicou*, a marsupial which is the local equivalent of the opossum. Other animals were brought to the island during the colonial era, and then multiplied. A notable example is the mongoose, a

Mongoose

sort of weasel imported from India by local planters in an effort to eliminate the deadly pit viper, nicknamed *fer-de-lance*, which had spread over agricultural land. The mongoose adapted well to the island, soon attacking not only the dreaded snakes, but the eggs of several different species of birds as well, so zealously that it wiped out a significant portion of Martinique's winged fauna altogether.

Birds

Fortunately, Martinique still has a few remarkable birds species sure to delight both amateur and professional ornithologists.

You are sure to see the **bananaquit** (known locally as the *sucrier fall' jaun'*), one of the most common birds in Martinique. These creatures can be spotted all over the island, and are easily recognizeable by their plumage, which is black on top and yellow underneath. In fact, the bananaquit is such a common sight here that the tourist office has made it the symbol of Martinique.

This choice, however, could be disputed, since one rare bird species is found only in Martinique: the **Martinique oriole**, a small, sedentary bird with a long tail and black and brownish-orange feathers.

The hummingbird is another species you are sure to see. There are actually several varieties of **hummingbirds** (the purple-throated, antillean crested, green-throated, and blue-headed). These minuscule birds have a unique method of flying that enables them to hover and move backwards.

The **rufous-throated solitaire** is another species found only on Martinique. Its melodious song is its trademark. It is small, grey-blue bird with black wings and a red throat, that lives in the forest.

Among the migratory birds that stop in Martinique, there are various species of **egret**, including the great egret, the snowy egret, the tricoloured heron and the little blue heron. These may be seen in mangrove swamps and marshes and around stretches of fresh water. Also noteworthy is the **black-necked stilt**, with its long, delicate legs and black and white plumage.

The **brown pelican** also lives along the shore. Its familiar silhouette features a long beak with a large bill, sturdy legs and palmed feet.

Near the shore, you might spot a **magnificent frigatebird**, a sea bird with a large wingspan, which catches its prey by skimming the surface of the water. This species is distinguished by its beak, which forms a hook at the end. Furthermore, at the base of its throat, the male has an orangish bill that becomes bright red during reproduction.

Birds of prey are plentiful on the island as well. One of these is the **broad-winged hawk**, found only in the mountains of Martinique, and the **peregrine falcon**, a migratory bird that stops along the coast and in the forest.

To find out more about Martinique's birds pick up the pocketbook *Birds of the West Indies*, published in Saint Barts by Éditions du Latanier.

Insects

In terms of insects, the island's most striking specimen is the *ravet*, a large tropical cockroach, which is, however, completely harmless. Then there is the *matoutou*, a big trap-door spider with hairy legs, which will certainly frighten anyone who happens upon it unexpectedly. And if you're lucky, you might see some beautiful butterflies, like the monarch or the mourning cloak (also known as the Camberwell beauty).

Marine Life and Crustaceans

Beautiful coral formations teeming with an incredible variety of marine fauna dot the sea bottom along the island's coast. If you go scuba diving, you'll probably come across surgeon fish, sergeant majors, boxfish, hatpin urchins (whose spines are dangerous), butterfly fish, parrot fish and angel fish, just to name a few. Farther out, you'll enter the territory of the larger, and sometimes more dangerous, species, like barracudas and, less frequently, sharks.

There is an abundance of crustaceans all along Martinique's coastline, including rock lobsters (*langoustes*) and crabs, which you'll often see on the beach. Turtles, which have been overhunted, can be spotted along river banks on rare occasions.

And last but not least, there are many varieties of crayfish thriving in the island's rivers.

HISTORY

Discovery of the Antilles

On the morning of August 3, 1492, Christopher Columbus prepared to set off on his first voyage westward, with the aim of discovering a new route to Asia. This journey led him to the Caribbean – more specifically, to the island of Hispaniola (today, the Dominican Republic and Haiti). Having discovered these magnificent islands, which he believed to be rich in gold, Columbus returned to Spain full of enthusiasm.

The success of his first voyage enabled him to embark on another, some time later. This second odyssey began with a stop at Hispaniola. Though the natives of the island, the Arawaks, told him there were ferocious "flesh-eating" tribes on other islands farther south, Columbus decided to continue exploring in that direction, and thus came across the chain of islands now known as the Lesser Antilles. He visited Dominica first, followed by Marie-Galante, which he named after his ship. Unable to find potable water on either of these islands, he continued on to Guadeloupe, where, having discovered fresh water, he stayed for a while before resuming his voyage once again.

In 1493, Columbus sailed to Matinino, the island known today as Martinique, but refused to set foot on its shores. The Ciguayo Indians he had met in northern Haiti had warned him that according to legend, the island, whose name meant "Island of Women," was inhabited by dangerous Amazons.

In June 1502, on his fourth voyage, Columbus finally alighted on the island's Caribbean coast, where the village of Le Carbet is now located. He then realized that the island was in fact inhabited by Caribs. These cannibalistic people probably came from South America and were descendants of the Galibi, who lived in the area between the Orinoco and Amazon Rivers. The Caribs settled in the Antilles during the 14th century, supplanting the Arawaks, who had already been living in the region for quite some time.

At the time of Columbus's arrival, the Caribs were already well established on fertile lands which provided them with an abundant supply of food. The men led a calm existence, especially as the division of labour between the sexes was hardly fair by today's standards. Each man owned several women, most of whom were Arawaks carried off from tribes on neighbouring islands. In addition to working in the fields, the women had to look after the house and the children. They also had to bathe the man and take care of his personal appearance. The man, meanwhile, would go hunting and fishing for part of the day and then while away the rest of his time indulging in various activities, such as meditating, playing the flute, making kitchen utensils or taming parrots. The Caribs were mighty warriors as well, and would occasionally launch an attack against one of the fearful neighbouring tribes.

For its part, Spain showed almost no interest in this little island which lacked mineral resources to recommend it, and thus never made any effort to establish a colony there.

French Colonization

The French appeared on the scene on June 25, 1635, when two gentlemen by the name of de l'Olive and du Plessis arrived in Martinique from Dieppe. This initial venture never got off the ground, though, for the two men deemed the island unfit for farming, claiming it to be infested with snakes and too mountainous (they, like Columbus, had landed near present-day Le Carbet, with the Pitons du Carbet and Montagne Pelé forming the horizon). Accordingly, they soon abandoned Martinique for Guadeloupe.

Shortly after, however, on September 15, 1635, Pierre Belain d'Esnambuc landed on the shores of Martinique, where the city of Saint-Pierre is now located, and claimed the island for France. When he died in 1637, his nephew Jacques du Parquet took over as Lieutenant-General of Martinique, and worked steadily to expand the colony. At the same time, he nurtured relations with the native population, in an effort to avoid what he viewed as futile confrontations. In 1650, du Parquet purchased Martinique, thus becoming its governor – a position he held until his death in 1658.

By introducing sugar cane, du Parquet set the island's agricultural development in motion. He also built Fort Royal, which would much later become Fort-de-France, and set up the Martinican militia.

After du Parquet's death, his wife took over control of Martinique. She struggled to stay in favour with the colonists and quell the fervour of those seeking

A Brief History of Martinique

1493 Christopher Columbus discovers the island of Martinique.

1502 On his second voyage to the New World, Columbus lands at Le Carbet, on the Caribbean coast, and claims the island for Spain.

1635 The French establish themselves on the island and Bélain d'Esnambuc founds the city of Saint-Pierre.

1637 Jacques du Parquet becomes Lieutenant-General of Martinique and starts expanding the colony. The following year, he orders the construction of Fort Royal, the origin of the city of Fort-de-France.

1642 Louis XIII authorizes the use of African slaves in the French Antilles.

1650 Jacques du Parquet purchases Martinique.

1660 The Carib Indians are exterminated.

1664 The *Compagnie des Indes Occidentales* purchases the island from du Parquet.

1685 Adoption of Colbert's *Code Noir* regulating slavery.

1717 The *Gaoulé* Revolt.

1762 The English occupy Martinique for the first time. Nine months later, under the terms of the Treaty of Paris, Martinique and Guadeloupe are restored to France in exchange for Canada.

1794 The English, joining forces with the royalists, recapture the island during the French Revolution.

1802 Napoleon Bonaparte recovers Martinique by means of the Treaty of Amiens.

1809 Once again, the English occupy the island, and remain there until the Treaty of Paris is signed in 1814.

1848 Slavery is permanently abolished.

1902 Montagne Pelée erupts, killing 30,000 people and completely destroying the city of Saint-Pierre.

1946 Martinique becomes a French *département*.

1983 Creation of the *Conseil Régional de la Martinique*. Aimé Césaire is elected as its first president.

1997 Alfred Marie-Jeanne becomes the first separatist candidate from Martinique to win a seat in the French general elections. The following year, he is elected president of the Conseil Régional.

to wage war against the Caribs. However, the mounting tension soon forced her to yield to their reasoning. The Martinican militia thus began attacking the Caribs, who were still living along the northern Atlantic coast. The colonists' goal was to take over the fertile lands of Cabesterre (as the region was known) in order to expand their settlement.

The church was also involved in conquering this new territory. The Jesuits joined forces with the colonists attacking from the sea, while the Dominicans allied themselves with those launching an invasion from inland. It was agreed that whichever of the two religious orders arrived first would be in charge of all future parishes in this part of the island. The Dominicans emerged victorious in this notorious pact.

In 1660, the French signed a "peace treaty" with the Caribs, virtually all of whom had either been exterminated or expelled from the island by that time anyway. Many of them had fled to St. Vincent and Dominica, which became their last two places of refuge when the French formally agreed to leave the two islands alone.

Meanwhile, in 1642, Louis XIII authorized the use of African slaves in the French Antilles to meet the urgent demand for labour. Thus was born a triangular trading route between France, Guinea and the Antilles. Black slaves were bought, just like cattle, by landowning colonists, and had to work under inhumane conditions in the sugar-cane fields.

Martinique's status, along with that of Guadeloupe, Marie-Galante, Grenada and the Grenadines, changed in 1664, when Louis XIV decided to restructure foreign commerce and ordered that the islands be purchased by the *Compagnie des Indes Occidentales*. Du Parquet's heirs were generously compensated for renouncing ownership of Martinique.

In 1669, Martinique was named capital of the French islands in the Caribbean, and the Marquis de Baas became Governor General of the French islands in America. It was he who ordered that Fort Royal be reinforced. In 1674, furthermore, Dutch troops led by Ruyter launched a futile attack on the fort. By this time, the French possessions in the Caribbean, which gave France a monopoly on sugar, otherwise known as "white gold", had become very desirable.

In 1675, all of the French colonies were ceded back to the Crown, which removed the authority of the *Compagnie des Indes Occidentales* and centralized the administration of foreign commerce. One offshoot of these changes was the initiation of Colbert's *Code Noir* (1685), which regulated the "use" of slaves, according them certain rights (limited working hours, restrictions on punishment, guaranteed food rations, etc.), but also imposing very strict constraints upon them.

By 1677, Charles de Courbon, Comte de Blénac, was governor of Martinique and Lieutenant-General (in the name of the King of France) of France's possessions in the Antilles. Upon his recommendation, the administration of Martinique was moved from Saint-Pierre to Fort-Royal in 1692.

The *Gaoulé* Revolt

In 1717, as part of France's efforts to centralize the administration of foreign commerce and ensure exclusive trade relations with its territories across the Atlantic, the Governor General of the islands, Antoine d'Arcy, Seigneur de La Varenne, was assigned the task of putting an end to illegal sugar trading between the French islands and their neighbours. In May, he and his steward, Louis-Balthazar de Rincouart d'Hérouville, arrived in Martinique. They were invited to a large banquet at the Bourgeot estate, near Pointe de la Chéry, not far from Le Diamant. To their surprise, they were held captive there by about a hundred furious colonists and then expelled from the island. In the following months, the commercial laws dictated by France were gradually relaxed enough to satisfy the Martinican planters.

The *béké* plantation owners' rebellion against the king's power became known as the *Gaoulé*. This term's origins remain uncertain, but some claim that it is a Carib word for "revolt".

The Battles of France and England

In 1762, the English captured Martinique for the first time by attacking Fort Royal from inland, cunningly taking advantage of the hills overlooking the fortress. The English occupation lasted nine months, until the Treaty of Paris restored Martinique to France, at the same time removing Canada from its possession. This incident led to a complete overhaul of the island's defense system, including the construction of Fort Bourbon (now Fort Dessaix) in the hills of Fort Royal.

From 1789 on, the French Revolution echoed through Martinique, sowing dissension among the islanders. On one side, there were the rural planters, who remained loyal to the monarchy; on the other, the merchants of Saint-Pierre, who became the Republic's faithful representatives in Martinique. In 1793, when Governor Rochambeau's republicans controlled both Fort Royal and Saint-Pierre, the royalists joined forces

with the English, who recaptured the island in 1794, and occupied it until 1802.

Napoleon Bonaparte used the Treaty of Amiens (1802) to recover Martinique for the French. In 1796 he had married a Martinican Creole named Marie-Josèphe Rose Tascher de la Pagerie, who would become Empress Josephine. It was supposedly on her insistence that he officially reintroduced slavery. In fact, all he did was cancel the law passed by the republicans in 1794, which had actually never been applied in Martinique, as the island had fallen into the hands of the English, who, like their royalist allies, were in favour of slavery.

In 1809, the English returned and conquered Martinique once again. They controlled the island until 1814, when a new treaty was signed in Paris. France recovered Guadeloupe and Martinique, but lost St. Lucia and Tobago.

The Abolition of Slavery

In 1834, England abolished slavery in its colonies. France, however, did not do so until April 27, 1848, when an Official Decree was passed, the result of a long political war waged by a minister named Victor Schœlcher. At the time, there were more than 70,000 slaves in Martinique, out of a total population of 125,000.

In the period between 1834, when England abolished slavery, and 1848, when France did the same, a great many slaves fled from Martinique and Guadeloupe to the English Caribbean islands. In addition, whites had already had to suppress more and more slave revolts, such as the riots in Saint-Pierre (1831) and Grande Anse (1833). Unrest was brewing, and it was becoming clear that the system couldn't hold out much longer.

Despite colonists' opposition, the government of the Second Republic opted for the immediate abolition of slavery on March 4, 1848. Victor Schœlcher, the driving force behind this reform, was named Under-Secretary of the Colonies. He also presided over a commission for the abolition of slavery and signed the Official Decree on April 27, 1848.

In addition to granting slave-owners compensation, the decree stipulated that the law would not be formally issued in the colonies until two months later. However, when a general revolt broke out in Saint-Pierre, the governor of Martinique had no other choice but to announce the abolition of slavery on May 22, 1848.

In an effort to make up for the work force that was lost when the slaves left the plantations, more than 25,000 East Indians were hired at very low wages between 1852 and 1884.

The compensation awarded to former slave-owners gave them basic capital permitting them to reorganize their production system, by developing large, centralized sugar factories. There were 25 of these on the island by the end of the 19th century. Before long, however, international competition and the collapse the world sugar market weakened the industry, and by the beginning of World War II, only about 15 factories were still functioning on the island. Between 1970 and 1980, one after another of these was shut down, too, until only one sugar factory, which is still in operation, remained.

The 20th Century

In Martinique, the 20th century was ushered in by the eruption of Montagne Pelée on May 8, 1902. Thirty thousand people lost their lives in the catastrophe, which completely destroyed the city of Saint-Pierre.

The rest of the first half of the century was marked by Caribbean participation in the two World Wars, with 52,000 citizens taking part in the Great War. Then, during the Second World War, gold from the Bank of France was stored in Martinique, which the Vichy government had placed under Admiral Robert's supervision. The island was consequently placed under blockade, which made fresh supplies very hard to come by. Finally, on June 30, 1943, Martinique rallied to the cause of General de Gaulle's Free France.

On March 19, 1946, Martinique, like Guadeloupe, French Guyana and Reunion, had its status as a colony changed to that of a French *département d'outre-mer* (DOM), or overseas department. The Antillean political left, of which poet Aimé Césaire (see p 27) was already a very active member, had demanded this total assimilation, viewing it as a means of eliminating the vestiges of colonialism by putting everyone on an equal footing and promoting greater social justice.

Today, however, these same leftists criticize the "failure" of departmentalization, which, in their view, was actually an effort to keep former colonies dependent on France.

Meanwhile, in March 1958, Aimé Césaire founded the *Parti Progressiste Martiniquais* (PPM). A man of letters, Mayor of Fort-de-France and Deputy of

PORTRAIT

Martinique, he became a political leader of great stature. His enlightened leadership prevented Martinique from falling into the same trap as Guadeloupe, whose independence movement led to outbreaks of violence in the 1980s. In 1983, after a decentralization bill was passed granting more wide-ranging powers to the *départements*, Césaire was elected as the first president of the *Conseil Régional de la Martinique*.

In 1994, Claude Lise of the PPM was elected president of the *Conseil Général de la Martinique*, while Aimé Césaire was voted back into power at the age of 82 in Fort-de-France's municipal elections in June 1995. Césaire has been the city's mayor since 1945. In France's presidential elections of April and May 1995, 59% of the population voted for the political left, favouring socialist Lionel Jospin over the future president of the French Republic, Jacques Chirac.

In the French general elections of 1997, Jospin was elected prime minister, and much to everyone's surprise, Alfred Marie-Jeanne becomes Martinique's first separate to win a seat in the legislature. Besides the *Mouvement Indépendentiste Martiniquais* (MIM) leader, two right-wing representatives and one from the left PPM are also elected.

The separatists gains did not end here, however: in the regional elections of March 1998, Marie-Jeanne is also elected president of Martinique's *Conseil Régional*.

POLITICS

Martinique has been a *département d'outre-mer français*, or overseas department since March 19, 1946. In accordance with its Constitution, it has two political assemblies, the *Conseil Régional* (Regional Council), elected according to a system of proportional representation, and the *Conseil Général* (Departmental Council), elected on a majority basis in two rounds. The former deals with matters relating to economic and territorial development and workforce training, while the latter handles social issues. These two assemblies have the power to pass legislation in their respective spheres and, of course, to allocate budgets.

In addition to the two Councils, Martinique has a *Comité Économique Social* (Economic and Social Committee) and a *Comité de la Culture et de l'Environnement* (Committee on Culture and the Environment). The island is represented in the French National Assembly by four deputies, and has two representatives in the Senate. Martinicans enjoy the same social programs as residents of metropolitan France, notably, old age pensions, unemployment insurance and health insurance. These programs are not, however, always instituted in Martinique according to the same standards as in France.

In terms of local administration, Martinique is divided into 34 *communes* (see map, p 23), each administered by a mayor and his assistants and advisors, who make up the *Conseil Municipal*. These individuals are voted into power in municipal elections held every six years; the last ones took place in 1995.

Fort-de-France is the main city, or seat of the prefecture, of the department of Martinique. Its *arrondissement* (district) also includes Bellefontaine, Le Carbet, Case-Pilote, Fonds-Saint-Denis, Grand'Rivière, Le Lamentin, Morne-Rouge, Morne-Vert, Le Prêcheur, Saint-Joseph, Saint-Pierre and Schœlcher.

The *Communes* of Martinique

Commune	Population	Area
Ajoupa-Bouillon	1,745 *Ajoupa-Bouillonais*	1,230 ha
Anses-d'Arlet	3,245 *Arlésiens*	2,592 ha
Basse-Pointe	4,454 *Pointois*	2,795 ha
Bellefontaine	1,530 *Bellefontainois*	1,189 ha
Carbet	3,022 *Carbétiens*	2,022 ha
Case-Pilote	3,657 *Case-Pilotins*	1,844 ha
Diamant	3,351 *Diamantinois*	2,734 ha
Ducos	12,536 *Ducossais*	2,904 ha
Fonds-Saint-Denis	82 *Denisiens*	2,428 ha
Fort-de-France	101,540 *Foyalais*	4,308 ha
François	17,065 *Franciscains*	5,393 ha
Grand'Rivière	959 *Riverains*	1,660 ha
Gros-Morne	10,197 *Gros-Mornais*	4,611 ha
Lamentin	30,696 *Lamentinois*	6,232 ha
Lorrain	8,116 *Lorinois*	5,033 ha
Macouba	1,502 *Macoubétins*	1,693 ha
Marigot	3,609 *Marigotins*	1,163 ha
Marin	6,429 *Marinois*	3,151 ha
Morne-Rouge	5,363 *Péléens*	3,764 ha
Morne-Vert	1,838 *Verdimornais*	1,337 ha
Prêcheur	2,051 *Prêchotins*	2,992 ha
Rivière-Pilote	12,678 *Pilotins*	3,578 ha
Rivière-Salée	8,785 *Saléens*	3,938 ha
Robert	17,746 *Robertins*	4,487 ha
Saint-Esprit	7,799 *Spiritains*	2,346 ha
Saint-Joseph	14,054 *Joséphins*	4,329 ha
Saint-Pierre	5,045 *Pierrotins*	3,858 ha
Sainte-Anne	3,883 *Saintannais*	3,842 ha
Sainte-Luce	5,978 *Lucéens*	2,802 ha
Sainte-Marie	19,760 *Samaritains*	4,456 ha
Schœlcher	19,874 *Schœlcherois*	2,117 ha
Trinité	11,392 *Trinitéens*	4,577 ha
Trois-Îlets	4,492 *Iléens*	2,731 ha
Vauclin	7,769 *Vauclinois*	3,906 ha

Source: *Mise à jour*, April-June 1995

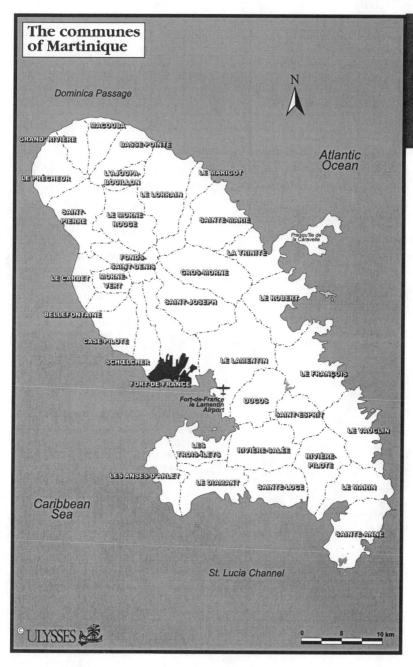

The communes of Martinique

Dominica Passage

N

Atlantic Ocean

MACOUBA

GRAND'RIVIÈRE

BASSE-POINTE

LE PRÊCHEUR

L'AJOUPA-BOUILLON

LE MARIGOT

LE LORRAIN

SAINT-PIERRE

LE MORNE-ROUGE

SAINTE-MARIE

FONDS-SAINT-DENIS

LA TRINITÉ

Presqu'île de la Caravelle

LE CARBET

MORNE-VERT

GROS-MORNE

BELLEFONTAINE

SAINT-JOSEPH

LE ROBERT

CASE-PILOTE

SCHŒLCHER

LE LAMENTIN

FORT-DE-FRANCE

LE FRANÇOIS

Fort-de-France le Lamentin Airport

DUCOS

SAINT-ESPRIT

LE VAUCLIN

LES TROIS-ÎLETS

RIVIÈRE-SALÉE

RIVIÈRE-PILOTE

LES ANSES-D'ARLET

LE DIAMANT

SAINTE-LUCE

LE MARIN

Caribbean Sea

SAINTE-ANNE

St. Lucia Channel

© ULYSSES

0   5   10 km

Martinique has two sub-prefectures as well. Le Marin, the south sub-prefecture, encompasses the *communes* of Anses-d'Arlet, Le Diamant, Ducos, Le François, Rivière-Pilote, Rivière-Salée, Saint-Esprit, Sainte-Anne, Sainte-Luce, Trois-Îlets and Le Vauclin, while La Trinité, the north sub-prefecture, is made up of Ajoupa-Bouillon, Basse-Pointe, Gros-Morne, Le Lorrain, Macouba, Marigot, Le Robert and Sainte-Marie.

ECONOMY

Martinique's gross domestic product totals $4,058,000,000 US for a population of 384,000 (*État du Monde*, 1998), which comes to about $10,760 US per capita. In comparison, Guadeloupe's GDP adds up to $8,215 US per capita, France's to about $20,510 US, Canada's to $21,520 US and the United States' to $24,750 US.

Martinique imports $1,975,000,000 US worth of goods annually, and only exports $212,000,000 US worth. Its main supplier (71%), as well as its most important client (49.5%), is metropolitan France. The total value of the goods imported by all *départements français d'Amérique*, or French departments in the Americas, comes to $5.3 billion US (32 billion francs), making them France's 11th most important market. About 2.7 million tons of merchandise passes through Fort-de-France's port, ranking it 7th among the ports in the Caribbean zone, after New Orleans (USA) (which is in another category altogether), Tampa (US), Kingston (Jamaica), San Juan (Puerto Rico), Belém (Brasil) and Paramaribo (Surinam), and just in front of Guadeloupe (2.6 million tons).

Agricultural production, which was once very important to the island's economy, is in constant decline. Bananas (the country's number one export, accounting for 50% of its export earnings) are still one of the main crops, gradually supplanting sugar cane, which is used to produce rum. Pineapples are in third place, with an annual production of just under 25,000 tons.

Today, Martinique's annual production of sugar cane is barely 228,000 tons (compared with 514,000 tons in 1968), ranking it 20th among countries and territories in the Caribbean basin, behind Guadeloupe (748,000 tons) and Barbados (600,000) and light years behind Cuba (39,000,000 tons) and Brazil (280,900,000 tons), the respective Caribbean and world leaders.

In terms of banana production, Martinique ranks 9th in the Caribbean. Its output of 210,000 tons remains modest alongside that of the world's top producers, India (7,900,000 tons) and Brazil (5,840,000 tons), but is nonetheless appreciable when compared to that of Costa Rica (1,900,000 tons), which ranks first in the Caribbean basin and 7th in the world. An estimated 15,000 jobs are directly related to the banana industry, and nearly twice as many indirectly. However, a number of obstacles have hindered the growth of this industry over the past few years. There is even talk of a veritable crisis provoked by fierce competition from French-speaking African countries, with whom France is nurturing its diplomatic relations, and Latin America, whose production is controlled by powerful multinational American companies (Chiquita, Dole and Del Monte). As production costs are much lower in these countries (a day of work in Africa or Latin America costs between 20 and 40 francs, compared to 350 francs in the French An-

PORTRAIT

An Unwelcome Visitor

In December 1997, Jean-Marie Le Pen, president of the Front National, paid a very brief visit to the "Island of Flowers". The French far-right-wing leader was greeted by a horde of anti-racist militants as he stepped off his plane at the Lamentin airport. These demonstrators came to inform Le Pen that his racist speeches made him persona non grata in Martinique.

Shortly after, the crowd became even more worked up and a shoving match ensued. Le Pen was ultimately forced to change his vacation plans and set course for Puerto Rico. In the end, he stayed in Martinique for all of 35 minutes!

tilles), Martinique is having a harder and harder time competing on the market.

New crops have, however, been developed as well, including melons, eggplants, limes and avocados. Flowers (anthuriums) and plants are also cultivated.

Livestock breeding, which accounts for about 15% of Martinique's agricultural production, is divided into the following three categories: cattle breeding, which is mainly restricted to the southern part of the island, pig and sheep breeding, which are less structured, but more widespread.

Surprisingly, fishing is something of a cottage industry and there aren't any precise statistics regarding production levels. In 1993, 5,850 tons of fresh fish were officially registered, but some observers would add 6,000 to 7,000 tons to that figure. Furthermore, there are about 1000 declared fishermen, but the real figure probably stands somewhere around 2,000.

The industrial sector, for its part, is geared mainly toward energy production (48% of revenue and 25% of jobs), farm-produce (70% of all industrial plants) and the manufacturing of construction materials (cement, parpens, bricks, etc.). Industry employs about 16% (6,800) of wage-earning Martinicans, with its companies accounting for 8% (1,800) of the total number of firms in operation. An estimated 900 unsalaried, independent contractors work in the industrial sector. Martinique's major industrial firms are EDF, which has a monopoly on the distribution of electricity, SARA (refining crude oil, imports and storage), Biométal (sheet metal, insulation panels, concrete forms), Batimat (concrete, gravel, sand) and SCIC (Société Caraïbe d'Industrie Chimique).

The service sector (shops, tourism, etc.) accounts for 83% of all wealth now produced in Martinique, versus 11% for industry and 6% for agriculture. Today, the state is the largest employer, and has actually become the driving force behind the island's economy, paying 40% of all salaries.

The tourism industry is thriving, with 880,000 visitors arriving on the island each year. It is important to keep in mind, however, that almost half of all visitors are passengers on cruise ships, and a fair number of these don't even set foot on the island, while the others only stay for four to eight hours. A little over 72% of the island's tourists come from metropolitan France, 11% from other European countries and 9% from other countries or territories in the Caribbean basin.

Small business also employs a large portion of the workforce. There are presently more than 1,500 retail establishments in Martinique.

Despite all of this, the job situation remains alarming. More than 50,000 potential wage earners are out of work, putting the unemployment rate at over 30%.

PEOPLE

The Carib Indians, who once inhabited the island, have long since been exterminated or they have fled to neighbouring islands, such as Dominica, where a few of them still live today. Previously, these same Caribs had wiped out the Arawaks, another, more peaceful indigenous people.

Today, the vast majority (90%) of Martinique's 384,000 inhabitants are black (descendants of the slaves brought over from Africa during the 17th and 18th centuries and at the beginning of the 19th century), or mulatto (a mix of European and African ancestry).

Only 1% of the total population is white. This tiny minority of *békés* (white Creoles directly descended from the first French colonists) controls a significant share of the island's economy, however, and is involved in many different spheres, such as agriculture, real estate, tourism, banking, etc.

The population also includes a significant number of *métros*, whites who have come from France to work in administration. It is very hard to determine exactly how many there are, because any French citizen with proper identification can move to Martinique without following any immigration procedures. This group could be made

of anywhere between 10,000 and 35,000 people.

There is also a small Hindu, and an even smaller Chinese community who came to the island in the second half of the 19th century immediately following the abolition of slavery, when there was a growing need for labour. And finally, there are the more recent Lebanese and Syrian immigrants, who live mainly in Fort-de-France, where many of them own clothing and jewellery stores.

More than three quarters of the island's inhabitants are Catholic, and while French is the official language, Creole is still widely spoken. Literacy, infant mortality and life expectancy are at about the same levels as in metropolitan France. Barely 5% of Martinicans are presently over the age of 65, while children under the age of 15 make up more than a third of the population.

Creole

Martinique, like other islands of the Antilles, including Guadeloupe and Haiti, was inhabited first by Amerindians, and then by immigrants from various European and African countries. These men and women, who lived together on plantations and thus found it necessary to communicate with each other, eventually created a common language, Creole, which is derived not only from French, but also from Spanish, Portuguese, assorted African dialects, and a few Carib words. As the language of the slaves, Creole was considered for a long time to be a bastardized version of French. Little by little, though, its recognition as not only a true language, both written and spoken, but also as an element of the Caribbean identity, led people to a more widespread appreciation of its worth.

ART AND CULTURE

Literature

Père du Tertre's *Histoire générale des îles de Saint-Christophe, de la Guadeloupe, de la Martinique et autres dans l'Amérique* (1654) and **Père Labat**'s *Nouveau voyage aux îles de l'Amérique* (1722), both descriptions of life in the Caribbean colonies, were probably the first pieces of writing to come out of the Antilles. Essentially eye-witness accounts, their interest lies mainly in their historical value. The colony continued to develop, but West Indian literature, hindered by the region's economic crises and political instability, did not start to flourish until the 20th century.

In the early 20th century, an Antillean literature reflecting the character of these sun-drenched islands began to thrive. **Daniel Thaly** (1880-1952), a native of Martinique's English neighbour to the north, Dominica (whose inhabitants also speak Creole), was the first Caribbean poet to be recognized.

Joseph Zobel (1915-), born in Rivière-Salée on Martinique, wrote a distinctively Caribbean novel called *Rue Case-Nègres*, which evokes the difficult conditions faced by blacks working on sugar-cane plantations. In 1983, **Euzhan Palcy** made this book into a film, which won the Silver Lion at the Venice Film Festival.

Little by little, West-Indian literature advanced, and a movement concentrating above all on the distinctive characteristics of the West Indian peoples took shape. The writings of **Aimé Césaire**, a Martinican born in Basse-Pointe (1913-), reject the canons of white literature, while focusing on and defending *"négritude,"* a term he uses to designate black culture as a whole.

"And mine the dances,
dances of the bad Negro
mine the dances
the dance which breaks the iron-collar
the dance which opens the prison
the dance it-is-good-and
right-and-glorious-to-be-a-Negro"

Césaire's work has had a considerable influence on French West Indian and African literature. Three of his most memorable works are *Cahier d'un retour au pays natal* (*Return to My Native Land*), from which the passage quoted above was taken; 1984's *Soleil cou coupé* (*Solar Throat Slashed*) and 1964's *La tragédie du roi Christophe* (*The Tragedy of King Christopher*).

Later, West-Indian writers stopped turning to Africa for inspiration and began concentrating on their own countries. This trend, known as *antillanité*, made rapid strides, with authors striving to evoke realities unique to island life. The father of this school was **Édouard Glissant** (1928-) of Sainte-Marie, whose novel *La Lézarde* won him the Prix Renaudot in 1958.

Antillanité has gradually given way to *créolité*, a movement focusing on Creole culture and language. Its leading figure is **Patrick Chamoiseau** (1953-), a Martinican whose novel *Texaco*, an extraordinary saga tracing the entire history of the island, was awarded the 1992 *Prix Goncourt*, thus bringing the movement public recognition. Chamoiseau was also one of the authors of *Éloge de la Créolité* (1989), along with linguist **Jean Bernabé** and novelist **Raphaël Confiant**, himself the author of several novels written entirely in Creole. Confiant also wrote the wonderful novel *L'Allée des Soupirs*, which

PORTRAIT

was nominated for the *Prix Goncourt* in 1994.

Music and Dance

From wild rhythms to romantic melodies, music breathes energy into every event in Martinique. It is an integral part of Martinican life and has taken on many different forms over the years, reflecting the island's cultural blend.

Of all the types of dance music found in the Antilles, one has made a name for itself around the world since the 1980s: *zouk*. Many consider *zouk* to be the first real trend in popular music to have originated in the French Antilles. Lively, even boisterous, and distinctly modern, this form of musical expression nevertheless has its roots in Antillean history and tradition.

These roots are evident in *gwo ka*, a form of music born in the hills of Guadeloupe, which bursts forth from wooden drums (up to 10 at a time!) and other percussion instruments made with shells. *Gwo ka* is still very much a part of the culture, enlivening the streets during Carnival, and generating celebrities like **Ti-Céleste**, **Esnard Boisdur**, **Eugène Mona**, etc.

Another forerunner of *zouk*, also heard often at Carnival time, is *chouval bwa*, which actually originated in Martinique. It is played on a battery of drums, the largest of which is known as a "bel-air". The group **Marcé et Tumpak** is considered the best representative of this form of music.

The *biguine* is definitely one of the most well-known types of music from the Antilles. A Martinican version of folk jazz, it dates back some 300 years. In the beginning, this music was only played on a few stringed instruments (guitars and banjos), and then drums borrowed from *chouval bwa* were used to punctuate its melodies. Later, clarinets and violins were added as well. The suggestive dance that grew up around this music is a blend of African dance steps and French ballroom dancing, and was all the rage in the twenties and thirties. In those years, clarinetist **Alexandre Stellio** was a major figure on the international jazz scene, as was **Sam Castandet**, who succeeded him as leader of the group **Orchestre Antillais**, which played in Paris up until the 1950s.

Cadence combines the strings of the *biguine* with the drums of the *chouval bwa* and *gwo ka*. Haitian musicians were mainly responsible for bringing this music to the public's attention. It was extremely popular throughout the Antilles in the fifties and sixties, and numerous Haitian *cadence* groups toured Martinique and Guadeloupe. In the seventies, *cadence* gradually evolved into what would later become *zouk*. The group **Exile One**, which moved to Guadeloupe from Dominica, added soul, rock, Latin and Afro-funk elements to traditional *cadence*. The singer of this group, **Gordon Henderson**, later founded a band called the **Vikings of Guadeloupe**. The name "viking" came to designate a musical style, which could be described as "progressive *cadence*" (there is another group known as the **Martiniquan Vikings**).

Perhaps the most noteworthy member of the Vikings of Guadeloupe is **Pierre Éduard Decimus**, one of the co-founders, along with heavy metal guitarist **Jacob Desvarieux**, of the group **Kassav'**, the dominant figure in the *zouk* movement. Founded in Paris in 1978, this legendary group originally consisted of only Guadeloupian musicians, but a number of Martinicans soon joined in, namely **Jean-Claude**

PORTRAIT

Naimro, **Claude Vamur**, **Jean-Philippe Martheny** and **Patrick Saint-Éloi**. It was Kassav' that put the French Antilles on the map as far as "world music" is concerned.

Since Kassav' disbanded, others have followed in the band's footsteps, like **West Indies Attitude** and **Kwak**, to name only two. One of Kassav's most important contributions was to renew interest in the roots of West Indian music. This revival benefitted musicians like **Kali** and his group **Patakak**, which play an interesting blend of *zouk* and modern jazz.

Other *zouk* and folk musicians have made a name for themselves in the wake of Kassav''s success, including flutists **Dédé Saint-Prix** and **Max Cilla**, pianist **George-Édouard Nouel**, radical nationalist singer **Joby Bernade** as well as **Sartana** and **Frankie Vincent**, also singers.

Perhaps most important of all are the extremely popular groups **Malavoi**, which has been playing a cheerful blend of *quadrille*, *gwo ka*, *zouk*, and *bossa nova* since the sixties, and **Zouk Machine**, which put out some smash hits in the late eighties. One of the three female singers from Zouk Machine's glory days, **Joelle Ursull**, is presently pursuing a brilliant solo career.

To learn more about West Indian music, or any other type of music from around the globe, we heartily recommend that you read *World Music*, a remarkable work published in England by Rough Guide.

Traditional Dress

Though today's young Martinican women follow the latest trends in fash-

ion, their ancestors used to dress according to a wide variety of clothing traditions. Spanish custom had them bare their shoulders, while their skirts were either cut in the French style, with a train, made of Indian madras (a brightly coloured fabric made of cotton and banana fibers) or decorated with English lace.

The traditional headdress, also made of madras, had different meanings depending on how it was tied. One point meant "I don't have a lover", two points, "My heart is taken", three points, "I'm married and don't need a lover" and four points, "I'm married, but you never know…"

Carnaval

Numerous competitions, including a beauty contest, take place in the month and a half leading up to *Carnaval*. The long-awaited festivities begin on the Sunday before Ash Wednesday, and liven up the streets for four days. *Carnaval* starts with a parade of floats, then musicians, peddlers, dancers, and of course residents flood into the streets and things really get going. On Wednesday, the festivities end with the burning of Vaval, an effigy of Carnival.

Cockfighting

Introduced to the West Indies by the Spanish, cockfights are held all over the island. Spectators gather around the *pitts* (packed dirt arenas) to watch two cocks battle it out. First, however, there is a ceremony in which the cocks are weighed and fitted with spurs and their owners are introduced. Then, each person in the audience places their bet on the one they think will win. Once the jury has decided which birds qual ify, the fight begins. In order to win, a cock has to kill its opponent.

ARCHITECTURE

First influenced by European models, West Indian architecture gradually forged its very own character, adopting, as is common worldwide, ways and forms to better withstand the particular climatic conditions and natural disasters likely to occur in the region.

Typical Martinican Houses

Martinique has seen a unique and greatly diverse residential architecture take shape on its territory. Nevertheless, if you look closely, these various kinds of houses – from the humble *case* (cabin or hut) to the *maison de maître* ("master's house") or the magnificent villa on Route de Didier – bare certain similarities .

These similarities are often dictated by climatic conditions. As such, certain basic principles must be respected in order to counter heat, rain and hurricanes. Hurricane-resistant features steep-sloping roofs are characteristic of all varieties of dwellings. Covered porches, partitions made of light materials, and full and slatted shutters, for their part, block the heat and the powerful rays of the sun.

Carbets and *Mouïnas*

None of the structures from Carib settlement circa European colonization remain in Martinique. Documents, however, reveal that the population resided in large communal cabins called *carbets* and that certain households lived in smaller cabins known as *mouïnas*. The first French colonists, for that matter, drew their inspiration from this architectural style when building their first homes, adopting the reed as a construction material and partitioning rooms in the same manner, separating the kitchen from the rest of the house for health and safety reasons.

The *Habitation* and the *Maison de Maître*

In the French West Indies, the term *"habitation"* refers to something more than a simple dwelling. In fact, it describes the whole estate, including the sugar-cane fields, the main house, the outbuildings (mill, sugar refinery, forge, stable, etc.) as well as the slave cabins, the latter set up along a part of the property known as "rues cases-nègres". It also housed the livestock, the tools – and the slaves themselves. As such, the "habitation", or plantation, consisted of all the planter's – or master's – "possessions".

In the heart of the plantation stood the *maison de maître*, or "master's house", where the landowner and his family resided. Though initially almost as modest as those of the workers and slaves, the "family mansion" became increasingly imposing and more and more complex in construction. Soon, more often than not, it became two-storied, with the upper floor usually set back, earning it the term "belvedere". Moreover, it borrowed architectural elements from regions whence the French colonists came from, while adapting them to the climatic conditions of the West Indies with four-sided and steep-sloping tiled roofs, full and slatted shutters.

Fine examples of such plantations and their master houses can be visited today. Notable among these are the **Habitation Pécoul** (1760) (see p 185) and the **Plantation de Leyritz** (see p 185), both located near Basse-Pointe,

Habitation Pécoul

as well as the **Domaine de Lajus** (1774) (see p 156), in Le Carbet, and the **Habitation Clément** (see p 130), in the vicinity of Le François.

The *Grand'case*

Across between the *maison de maître* and the *cases* is the *grand'case*, whose design was derived from African slaves. These buildings were made of indigenous wood, and sometimes materials imported from France were added to them, such as dressed stone. The tiled roof was steeply sloped and often graced with windows known as *chiens assis* (shed dormers). These openings, like those on the main floor, were covered with metal and full shutters as opposed to glass. The roof also had a wraparound shuttered porch. At the back, the house usually opened onto a large garden. The main house of the **Jardin de Balata** (see p 186) is an excellent example.

The *Case*

Common housing, known as *case* (hut or cabin) in the French West Indies, is symmetrical in design as far as the arrangement of doors and windows goes, and always 8 metres in width by 4 metres in depth. Most often painted in bright colours, the *case* generally consists of a single room.

In the past, particularly in southern Martinique, the walls of the *case* were made of poles, known here as *bois ti-baume* (type of spurge plant), coated with a cob of mud and even cow dung. Planks of indigenous wood, then concrete and fibrocement walls eventually replaced shingles. The two-sided roof, formerly composed of dried sugar-cane leaves, is now generally made of reeds, corrugated iron or tiles.

Case

Urban Housing

Martinique's cities, like most around the world, were built in order to meet the demands of growing economic activity. Thus, from the 19th century on, the expansion of cities and villages became inevitable, giving rise to the development of a type of housing specific to the inner city. At first, the farmers who came to settle in the city brought elements of rural architecture with them. The town centres nevertheless saw a new form of housing originate in the form of tall buildings, on account of the high value of the land. The main floor of these city dwellings, which consists of the living room and dining room, is made of stone, brick or concrete, for fire prevention. The upper floor, usually made of wood, is reserved for the bedrooms. This floor is most often graced with a wooden or cast-iron balcony, which also acts as a porch roof to the main floor. A side corridor leads to an indoor courtyard where the annexes are located, including the kitchen.

The Creole House

A typically West Indian type of housing emerged at the turn of the century: the Creole house. These are majestic wooden villas with classic lines, usually painted white and ideally suited to the tropical climate. A veranda surrounds the ground floor, serving as extra space and protecting the house from both rain and intense heat. Finally, a balcony gracefully adorns the top floor. The Plateau Didier district, in the hills of Fort-de-France, boasts magnificent examples of these charming houses.

To get a general idea of the various types of housing in Martinique, we recommend the very beautiful book *Maisons des Îles: Martinique*, by Brigitte Marry, Roland Suvélor and Jean-Luc de

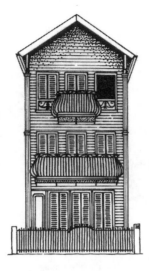

Urban house

Laguarine, co-published by Éditions Arthaud and the Fondation Clément.

Religious Architecture

All the churches in Martinique are of relatively recent construction, going back no further than the 18th century. Even those that old are usually only partly so. Fact is, churches have a hard life in Martinique, victims of numerous fires, past colonial wars, hurricanes, volcanic eruptions, earthquakes, etc.

Several of them are reminiscent of, though less elaborate than, 17th-century European churches. Their masonry façades were built on a wooden framework up until the mid-19th century. From then on, a metal substructure was more often used, particularly for bigger churches, as is the case with the **Cathédrale Saint-Louis** in Fort-de-France (1895) (see p 77), by architect Henri Picq.

In the majority of cases, Martinique churches are equipped with a single bell tower on the main structure itself and, more often than not, above the main door. Church design varies throughout the island – in towns such as **Le Carbet**, **Sainte-Anne**, **Diamant** and **Trois-Îlets** – and borrows from different styles (baroque, neoclassicism, etc.), but systematically follows the basic bell-tower pattern. This pattern runs counter to the Guadeloupian model, where the bell tower is built next to the church so that the whole better withstands hurricanes and earthquakes. Martinique nevertheless boasts a few churches built according to the latter principle, in the towns of **Grand'Rivière**, **Le Marin** and **Ajoupa-Bouillon**.

Martinique's modern churches, however, have broken away from these standard designs and display a harmonius combination of forms and styles. Among these is the stunning **Église de Balata** (1926; Charles-Albert Wulfleff, architect) (see p 182), a

Creole house

scaled-down replica of the famous Basilique du Sacré-Cœur in Paris, and the futurist **Église Saint-Michel-du-François** (1973) (see p 129), by Martinican architect Marc Alie.

Institutional Architecture

In Martinique, the architecture of official buildings draws heavily from French metropolitan models. Such buildings are thus often graced with lines characteristic of French-style classicism. Among these are the **former Hôtel de Ville** (1901) (see p 78), the **Palais de Justice**, or courthouse, (1907) (see p 78) and the **Hôtel de la Préfecture** (1925-1928; Charles-Albert Wulfleff, architect) (see p 77), all in Fort-de-France.

Architect Henri Picq, however, took an altogether different approach with his unclassifiable **Bibliothèque Schœlcher** (1889-1893) (see p 76), also in Fort-de-France. Picq gave this magnificent building that rests on a metal substructure, a more unique style by cleverly employing innovations from the Industrial Revolution. The **central factories** that were built in Martinique in this era, as well as the **covered markets** (Saint-Pierre, Lamentin, etc.), were also similarly constructed.

More recently, attempts to modernize institutional architecture have not always been the greatest success stories. One example is the **Centre Administratif et Culturel de Fort-de-France** (1990; Marc Alie, architect) (see p 79). On the other hand, the newly built **air terminal of the Lamentin airport** (1995; Dominique Chavanne architect) is a brilliant triumph.

PRACTICAL INFORMATION

T his chapter is intended to provide you with all the information you will need to prepare for your trip to Martinique.

ENTRANCE FORMALITIES

Passport and Visa

You must have a valid passport to enter Martinique. This requirement does not apply, however, to French tourists, who need only present their national identification card.

Canadians, Americans and members of the E.E.C. are admitted without a visa for stays of up to three months.

In addition, all travellers except French citizens must have an ongoing or return ticket.

As these regulations are subject to change at any time, we recommend that you verify them with the French embassy or consulate nearest you before leaving on your trip.

Customs

North Americans over the age of 18 are allowed to bring one litre of liquor containing over 22% alcohol and two litres of wine into the country, as well as 200 cigarettes, 100 cigarillos, 50 cigars, or 250 g of tobacco.

Tourists from the E.E.C. are allowed to bring in 1.5 litres of alcohol, four litres of wine and 300 cigarettes, 150 cigarillos, 75 cigars, or 400 g of tobacco.

EMBASSIES AND CONSULATES IN MARTINIQUE

Not every country is represented in Martinique, in this case the closest representation is given.

Australia
Australian High Commission: Bishop's Court Hill, St. Michael, PO Box 396, B r i d g e t o w n ,   B a r b a d o s , ☎(246) 435-2834, ◄(246) 435-2896..

Belgium
Belgian Consulate: Immeuble UAP, Centre Dillon Valmenière, Fort-de-France 97200, ☎05.96.59.50.50.

Canada
Canadian High Commission: Maple House, 3-3A Sweet Briar Road, PO Box 1246, Port-of-Spain, Trinidad and T o b a g o ,   ☎(868)   6 2 2 - 6 2 3 2 , ◄(868) 628-1830.

Denmark
13 Rue Victor-Sévère, 97200 Fort-de-F r a n c e ,   ☎0 5 . 9 6 . 7 1 . 3 8 . 8 6 , ◄05.96.60.48.43.

Finland
Goddard Enterprises, Carlisle House, Hincks Street, Bridgetown, Barbados, ☎(246) 436-1820, ◄(246) 436-8934.

Germany
Z.I. Mangles Acajou, 97232 Le Lamentin, ☎05.96.50.37.56.

Great Britain
British Consulate: Le Petit Pavois, 96 Route du Phare, 97200 Fort-de-France,   ☎05.96.61.56.30, ◄05.96.61.33.89.

Italy
28 Boulevard Allègre, 97200 Fort-de-France, ☎05.96.70.54.75.

Netherlands
Consulate: 44 Avenue Maurice-Bishop, 97200 Fort-de-France, ☎05.96.63.30.04, ◄05.96.63.42.65.

Norway
Royal Norwegian Consulate: Sodjm, Acajou, 97232 Le Lamentin, ☎05.96.58.91.02, ◄05.96.58.91.29.

Spain
Lotissement Hauts de Frégate, 97240 Le François, ☎05.96.54.27.79.

Sweden
Etablissement Louis Crocquet, Kerlys, Rue Saint Christophe, 97207 Fort-de-France,   ☎05.96.60.75.78, ◄05.96.73.54.94.

Switzerland
Centre d'Affaires Californie, ZI de la Jambette, 97232 Le Lamentin, ☎05.96.50.12.43.

United States
Embassy: 15 Queen's Park West, PO Box 752 Port-of-Spain, Trinidad and Tobago, ☎(809) 622-6362, ◄(809) 628-5462.

FRENCH AND MARTINICAN TOURIST OFFICES ABROAD

Australia
Maison de La France: BNP Building, 12th Floor, 12 Castlereagh Street, Sydney NSW 2000, ☎(2) 231.52.44, ◄(2) 221.86.82.

Belgium
Maison de la France: 21 Avenue de la Toison-d'Or, 1060 Bruxelles, ☎(02) 513.07.62, ◄(02) 502.33.75.

Canada
Martinican Tourist Office: 2155 Mackay, Montreal, Quebec, H3G 2J2, ☎(514) 844-8566, ◄(514) 844-8904.

France
Office de Tourisme de la Martinique: 2 Rue des Moulins, 75001 Paris, ☎01.44.77.86.00, ⇴01.49.26.03.63.

Antilles Voyages Atmosphère: Official travel agency for Martinique with central reservation service; 2 Rue des Moulins, 75001 Paris, ☎01.44.77.86.11, ⇴01.49.26.03.63.

Germany
Maison de La France: Westendstrasse 47, 60325 Frankfurt Am Main, ☎(69) 75.60.83.30, ⇴(69) 75.21.87.

Mailing address: Maison de La France, Postfach 100128, 60001 Frankfurt/Main.

Great Britain
Maison de la France: 178 Picadilly, London WIV OAL, ☎(171) 493.55.76, ⇴(171) 493.65.94.

Italy
Maison de la France: Via Larga 7, 20122 Milano, ☎(2) 58.31.66.10, ⇴(2) 58.31.65.79.

Netherlands
Maison de la France: Prinsengracht 670-1017 KX, Amsterdam, ☎(20) 627.33.18, ⇴(20) 620.33.39.

Norway
Maison de la France: Storgaten 10A, 0155 Oslo, ☎(22) 42.15.55, ⇴(22) 42.29.44.

Spain
Maison de La France: Gran Via de los Corts Catalanes 656, Barcelona 08010, ☎(3) 302.05.82, ⇴(3) 317.29.71.

Maison de La France: Alcala 63, Madrid 28014, ☎(1) 576.31.44, ⇴(1) 577.13.16.

Sweden
Martinique Commercial Representative Office: PO Box 4031 Fregattvägen 14, S.18.1.04 Lindingö Sueden, ☎(87) 65.58.65, ⇴(87) 65.93.60.

Maison de la France: Norrmalmstorg 1 Av., S11146 Stockholm, ☎(8) 679.79.75, ⇴(8) 611.30.75.

Switzerland
Maison de la France: 2 Rue Thalberg, 1201 Genève, ☎(22) 732.86.10, ⇴(22) 731.58.73

Maison de la France: Löwenstrasse 59, Postfach 7226, 8023 Zurich, ☎(1) 211.30.85, ⇴(1) 212.16.44.

United States
Martinique Promotion & Development Bureau: 444 Madison Avenue, 16th floor, N.Y. 10022, ☎(212) 838-7800, ⇴(212) 838-7855.

Maison de la France: 9454 Wilshire Boulevard, Suite 715, Beverly Hills, CA, 90212-2967, ☎(310) 271-6665, ⇴(310) 276-2835.

Maison de la France: 676 North Michigan Avenue, Suite 3360, Chicago, IL, 60611-2819, ☎(312) 751-7800, ⇴(312) 337-6339.

TOURIST INFORMATION

You will have no trouble finding all the tourist information you need in Martinique. Most villages on the island have a *syndicat d'initiative* (tourist office) to welcome visitors and provide them with information. Throughout this guide, we will provide you with the telephone number and address of the tourist office in the area being described.

In addition, the *Office Départementale du Tourisme de la Martinique* is located on the waterfront in Fort-de-France:

Office Départemental du Tourisme de la Martinique: Rue Ernest Deproge - Bord de mer, B.P. 520 - 97200 Fort-de-France, ☎05.96.63.79.60, ⊷05.96.73.66.93.

Martinique on the Web

There are several interesting Internet sites where you can find all sorts of information about Martinique. The French-language *Martinique; le guide* (www.sasi.fr/guidemartinique), has scores of hotels, restaurants, nightclubs, etc.

The trilingual (English, French, German) French West Indies Net (www.fwinet.com) has a major section on Martinique. Among its features is a click-on map providing information about the island's various communes.

New York's Martinique Promotion Bureau (www.martinique.org), in both English and French, can be regarded as Martinique's official web site. Historical outline; description of attractions; hotel, restaurant and nightclub listings.

Guided Tours

Some companies specialize in organizing guided tours all over the island, as well as arranging sea excursions. Here are a few:

STT Voyages: 23 Rue Blénac, Fort-de-France, ☎05.96.71.68.12 or 73.32.00.

Caribjet: Lamentin Airport, ☎05.96.51.90.00.

Caribtours: Marina Pointe du Bout, Trois-Îlets, ☎05.96.66.04.48, ⊷05.96.66.07.06.

Madinina Tours: 89 Rue Blénac, Fort-de-France, ☎05.96.70.65.25, ⊷05.96.73.09.53.

 GETTING TO MARTINIQUE

By Plane

Most tourists arrive in Martinique by plane. The island has only one international airport, located southeast of the departmental capital, Fort-de-France.

Lamentin Airport
☎05.96.42.16.00

In the airport lobby, you'll find a branch of the **Office Départemental du Tourisme** *(☎05.96.42.18.05 or 05.96.42.18.06)*, a counter of **Caribjet** *(☎05.96.51.89.80 or 05.96.51.90.00)* where you can inquire about guided tours, and an information centre run by the **Chambre de Commerce et d'Industrie** *(☎05.96.51.56.26)*.

You'll also find a foreign exchange office, **Change Caraïbes** *(☎05.96.42.17.11)*, as well as a **baggage-check counter and lockers** *(☎05.96.42.18.70)*.

The following car rental agencies also have offices at the airport:

Avis Lam	☎05.96.42.16.92
Budget	☎05.96.42.16.79
Carib Rent A Car	☎05.96.51.15.15
Europcar	☎05.96.42.16.88
Hertz	☎05.96.42.16.90
Pop's Car	☎05.96.42.16.84
Thrifty	☎05.96.42.16.99

You can take advantage of a variety of telephone information services whose recorded messages change from one day to the next. The following two might be useful:

Arrivals/Departures: all destinations, ☎08.36.68.43.14.

Departures: domestic and international flights ☎08.36.68.43.12.

Arrivals: domestic and international flights, ☎08.36.68.43.13.

The Lamentin airport was thoroughly restructured over the last few years. The run-down air terminal built in 1965 was replaced by a modern and considerably more spacious (28,000 square metres) building, which officially opened on July 12, 1995. Built in 25 months at a cost of 632 million francs, this new terminal building has enabled the airport to accommodate twice the number of passengers, up to 2,5 million per year.

Lamentin Airport is no longer served by Air Canada, which up until a few years ago offered daily flights between Montreal and Toronto and Fort-de-France. There is, however, a weekly flight to Point-à-Pitre in Guadeloupe, which can be taken with an inter-island connection (on Air Guadeloupe, for example). North Americans can also fly to Martinique on Air France, via Miami, or on American Airlines, from New York via San Juan, Puerto Rico. BWIA and Air Martinique jointly offer flights from New York as well. During the high season, charter companies like Air Transat and Royal provide direct flights from Canada. American FlyAway Vacations and Jet Vacations both offer packages from the U.S.

Air France, Air Liberté and Corsair offer daily flights between Paris and Fort-de-France, whereas the latter also offers flights from other cities in France (Bordeaux, Lyon, Lille, etc.) depending on the time of year. The company AOM provides regular service to Fort-de-France from Orly-Sud.

Air Guadeloupe, American Airlines and Liat are the other airlines serving Lamentin Airport. Air France, Air Guadeloupe and Liat also provide service between Martinique and other Caribbean islands.

Air Guadeloupe even offers a 7-day (1,490F) or 14-day (1,990F) *Pass Caraïbes*, so you can explore several Caribbean islands (Martinique, Guadeloupe, Saint-Martin, Saint-Barts, Les Saintes, Marie-Galante, Puerto Rico, Hispaniola, etc.) provided you have first taken a transatlantic flight to Fort-de-France, Pointe-à-Pitre or Saint-Martin.

Aside from taxis and shuttles intended for travellers with all-included vacation packages, there is no public transportation from the airport to Fort-de-France or anywhere else on the island. As taxis can prove very expensive (80F to Fort-de-France, 160F to Trois-Îlets or Le Diamant, 270F to Saint-Anne, 160F to Trinité; rates are higher in the evening), many travellers heading elsewhere than Fort-de-France rent their own car, which is in many ways a more practical option, even for a day. The other solution is to hitchhike, but there is stiff competition.

By Boat

Another increasingly popular way of visiting Martinique is by cruise ship. Many of these, usually based in New York or Florida, crisscross the Caribbean, and one of their ports of call is of course Fort-de-France. Among these cruise lines, you might try Celebrity

PRACTICAL INFORMATION

Cruises, Costa Cruises, Cunard Lines, Fantasy Cruises, Holland America Lines, Norwegian Cruise Lines or Royal Caribbean Cruise. Ask your travel agent about air/sea packages.

There is also a rather original way of getting to Martinique from France – aboard a banana ship that can accommodate about ten passengers. The trip takes seven days and there are weekly departures. For more information, call the Société Sotromat in Paris (☎01.49.24.24.00).

Finally, ferries shuttle back and forth between Fort-de-France and Guadeloupe, Dominica, Les Saintes and St. Lucia. Rates for adults range from 305F to 450F one-way. In Fort-de-France, the boats set out from the Quai Ouest, at the entrance of the dry dock. For departure times and exact fares, contact **L'Express des Îles** (☎05.96.63.12.11, ☎05.96.63.34.47).

INSURANCE

Cancellation Insurance

Your travel agent will usually offer you cancellation insurance when you purchase your airplane ticket or vacation package. This insurance guarantees reimbursement for the cost of the ticket or package in case the trip has to be cancelled due to serious illness or death. Travellers with no health problems are unlikely to require such protection, and should weigh its advantages carefully.

Theft Insurance

Most homeowner's insurance policies in North America cover some personal possessions, even if they are stolen abroad. In order to file a claim, you must have a police report. Depending on what is covered in your policy, it is not always necessary to take out additional insurance. European travellers, on the other hand, should make sure their policies protect their property in foreign countries, as this is not always the case.

Health Insurance

This is without question the most useful kind of insurance for travellers, and should be purchased before leaving. Look for the most complete coverage possible, because health care costs in foreign countries can add up quickly. When you buy your policy, make sure it provides adequate coverage for all types of potentially costly medical expenses, such as hospitalization, nursing services and doctor's fees. It should also include a repatriation clause in case necessary care cannot be administered on site. In addition, as you may have to pay upon leaving the clinic, you should check your policy to see what provisions it includes for such cases. During your stay in Martinique, you should always keep proof that you are insured on your person, as it will save you a lot of trouble if you are unlucky enough to require health care.

Life Insurance

Many credit cards offer life insurance when used to buy plane tickets. In addition, many travellers already have a life insurance policy. In these cases it is not necessary to obtain life insurance coverage.

CLIMATE

The average temperature in Martinique is around 26°C. The heat is never oppressive, as it is tempered by the steady, refreshing *alizés*, or trade winds, from the east and northeast. The most popular tourist period is roughly from December to May, when the temperature is pleasantly mild. This is known as the *carême* or dry season, as opposed to the rainy season, which lasts from June to November.

The rainy season, though marked by heavy downpours, is the hottest time of the year, with an average temperature of 30°C. Oddly, this season is also known as the *hivernage* (wintering). The hurricane risk is much higher during this period, especially in August and September. Fortunately, these storms are rare, but the extensive damage caused by hurricane David in August 1979 and hurricane Klaus in October 1990 is proof of their devastating force.

Ocean swimming is possible year-round in Martinique, as the water temperature (27°C on average) fluctuates only two or three degrees from one season to the next.

Packing

Regardless of the season, pack loose, light cotton clothing. A bathing suit is of course essential, and if you plan on exploring the tropical rainforest or climbing Montagne Pelée, bring a pair of walking shoes. A light sweater for air conditioned rooms and high altitudes, and a raincoat, especially if you're visiting Martinique during the rainy season, might also prove useful. Bring some more formal clothes for evenings out, in restaurants or at the casino.

Finally, make sure to bring a pair of sunglasses, some sunscreen and a hat.

HEALTH

Vaccinations are not necessary before entering Martinique. Tourists arriving from regions contaminated by yellow fever are, however, required to be immunized against this disease.

Martinique has modern sanitary facilities, so it is generally safe and easy to obtain medical care in one of the island's 18 hospitals or numerous clinics.

Illnesses

The water is potable all over the island, and thus poses no risk to your health.

If you do get diarrhea, though, there are several means of treating it. Try to soothe your digestive system by avoiding solids and drinking carbonated beverages, bottled water, tea or coffee (with no milk) until your symptoms ease up. Drink a lot of liquids to avoid dehydration, which can be dangerous. To remedy severe dehydration, try drinking a solution made up of one litre of water, three teaspoons of salt and one of sugar. You can also find ready-made preparations in most pharmacies. Next, gradually start reintroducing solids into your diet by eating easy-to-digest foods. Medications like Imodium can help control some intestinal disorders. If your symptoms are severe (high fever, violent diarrhoea) you may need antibiotics, so consult a doctor. Food and climate can also cause various problems. You should always make sure that food, especially meat or fish, is fresh and that the preparation area is clean. It is highly unlikely, however, that you will encounter any problems of this sort in Martinique. Proper hygiene, such as washing your hands frequently, will help keep you healthy.

In the tropics, still bodies water are often contaminated with the bacteria that causes schistosomiasis. This illness, caused by a parasite which invades the body and attacks the liver and nervous system, is difficult to treat. Swimming in unmoving fresh water should be avoided to minimize the chances of being infected.

Remember that excessive alcohol consumption can cause severe dehydration and lead to health problems, especially when accompanied by lengthy exposure to the sun. Consequently, it is advisable to drink only in moderation.

Furthermore, here as in other places, cases of AIDS and certain venereal diseases have been reported. It is therefore wise to take the necessary precautions.

Manchineel Trees

The gorgeous beach at Grande Anse des Salines, on the southernmost part of the island, is what attracts most visitors to Martinique. However, one of the plant species that grows along this beach is the dangerous manchineel tree (in French, *mancenillier*), which belongs to the spurge family. The sap of this tree is highly poisonous and can cause serious burns. Be especially careful to avoid the liquid that comes out when one of its leaves or branches is broken or its fruit, which looks like a small apple, is split open.

Also, don't make the mistake of standing under this tree to shelter yourself from the sun or, even worse, the rain.

Manchineel trees are usually marked with a red paint stripe, which makes them easy to spot. The *Office National des Forêts* has not, however, marked all of them. You should therefore to take a good look at those bearing the stripe so you'll be able to recognize the others. It can be identified by its small round green leaves bisected by a yellow vein. If, in spite of taking all the necessary precautions, you burn yourself on manchineel sap, consult a doctor immediately.

Insects

All over the island, you'll find a great many insects, which can be very unpleasant. A good insect repellent is essential. To reduce the risk of being bitten, cover up well, avoid brightly coloured clothing and don't wear perfume. Insects are more active at sundown. Shoes and socks that protect your feet and legs are very practical for hiking in the forest and mountains. It's also advisable to bring along ointment to relieve irritation caused by insect bites.

The Sun

In spite of its benefits, the sun can cause numerous problems. Always take along sunblock to protect yourself from the sun's harmful rays. Many of the sunscreens available on the market do not provide adequate protection, so before setting off on your trip, ask your pharmacist which ones are truly effective against the dangerous rays of the sun. Overexposure to the sun can cause sunstroke, which is characterized by dizziness, vomiting and fever. Cover yourself well and avoid prolonged exposure, especially for the first few days of your trip, as it takes a while to get used to the tropical sun. Even once you are used to the sun's intensity, moderate exposure is best. Wearing a hat and sunglasses can help shield you from the harmful effects of the sun. Lastly, don't forget that sunscreens are most effective when applied 20 to 30 minutes before exposure to the sun.

The First Aid Kit

A small first aid kit can help you avoid many difficulties. It is best to prepare it carefully before setting off on your trip. Make sure to take along a sufficient supply of all medicines you take regularly, as well as a valid prescription in case you lose them. Other medicines, such as malaria pills and Imodium (or its equivalent) should be purchased before leaving. In addition, don't forget to bring adhesive bandages, a disinfectant, pain relievers, antihistamines, condoms, an extra pair of prescription glasses and medicine for stomach upsets.

SAFETY AND SECURITY

You should take the same precautions in Martinique as you would anywhere else. Keep your passport, traveller's checks and credit cards with you at all times. Avoid bringing valuables to the beach, but if you must, keep an eye on them. Most hotel rooms are, however, equipped with a small safe in which you can store valuable objects and papers.

You should pack a copy of your passport and your traveller's itinerary, as well as a list of the serial numbers of your traveller's checks. If ever the originals are lost or stolen, knowing their reference numbers will make it much easier to replace them.

Although Martinique is not a dangerous country, it has its share of thieves. Don't forget that to many people, your camera equipment, leather suitcases, jewellery and other possessions represent a lot of money. A certain degree of caution can save you a lot of trouble, it's in your best interest to wear little or no jewellery, keep your electronic equipment in a plain bag slung across your shoulder and avoid showing the contents of your wallet when paying for a purchase. You can conceal your traveller's checks, passport and some of your cash in a money belt. Remember, the less attention you attract, the less you risk being robbed.

MAIL AND TELECOMMUNICATIONS

You can buy stamps at any post office, and also at the major hotels. Airmail is collected on a daily basis.

Martinique has a well-developed telephone system. You'll have no trouble finding public telephones which operate with coins or, more often, cards. These cards, known as *télécartes*, are available at the post office and at easily identifiable shops.

To call Martinique from Canada or the States, dial 011 596 and then the local number; from France, 05.96 and then the number; from Great Britain, 010 596 and then the number, and from Belgium, the Netherlands or Switzerland, 00 596 and then the number.

Discount rates are available at certain times of the day. These are usually late in the evening and early in the morning. Check with your phone company.

To call Canada from Martinique, dial 001, the area code and then the local number. The United States can be reached by dialing 001, the area code and then the local number. If you're calling Belgium, dial 00 32 and then the number. For Switzerland, dial 00 41 before the number. Dial 00 31 and the number if you wish to call the Netherlands. To reach France, simply dial the 10-digit number that begins either with 01 (Paris and greater Paris), 02 (northwest), 03 (northeast), 04 (southeast) or 05 (southwest). Finally, British citizens can call home by dialing 00 44 and the number.

Useful Numbers	
Emergency	☎17
Fire Department	☎18
Information	☎12
Lamentin Airport	☎42.16.00
Sea-rescue	☎71.92.92
Telephoned Telegrams	☎36.55
Time	☎36.99
Weather (Airport)	☎08.36.68.97.20

Canadian travellers can also call home through Canada Direct and pay cheaper rates than regular long distance. To reach this service in Martinique, dial ☎0.800.99.00.16. A Canadian operator will then direct your call. Rates and access numbers are subject to change at any time, so check them with Canada Direct before leaving at ☎1-800-561-8868, or by visiting www.stentor.ca/canada_direct.

In addition, most hotels offer fax and telex services.

TRANSPORTATION

Roads

Martinique's roads are extremely well-maintained and extend to most points on the island. You will, however, come across some very narrow, winding roads, which can be somewhat disconcerting, especially because islanders accustomed to these conditions, often drive very quickly.

The only really poorly maintained roads on the island are the ones leading to some of the lovely properties on the Atlantic coast (Le François, Le Robert). Supposedly, this neglect is intentional on the part of the owners, who wish to discourage curious passersby from poking around their homes. These roads are therefore known as *chemins de békés* (*béké* roads).

There are two main kinds of roads, *Routes Nationales*, which usually have several lanes, and *Routes Départementales*, which are narrower, with only one lane in each direction. In addition, some of the secluded beaches of the southeast coast and a few of the more isolated spots on the island are only accessible on dirt roads, for which all-terrain vehicles are more appropriate than standard automobiles. In most cases, the roads are not lit at night.

The road signs are also good, although some are hidden behind branches, which is clearly the price Martinicans have to pay for living on an island with such spectacular vegetation. In addition, signs for some sights, including a few of the most interesting ones, are missing. Throughout this guide, we will try to make up for these minor shortcomings.

A Few Tips

Driving and the Highway Code: North Americans are advised that at intersections, priority is given to cars arriving on the right, regardless of which driver stopped first. Stop signs and traffic lights are rare; however, major roads are served by round-abouts and cars

Table of Distances (km)
Via the shortest route

	Trinité	Sainte-Anne	Saint-Pierre	Morne-Rouge	Le François	Grand'Rivière	Fort-de-France	Diamant	Anses-d'Arlet	
										Anses-d'Arlet
									7	Diamant
								26	32	Fort-de-France
							44	70	74	Grand'Rivière
						52	21	28	34	Le François
					42	23	22	48	54	Morne-Rouge
				7	43	30	22	48	54	Saint-Pierre
			65	65	28	74	43	28	36	Sainte-Anne
		42	45	32	18	32	23	38	44	Trinité
Trois-Îlets	36	33	46	46	25	68	24	15	10	Trois-Îlets

Example: The distance between Le François and Sainte-Anne is 28km.

within them always have priority. Therefore, wait for the way to completely clear before entering the roundabout.

A road map will make it easier for you to find your way around the island. The best one available, by far, is published by the *Institut Géographique National* (IGN), and is available in travel bookstores (scale: 1:100 000).

Watch out for the numerous speed bumps (*dos d'ânes* – or donkey's backs) on the roads both near and in the cities, which serve the laudable purpose of slowing down traffic to protect pedestrians. If you're not careful, however, you won't see the sign warning you to slow down until after you've hit the speed bump, which is obviously a little hard on your car. If you have your wits about you, you'll have just enough time to slam on the brakes at the last second.

You might also encounter various domestic animals on the road, not only cats and dogs, but quite often goats, hens and roosters as well. Again, a minimum of caution can prevent an accident.

A litre of gas costs about 6.10F in Martinique. By North American standards, this is expensive, so you're bound to be surprised by the bill the first time you fill up your tank. For Europeans, however, this is the regular price.

Car Rentals

All international car rental agencies have branches in Martinique, and you can find most of them at Lamentin Airport (see p 38). You can also rent a car wherever you happen to be on the island. Throughout this guide, we'll do our best to provide you with the names and addresses of car rental agencies all over Martinique. You'll find this information in the "Finding Your Way Around" section of each chapter.

In addition to standard automobiles, several agencies (including Hertz) rent four-wheel drive vehicles, often convertibles. It can be very pleasant to drive along the island's winding roads in one of these, the wind in your hair and the sun warming your skin. Having four-wheel drive also makes it easier to reach isolated areas, such as the beaches on the southeast coast, certain spots in the north, and inland, in the heart of the tropical rainforest.

All you need to rent a car in Martinique is your country's driver's license. You must, however, be 21 or older.

Renting a small car costs about 360F per day (unlimited mileage) or 2,160F per week.

Motorcycle and Scooter Rentals

The idea of travelling the island's roads on a motorcycle or a scooter appeals to many people. Doing so will cost between 115 F and 210 F per day. You are required by law to wear a helmet. The following agencies specialize in renting this type of vehicle:

Funny
80 Rue Ernest Deproge, Fort-de-France
☎05.96.63.33.05.

Discount
Pointe du Bout - 97229 Trois-Îlets,
☎05.96.66.05.58.

Sud Loisirs
Sainte-Anne, ☎05.96.76.81.82.

Sainte-Luce Location
Sainte-Luce, ☎05.96.62.49.66.

Public Transportation

There are two kinds of public transportation in Martinique : buses and collective taxis.

Buses

Buses only serve the immediate outskirts of Fort-de-France, mostly via Boulevard du Général-de-Gaulle.

Collective Taxis

Collective taxis are without question more versatile and more colourful than buses. These vehicles, nicknamed "weed-killers", serve every village on the island. A number of them leave from the Pointe Simon station on the waterfront in Fort-de-France and then stop when signaled, while the different villages are linked by other routes.

There are shelters all along the road where you can wait for a collective taxi to pass. You can catch one anywhere, however, simply by waving to the driver, who will pull over if there is enough room for you, which is often not the case.

Collective taxis start running very early in the morning, but stop at 6pm. To give you an idea of the prices, it costs 17F to go from Fort-de-France to Trois-Îlets, 19F to Le Diamant, 31F to Saint-Anne, 18F to Saint-Pierre and 40F to Grand-Rivière.

Hitchhiking

Hitchhiking is one of the most popular means of transportation on the island, most probably because collective taxis don't really follow any fixed schedule and are often overcrowded. Furthermore, as islanders often stick out their thumb while waiting for a collective taxi to pass by, these two ways of getting around are in fact complementary.

Hitchhiking can be an interesting way of meeting people while travelling. Unfortunately, this practice is also fraught with obvious risks. Indeed, attacks are an all-too-common occurrence, particularly on women travelling alone. Exercising caution is therefore absolutely necessary at all times.

Taxis

Taxis are a perfectly good alternative to other types of transportation, especially for short trips. They tend to be a little expensive for travelling from one city to another (for an idea of prices leaving from the airport, see p 39).

Taxis are obviously easy to find at the airport, and near the major hotels. As well, in Fort-de-France, they are available near the sea or near Place de la Savane.

Ferries

Ferries run regularly between Fort-de-France and the main resorts on the island, thus avoiding the heavy traffic both coming and going from Martinique's departmental capital. On top of this advantage, taking the ferry is a different way to discover the island, almost an attraction in itself.

As well, four ferries (pedestrians only) run between Quai Desnambuc in Fort-de-France and the marina in Pointe du Bout. This service is managed by the *Société Somatour* (☎05.96.75.05.53). The fares are as follows:

adults (one-way)	19F
children (one-way)	10F
adults (round trip)	29F
children (round trip)	15F

From Fort-de-France to Pointe du Bout: 6:30am, 8am, 9am, 10am, 11am, 12:15pm, 1:15pm, 3pm, 4pm, 5pm, 6pm, 7pm, 8pm, and 11:15pm

From Pointe du Bout to Fort-de-France: 6:10am, 7:15am, 8:30am, 9:30am, 10:30am, 11:30am, 12:45pm, 2:30pm, 3:30pm, 4:30pm, 5:30pm, 6:30pm, 7:30pm, 10:45pm, and 11:45pm

The **Société Madinina** *(☎05.96.63.06.46)* has three ferries which run between Fort-de-France,

l'Anse Mitan and l'Anse à l'Âne. During the July and August vacations, a boat links Fort-de-France and Sainte-Anne. Schedule varies, prices are similar to Somatour.

Sailing fans will find boat rental possibilities all over the island, varying from little ships to yachts with skippers.

 MONEY AND BANKING

The local currency is the French franc (F), equal to 100 centimes. There are 5, 10 and 20 centime pieces in circulation, as well as and 1/2, 1, 2, 5, 10 and 20 F coins and 20, 100, 200 and 500 F bills.

All prices in this guide are quoted in French francs.

Banks

Banks usually offer the best exchange rates when converting foreign currency into francs. Most banks in Martinique are open Monday to Friday from 8am to noon and 2:30pm to 4:30pm and are closed in the afternoon preceding any public holiday (see list, p 58).

Foreign Exchange Offices

You can also exchange money at one of Change Caraïbe's two branches. One is located at Lamentin Airport (see p 38), and the other on Rue Ernest-Deproge in Fort-de-France.

If the banks and exchange offices are all closed, you can always exchange money at one of the major hotels, though the rates won't be nearly as good.

Exchange Rates

$1 CAN	= 3.69 F	1 F =	$0.27 CAN
$1 US	= 5.64 F	1 F =	$0.17 US
1 Euro	= 6.58 F	1 F =	0.15 Euro
£1	= 9.50 F	1 F =	0.11 £
$1 Aust	= 3.30 F	1 F =	$0.30 Aust
1 DM	= 3.35 F	1 F =	0.29 DM
1000 lire	= 3.39 F	1 F =	294.44 lire
100 pesetas	= 3.94 F	1 F =	25.31 pesetas
1 SF	= 4.06 F	1 F =	0.24 SF
1 BF	= 0.16 F	1 F =	6.15 BF
1 fl	= 2.97 F	1 F =	0.34 fl

Credit Cards and Traveller's Cheques

Major credit cards are accepted in the vast majority of shops, restaurants and hotels in Fort-de-France, as well as in popular tourist areas (except in some of the more modest establishments). Elsewhere on the island, however, the situation can be otherwise. You should therefore never assume you can pay by credit card without asking first.

It is not always easy to pay with travellers' cheques, since some shops have a policy of refusing them. Nevertheless, they can come in handy. Keep in mind, though, that you have to cash them at the bank or in a currency exchange office.

Most bank machines also accept Visa and MasterCard; small charges do apply, but you will usually receive a better exchange rate than in the banks or at exchange offices. And, you can get money whenever you want, since these machines are open all day, every day. Also, you can use your bank card to withdraw money from any automatic teller machine with the Interac, Cirrus or Plus logo.

TAXES AND TIPPING

Service charges and taxes are always included in the bill, whether it be in a restaurant, at a hotel or for a taxi. It is nevertheless polite, especially at a restaurant, to leave a tip, depending of course on the service.

 ACCOMMODATIONS

There are all sorts of accommodations in Martinique, from "Club Formula" vacation villages to *gîtes ruraux*, from luxury hotels to furnished lodgings and *Relais créoles*.

In this guide, we have listed what we believe to be the best accommodations in each category. The prices quoted were in effect during high season when this guide went to press, and are clearly subject to change at any time. Unless otherwise indicated, these rates apply to the cost of a room for two people, taxes included.

Each listing also includes a complete address, telephone number and fax in order to assist you in making reservations from home.

You can, however, always call on the services of the *Centrale de Réservation de la Martinique*, which can also arrange car rentals and make reservations for a variety of excursions:

Reservations: B.P. 823 - 97208 Fort-de-France Cédex, ☎05.96.71.56.11 or 05.96.63.79.60, ⌐05.96.63.11.64.

Luxury Hotels

There are several luxury hotels on the island, many located in the Fort-de-France area (the Batelière, the Squash, the Valmenière) and, above all, in the south (the Méridien, the Bakoua, the Novotel, the Frantour, Manoir Beauregard). These three- and four-star hotels meet all the international standards of comfort and convenience.

Some of these hotel complexes are practically luxury vacation villages, following the example of the extremely well-known Club Med Les Boucaniers at Pointe Marin in Sainte-Anne. Club Med, like a few other places on the island, offers its clientele the "Club Formula" – an all-inclusive rate covering a wide range of activities, meals and even drinks.

Small and Medium-Sized Hotels

There are a large number of small and medium-sized accommodations scattered all over the island, a number of which are known as *Relais créoles*. These are often as well-located as the luxury hotels (near the beach, with lovely views, etc.), but are more of a bargain. In some cases, the rooms or bungalows include kitchenettes.

Furnished Lodgings and Residential Hotels

These are two very similar options. In both instances, guests stay in fully equipped (kitchenette, refrigerator, dishwasher, etc.) studios or apartments.

Residential hotels have some of the characteristics of traditional hotels, such as private bathrooms, televisions and telephones, but are usually located in large, private homes, and guests are welcomed by the owners themselves. This type of hotel is especially common in the Sainte-Luce area, where more and more are popping up all the time.

You should, however, inquire about reservation requirements, as some of these places are only available by the week.

Gîtes Ruraux

There are over 200 *gîtes ruraux* (house rentals) and *chambres d'hôte* (bed and breakfasts) in Martinique. This type of accommodation enables visitors to get to know some of the people who live in the island's rural areas and see how they live.

Some *gîtes* are independent units, while others adjoin the owner's residence. They are completely furnished and equipped with appliances. As a general rule, *gîtes* are rented by the week, but a few also offer weekend rates. *Chambres d'hôtes*, which are much rarer in Martinique, are like bed-and-breakfasts : overnight accommodations in the owner's home, breakfast included.

All of these establishments must meet certain specific standards of quality

PRACTICAL INFORMATION

before being listed as *Gîtes de France*. In addition, the following rating system has been developed to assist visitors in their choice of a place to stay:

    ordinary
    comfortable
    very comfortable

We have provided listings for a few *gîtes*, including their official ratings, in the "Accommodations" section of each chapter of this guide. Those who would like a complete list can obtain a copy of the annual directory of *Gîtes de France en Martinique* by contacting the *Association Martiniquaise pour le Tourisme en Espace Rural*:

Relais des Gîtes de France - Martinique: Maison du Tourisme Vert, 9 Boulevard du Général-de-Gaulle, BP 1122 - 97248 Fort-de-France Cédex, ☎05.96.73.67.92, ≠05.96.63.55.92 .

Villa Rentals

Renting a villa that can accommodate 2 to 10 people is becoming an increasingly popular option. The Office de Tourisme de la Martinique (see p 38) can provide you with a repertoire of about one hundred of these types of houses.

Séjours Antilles *(Domaine de Belfond, 97227 Sainte-Anne, ☎05.96.76.74.31, ≠05.96.76.93.22)* also rents out villas that can accommodate up to eight people in the region of Sainte-Anne.

If you like to do things at the last minute, check out **Logis Vacances Antilles** *(☎05.96.42.18.63)*, an organization based at the Lamentin airport.

Villages Vacances Familles

Villages Vacances Familles were designed to offer local families somewhere other than their homes to spend their vacations, but foreign visitors are welcome, too, if there are any vacancies. The only time there might not be any room is in July and August, during the school vacation.

A *Village Vacances Familles* is usually a group of seaside bungalows, each one containing simple but clean rooms, a kitchen and a bathroom. There are a few in Martinique, including one in Tartane and another in Sainte-Luce (closed for renovations during our visit in March 1998). In some cases, the minimum stay is a week or longer. Furthermore, guests are responsible for their own housekeeping (except in Tartane).

You can camp at some of these villages, including the one in Sainte-Luce. In short, Villages Vacances Familles provide an inexpensive, interesting alternative to traditional hotels.

 ## Camping

There are a few campgrounds scattered across the island, in Anse à l'Âne, Sainte-Luce, Sainte-Anne and Le Vauclin. You can pitch your tent on public land, too, but you must first obtain authorization from the local town hall. The appropriate telephone numbers are listed in the "Practical Information" section of each chapter.

Also, during summer vacation, camping is permitted along a few of the island's most beautiful beaches, including Grande Anse des Salines and Cap Chevalier.

RESTAURANTS AND FINE FOOD

Martinique is overflowing with good places to eat, so you can enjoy excellent food all over the island. Indeed, this is without question one of the best things about this "sun destination". Many of Martinique's wide variety of top-notch restaurants have a blend of French and Creole culinary traditions, but various other kinds of food (Chinese, Italian, Vietnamese, etc.) add to your dining options.

As a general rule, restaurants are open from noon to 3pm and from 7pm to 10pm. A few serve dinner only, starting at 7pm, and most are closed one day a week. We strongly recommend, therefore, that you make reservations, especially at the height of the tourist season. When reserving, ask if the restaurant accepts credit cards.

In this guide, we have tried to provide you with the best possible selection of restaurants, for all budgets, and in every part of the island. Each listing includes the restaurant's telephone number, which will make it easy for you to call for reservations. **The prices quoted are intended to give you an idea of the cost of a meal for one person, tax and tip included, but excluding drinks.** Furthermore, in Martinique, tax and service are included in the prices on the menus. Nevertheless, it is customary to leave a bit extra in recognition of good service (see "Tipping" p 48).

More often than not, you'll be able to enjoy your meal on a large outside terrace affording a view of a valley (in the mountains) or, more commonly, the sea. In addition, the expression *les pieds dans l'eau* (which means "on the waterfront", though the literal translation is "feet in the water") is used, as you've probably already guessed, to describe restaurants with a waterfront terrace. Some beach restaurants, especially those right on the water, are only open during the day.

Considering the growing popularity of rental villas, studios and rooms equipped with kitchenettes, the "Restaurants" sections throughout this guide also include places where you can stock up on the necessary provisions to prepare your own meals.

Creole Cuisine

Your stay in Martinique will give you a chance to familiarize yourself with Creole cuisine, which is both varied and delicious. Several good restaurants on the island still serve **traditional Creole cuisine**, born of a mixture of African, Indian, French and Caribbean influences, while a few others have ventured into the realm of **nouvelle cuisine Créole**, which draws inspiration from the most recent French trends, while continuing to make use of local foods.

Creole cuisine gives top billing to fish and shellfish, such as **red snapper** (*vivaneau*), **bass** (*bar*), **shark** (*requin*), and *lambi* (an edible shellfish), **rock lobster** (*langouste*), **crab**, **sea urchin** (*oursin*) and **crayfish** (usually *écrévisses*, but known here as *z'habitants*). Some kinds of meat also appear on the menu, including **goat** (*cabri*), **lamb**, **pork** and poultry, most often **chicken**.

The flavour of all these foods is heightened by the use of a wide range of seasonings, including **nutmeg**, *bois d'Inde* (a spice derived from a small evergreen tree), **cinnamon**, and various different **peppers**.

A surprising number of vegetables native to the Antilles, such as ***christo-***

PRACTICAL INFORMATION

Glossary

Accras: Fritters made of cod, seafood (shrimp, crayfish) or vegetables.

Bébélé: Boiled sheep tripe.

Blaff: Fish or seafood boiled in spicy water. The word itself is an onomatopoeia of the sound the fish makes when it's plunged into the boiling water.

Blanc-manger: Blancmange; a coconut-based gelatin dessert.

Cabri: Type of goat used instead of lamb in Creole cooking.

Calalou: Soup made with herbs and vegetables, which contains pieces of crab and pork.

Chatrou: A small octopus.

Chou coco: The heart of the coconut tree, eaten raw; a very rare dish, as it can only be obtained by cutting down a coconut tree.

Chou-pays: An edible tuber.

Christophine: A vegetable, particularly delicious au gratin.

Cirique: A small crab.

Colombo: Curry-like mixture of spices served on meats, poultry and fish.

Corossol: A fruit with creamy-white flesh.

Court-bouillon: Tomato, pepper and onion mixture used with fish.

Féroce: Mixture of avocado, cod, manioc flour and peppers.

Fricassée: Fricassee; fish or meat browned and stewed in a frying pan.

Fruit à pain: Breadfruit; a large, melon-like fruit.

Giraumon: Pumpkin.

Igname: Any of a wide variety of yams.

Lambis: Large, edible shellfish.

Manioc: Cassava, tapioca flour

Maracudja: Passion fruit.

Matoutou: Crab fricassee.

Pâté en pot: A thick soup made with goat offal, vegetables, capers, which wine and occasionally rum.

Patate douce: Sweet potato.

Planteur: Planter's punch; cocktail composed of rum, fruit juice and cane syrup.

Schrub: Liqueur made with oranges soaked in rum.

Soudons: Clams.

Ti-nain: Small banana, which is not as sweet as the larger variety, and is used as a vegetable.

Ti-punch: Apéritif containing rum, cane syrup and zest of lemon or lime.

Titiris: Tiny fish.

Touffé: Braised.

Z'habitants: Large crayfish.

PRACTICAL INFORMATION

phine, **yams**, **manioc** and **ti-nain** are also used in Creole cuisine, adding to its unique character.

A common way to start off a good Creole meal is with a plate of **accras**, mouth-watering fritters made with fish, seafood or vegetables, which are served at the same time as your apéritif, usually punch. Other traditional appetizers include **féroce** (avocado purée mixed with cod), **pâté en pot** (a thick soup made with sheep offal and vegetables), **blood pudding** (*boudin*), **stuffed crab** and fish or **z'habitants soup**.

A few of the most popular main dishes are **blaffs** (white fish or shellfish immersed in boiling water), **court-bouillon** (red fish cooked in a sauce of tomatoes and peppers) and goat, chicken, crab, fish or turtle **colombos** (the local equivalent of curries, of Indian origin).

For dessert, treat yourself to a delicious **blancmange** or some luscious **tropical fruit sorbet**.

Creole Menu

Cod Accras (8 servings)

250 g (8.75 oz, just over ½ lb) salted cod
2 chopped onions
2 chopped scallions
3 cloves garlic
45 ml (3 tablespoons) chopped parsley
1 pepper
1 bay leaf
5 ml (1 teaspoon) thyme
15 ml (1 tablespoon) butter and a little oil
500 ml (2 cups) flour
5 ml (1 teaspoon) baking powder
5 ml (1 teaspoon) salt
2 eggs
310 ml (1 ¼ cups) milk
oil for frying

•Soak the cod in cold water for 8 hours. Drain, then crumble after removing skin and bones.

●Brown the cod and onions in the oil and butter. Add the scallions, garlic, parsley, pepper, bay leaf and thyme. Mix well and let cool.

●Combine the flour, baking powder, salt, eggs and milk, then add the cod mixture.

●Using a spoon, shape batter into small fritters, and drop them into hot oil. Fry for about 5 minutes or until golden, turning them as they cook.

●Remove fritters and place them on a paper towel to absorb excess oil. Serve immediately.

Court-Bouillon for Fish (4-6 servings)

1 kg (2.2 lbs) fish (sea or any other)
juice of 2 lemons
chopped pepper, to taste
2 crushed cloves garlic
salt and pepper
1 sliced onion
3 chopped scallions
45 ml (3 tablespoons) oil
30 ml (2 tablespoons) butter
15 ml (1 tablespoon) tomato paste
1 pinch thyme
15 ml (1 tablespoon) parsley
375 ml (1 1/2 cups) water
the juice of 1 lemon
1 crushed clove garlic
2 ml (1/2 teaspoon) pepper
15 ml (1 tablespoon) oil

●Marinate the fish for approximately 1 hour in the juice of 2 lemons, chopped pepper, 2 cloves garlic, salt and pepper.

●Gently brown the onion and scallions in the oil and butter. Add the tomato paste, thyme and parsley. Stir in the water and bring to a boil.

●Add the fish, cover and simmer for 10 minutes.

●During the last minute of cooking, pour the juice of 1 lemon mixed with 1 crushed clove garlic, 2 ml (1/2 teaspoon) pepper and 15 ml (1 tablespoon) oil over the fish.

●Serve fish hot, in its own sauce, with Creole rice.

Coconut Ice Cream

2 coconuts
500 ml (2 cups) water
165 ml (2/3 cup) sugar
the milk from the 2 coconuts
5 ml (1 teaspoon) pure vanilla extract
1 small stick cinnamon
the zest of 1 lemon
1 can sweetened condensed milk
2 ml (1/2 teaspoon) almond oil
500 ml (2 cups) water (for half of the condensed milk)

●Drain the milk from the coconuts and set aside.

●Split and shell the coconuts, then grate them. Bring the water, sugar, coconut milk, vanilla, cinnamon and lemon zest to a boil. Place the grated coconut in a large bowl. Pour the boiling liquid over the coconut and let stand for 1 hour.

●Strain the liquid and set aside. Put the coconut shavings in a clean cloth and wring out into the strained liquid.

●Add the almond oil and half of the condensed milk to the liquid.

●Use a skimmer to remove the cinnamon and the zest.

●Mix the remaining condensed milk with 500 ml (2 cups) of water and add to the coconut milk.

●Pour this mixture into ice trays and leave in the freezer until hard, stirring occasionally.

Recipes graciously provided by Richard Bizier

DRINKS

Rum

The number one alcohol produced in Martinique is of course rum, which islanders rightly claim is the best in the Antilles, and on par with Haiti's. Closely linked to the island's history, the rum industry is steeped in tradition and plays an integral role in West Indian culture. What is more, Martinican agricultural rum was awarded the *Appellation d'Origine Contrôlée* (A.O.C.) label in the fall of 1996, a great first for a French product from overseas.

First of all, there is *rhum vieux*, aged in oak barrels, which give it its amber colour. Then there's *rhum blanc agricole*, or white rum, which is also made with cane sugar juice (*vésou*), but is not aged before being bottled.

There are many rum distilleries spread all over the island, most of which offer guided tours of their facilities and arrange tasting sessions. The most famous of these *rhumeries* is probably La Mauny, but a tour of one of the smaller distilleries, such as the one in Trois-Rivières, will also provide you with a good introduction to the techniques involved in rum-production. Some distilleries even include "mini-museums" intended to make it easier to understand their art (Plantations Saint-James).

Before meals, you'll be offered a *ti-punch*, a traditional island drink with three parts white rum, one part cane syrup and a zest of lime or lemon. One of the most highly-rated cocktails, however, is the smoother, fruitier *planteur* (planter's punch), made of four parts each of aged rum, orange juice and pineapple juice; one part cane syrup; nutmeg and cinnamon. As far as after-dinner drinks go, **aged rum** is as highly prized here as any of the best cognacs. **Schrub**, an orange, rum-based liqueur, is another purely Martinican digestif.

Beer

Several European beers are available on the island, including Heineken. Real beer lovers, however, will be thrilled to discover **Lorraine**, a thirst-quenching local beer brewed in Le Lamentin. It is a pale ale with a crisp, delicious taste and a low alcohol content.

Wine

As a general rule, restaurant wine cellars are very small in Martinique. After all, this is not quite France! Nevertheless, a well-chilled rosé goes very nicely with Creole food.

  ENTERTAINMENT

Contrary to what you might be inclined to believe, Martinique is relatively quiet after dark. In Fort-de-France there's always something to do in the evening (nightclubs, movies, theatre, etc.), but elsewhere on the island the nights are fairly calm. The exception is the luxury hotels, where you'll occasionally find a discotheque (the Méridien, the Carayou and the Batelière) or a casino (the Méridien and the Batelière).

The Rum Route

Each of Martinique's *rhumeries* has its own special product, its own history and its own secrets. These distilleries are briefly described below.

Fort-de-France and Area

Around Fort-de-France, you can visit the **Dillon** and **La Favorite** distilleries, which produce a wide range of rums, a number of which are exported to Europe, where they are very popular. The latter was named as such, supposedly because Louis XV's preferred mistress, Madame de Pompadour, was particularly fond of the rum made here. Finally, there is the **Bernus** distillery, which is highly regarded, but maintains a low-profile.

The Northwest Coast

Bally rum was produced on the Lajus plantation in Le Carbet until 1978. Today, even though production has been moved to Le François, the rum bottle still has its square shape and label designed by Jacques Bally in 1924. The distillery is renowned for some of its vintage rums (1982, 1975, 1970, 1966 and 1957). The small-scale **Neisson** distillery, also located in Le Carbet, puts out an other high-quality rum that, in the last few years, has claimed several prizes in international competitions.

Victor Depaz returned home to Martinique from Europe, where he had been studying, after the eruption of Montagne Pelée in 1902, which destroyed Saint-Pierre and wiped out his family, and began rebuilding the family estate, the Habitation Pécoul La Montagne. The **Depaz** "special reserve" is a favourite among connoisseurs.

The South

You will find an attractive small-scale distillery in **Trois-Rivières**, in the Sainte-Luce area. In 1635, Louis XIV's superindendent of finance, Nicolas Fouquet, built a veritable château on what are now the grounds of the distillery, using the fortune he had fraudulently amassed in the course of performing his duties. Colbert denounced him to the king, who consequently ordered the demolition of the scoundrel's luxurious retreat. The distillery's white rums, which have a vanilla flavour, are particularly well-reputed.

The **La Mauny** distillery is located near Rivière-Pilote. It is one of the largest *rhumeries* in Martinique, and produces the island's most famous rum. In 1749, the La Mauny estate was given its present name by Joseph Ferdinand Poulain, Comte de Mauny, of Normandy. La Mauny rum now accounts for 50% of the island's domestic market, and is setting sales records in Europe (1,000,000 bottles a year), where it is distributed by Barton & Guestier.

Near the village of Le François, on the road to Saint-Esprit, you can visit the Domaine de l'Acajou, also known as the Habitation **Clément**, founded in 1907 by Dr. Homère Clément, deputy and mayor of Le François. This, along with La Mauny, is where the most prestigious Martinican rums were produced until 1988. These rums are now produced in a more modern facility. Vieux Clément is particularly prized by connoisseurs; 1952 and 1970 are superb vintages. There is a beautifully restored 18th-century residence on the grounds. Visitors are also shown a film on the history of rum in Martinique.

The Northeast Coast

On Presqu'île de la Caravelle, in the charming fishing village of Tartane, you will find the **Hardy** distillery, the smallest on the island. Limited quantities of white, aged and pale rums are produced here.

On the way out of the village of Sainte-Marie, make sure to stop at the **Saint-James** distillery. This *rhumerie*, originally founded in the hills of Saint-Pierre, was moved here after Montagne Pelée erupted in 1902. It produces a pale rum and a number of liqueurs. More importantly, though, you can purchase a bottle of century-old rum here. Saint-James is Martinique's oldest brand of rum, and its elegant square bottle enhances its prestige. At the distillery's Musée du Rhum, you can learn about the history of sugar cane cultivation from 1965 to the present day.

Finally, in Basse-Pointe, you'll find the **JM** distillery, known mainly for its excellent aged rums, produced on one of the oldest *habitations* in Martinique.

Chouboulote, a small, free biannual magazine (published in January and June) available all over the island, will give you an overview of the island's nightlife and cultural events. It's also worth picking up a copy of *Ti-Gourmet*, an annual guide available for free at local tourist offices, among other places. Inside, you'll find information on restaurants and a section entitled "Martinique By Night", which includes a fairly comprehensive list of local bars, theatres, movie theatres, and discotheques. In addition, by presenting a copy of *Ti-Gourmet* at some of the places mentioned in it, you'll usually receive a free cocktail, a discount, or some other bonus. Both these guides are bilingual (French and English).

 SHOPPING

If you love shopping and beautiful boutiques, you'll be in heaven in Fort-de-France, where you'll find nearly all the famous European names in perfume, crystal, watches, haute couture, leather goods, etc. European tourists, especially the metropolitan French, will find the prices a little high, due, of course, to the transportation costs of bringing the merchandise all the way to heart of the West Indies. North Americans, on the other hand, can sometimes find bargains.

Shops are open Monday through Friday from 9am to 1:30pm and 3pm to 6pm, and on Saturday from 9am to 1pm. In addition to the major shopping streets in Fort-de-France, there are also several shopping centres in the suburbs (Cluny, Dillon, Bellevue, Le Lamentin, etc.). Remember that you can sometimes get a discount by paying with travellers' cheques in foreign funds. Personal cheques, however, are accepted in fewer and fewer shops and restaurants on the island.

More typically Martinican products make nice souvenirs. These include coral and gold jewellery, articles made of bamboo, Creole dolls in traditional madras head scarves, pottery and of course rum.

Fort-de-France's *Centre des Métiers d'Art* (Crafts Centre) has a lovely selection of local handicrafts. In addition, experienced bargainers will enjoy visiting the craft market on Place de la Savane. Similar markets can be found in other spots on the island as well, including Sainte-Anne and Saint-Pierre.

CALENDAR

Public Holidays

New Year's Day	January 1
Lundi gras	(varies)
Mardi gras	(varies)
Ash Wednesday	(varies)
Good Friday	(varies)
Easter Monday	(varies)
Labour Day	May 1
1945 Armistice Day	May 8
Slavery Abolition Day	May 22
Pentecost Monday	(varies)
Bastille Day	July 14
Assumption Day	August 15
All Saints' Day	November 1
All Souls' Day	November 2
1918 Armistice Day	November 11
Christmas Day	December 25

Holidays Honouring Patron Saints

Each of Martiniques 34 *communes* holds annual festivities in honour of its patron saint. The celebrations usually go on for several days, often over the weekend immediately following the official date.

Ajoupa-Bouillon	December 8
Anses-d'Arlet	July 15
Basse-Pointe	June 24
Bellefontaine	August 1
Carbet	July 25
Case-Pilote	August 15
Diamant	December 21
Ducos	September 8
Fonds-Saint-Denis	October 9
Fort-de-France	August 25
François	September 29
Grand'Rivière	November 25
Gros-Morne	July 2
Lamentin	August 10
Lorrain	August 15
Macouba	July 26
Marigot	June 29
Marin	December 26
Morne-Rouge	December 8
Morne-Vert	November 11
Prêcheur	March 19
Rivière-Pilote	December 8
Rivière-Salée	June 24
Robert	August 30
Saint-Esprit	Pentecost
Saint-Joseph	March 19
Saint-Pierre	June 29
Sainte-Anne	July 26
Sainte-Luce	December 13
Sainte-Marie	August 15
Schœlcher	September 8
Trinité	June 16
Trois-Îlets	February 2
Vauclin	June 24

Annual Events

February
Semaine Nautique Internationale de Schœlcher (International Nautical Week)

March
Carnaval (the four days leading up to Ash Wednesday)
Semaine Internationale de la Voile à Fort-de-France (International Sailing Week, ☎05.96.63.26.76)

April
Aqua-Festival in Le Robert (Nautical Festival)
Salon du Tourisme de la Caraïbe (Caribbean Tourism Show)

May
Championnat de Tennis de la Caraïbe et des Amériques in Le Lamentin (Caribbean and American Tennis Championship ☎05.96.51.08.00)
Mai de Saint-Pierre (commemoration of the eruption of Montagne Pélée)
Anniversaire de l'abolition de l'esclavage (commemoration of the end of slavery)

June
Salon de l'Environnement (Environment Show)
Festival de Jazz at the Plantation Leyritz

July
Festival Culturel de Fort-de-France (Cultural Festival, ☎05.96.71.66.25 or 05.96.60.48.77)
Festival Culturel de Sainte-Marie (Cultural Festival, ☎05.96.69.89.78)
Tour Cycliste de la Martinique (Martinique's Cycling Tour)

August
Festival culturel du Marin (Cultural Festival, ☎05.96.74.90.74)
Tour de la Martinique des yoles rondes (sailing; ☎05.96.72.59.21)

October
Tournoi Intercaraïbe de Golf (Inter-Caribbean Golf Tournament)

November
Semi-Marathon de Fort-de-France (Half Marathon, ☎05.96.60.60.13)
Course Transat (every two years; ☎05.96.63.26.76)

December
Festival International de Jazz (even years) or *Carrefour Mondial de la Guitare* (odd years). Alternately; International Jazz Festival and World Guitar Forum ☎05.96.61.76.76
Journées Martiniquais du Tourisme (Matinican tourism days)

GENERAL INFORMATION

Time Zones

Martinique is in the Eastern Standard Time Zone. This means that when North America is not on daylight savings time, there is no time difference between Montréal, Toronto, New York and Martinique, and it is three hours ahead of Los Angeles. Martinique is five or six hours behind continental western Europe, depending on the time of year.

Electricity

Local electricity operates at 220 volts AC (50 cycles), so tourists from North America will need to bring along an adaptor with two round pins and a converter for their appliances. Continental European visitors need no converter, where as those from Great Britain will need an adaptor with two round pins.

Women Travellers

Women travelling alone in Martinique shouldn't have any problems. On the whole, islanders are friendly and not too aggressive, and women are treated with respect. Even though Martinican men enjoy flirting with unaccompanied women, harassment is relatively rare. Of course, a minimum amount of caution is required; for example, women should avoid walking alone through poorly lit areas late at night and avoid hitchhiking at all costs.

Newspapers

The one daily newspaper in the Antilles, *France-Antilles*, is published in Fort-de-France. There are also a few weekly papers, such as *Antilla*, *France-Antilles* magazine, *Question*, *Naïf*, *Justice* (put out by the communist party of Martinique) and *Le Progressiste* (put out by the *Parti Progressiste Martiniquais*)

Le Madras, a practical encyclopaedic dictionary published by *Éditions Exbrayat* in Fort-de-France, is a great source of information about Martinique. It is sold in bookshops for 245F. You can also subscribe to *Mise à Jour* (120F a year), a quarterly magazine that allows you to keep your *Madras* up to date.

Weights and Measures

Martinique uses the metric system.

Weights
1 pound (lb) = 454 grams (g)
1 kilogram (kg) = 2.2 pounds (lbs)

Linear Measure
1 inch = 2.54 centimetres (cm)
1 foot (ft) = 30 centimetres (cm)
1 mile = 1.6 kilometres (km)
1 kilometre (km) = 0.63 miles

Land Measure
1 acre = 0.4047 hectare
1 hectare = 2.471 acres

Volume Measure
1 US gallon (gal) = 3.79 litres
1 US gallon (gal) = 0.83 imperial gallon

Temperature
To convert °F into °C: subtract 32, divide by 9, multiply by 5
To convert °C into °F: multiply by 9, divide by 5, add 32.

OUTDOORS

 PARKS

A tropical forest to roam through, hills and mountains to climb, limpid waters to explore, long, tree-lined beaches to lie on... All of this makes Martinique a veritable paradise for people who enjoy outdoor activities.

In order to give you an overall idea of what is available in Martinique, we have included below a summary of the most popular outdoor activities. In subsequent chapters, each of which is devoted to a specific region, the addresses listed in the "Parks and Beaches" and "Outdoor Activities" sections will enable you to obtain further information.

Parc Naturel Régional de la Martinique

The *Parc Naturel Régional de la Martinique* (PNRM) is an organization for the protection of two-thirds of the island's land, which incorporates all rural areas. The PNRM is responsible for preserving, and at the same time promoting, the natural surroundings. It also organizes all sorts of activities ranging from guided walking tours (at least three times a week) to rallies, and including environment festivals, trail rides and expeditions at sea. The calendar of events is available throughout the island. You can also get a copy by contacting the PNRM or the *Association Martiniquaise pour le Tourisme en Espace Rural*:

Centre d'Information du Parc Naturel Régional de la Martinique *(Mon to Fri 8am to noon and 3pm to 6pm; Sat 8am to noon),* Maison du Tourisme Vert, 9 Boulevard du Général-de-Gaulle, 97205 Fort-de-France Cédex, ☎05.96.73.19.30.

Service Administratif et Technique du PRNM *(Mon, Thu, Fri 7:30am to 1pm and 2pm to 5:30pm; Tue and Wed 7:30am to 1:30pm),* Tivoli - Ex-Collège Agricole, B.P. 437, 97200 Fort-de-France, ☎05.96.64.42.59.

Association Martiniquaise pour le Tourisme en Espace Rural: Maison du Tourisme Vert, 9 Boulevard du Général-de-Gaulle, B.P. 1122, 97248 Fort-de-France, ☎05.96.73.67.92, ⊶05.96.63.55.92.

OUTDOOR ACTIVITIES

Hiking

This is probably the most well-organized outdoor activity on the island, as well as the one the island is trying the hardest to develop. It is certainly the best means of introducing visitors to some of Martinique's natural treasures, such as the tropical rainforest, the untouched beaches of the southeast, the rocky hills *(mornes)* and sharp peaks *(pitons)* studding the island and, of course, Montagne Pelée.

The *Office National des Forêts*, dedicated to managing Martinique's 15 000 hectares of woodland, has developed a network of 31 hiking trails (170 km), which it marks and maintains. The starting point of each of these trails is usually well-indicated, with a map showing the path to follow. The Office has also published an excellent guide entitled *31 Sentiers Balisés*

en Martinique (available only in French), which describes the various walking tours in detail and is available in bookstores and at newspaper stands all over the island at a cost of 60F.

Office National des Forêts: 3.5 km, Route de Moutte, 97200 Fort-de-France ☎05.96.60.70.70, ⊶05.96.63.56.67.

Detailed maps will prepare you even better for your outings. We suggest the *Institut Géographique National* (IGN) blue series (1:25 000), which is available in travel bookstores.

The hiking trails are briefly described in the "Outdoor Activities" section of each chapter. The classifications "easy", "average" and "difficult" will help you choose the trail best suited to your physical condition.

As a general rule, however, most of the trails fall in the first two categories. Nonetheless, hikers always face certain risks, such as sunstroke, snakes, or storms, which can render some trails impassable.

Sunstroke

Long sections of some trails are exposed to the sun, with no shady spots in which to take refuge. The risk of sunstroke is therefore considerable and threatens all hikers enjoying this activity in the tropics. Cramps, goose bumps, nausea and loss of balance are the initial symptoms. If these symptoms arise, the victim should be moved quickly into the shade, fanned and given something to drink.

To avoid this problem, always wear a hat and arm yourself with a good sunscreen. You are also strongly advised to go hiking early in the morning.

Snakes

There is only one dangerous animal in Martinique the *trigonocéphale*, or pit viper, whose bite can be fatal. You should not, however, develop an exaggerated fear of this snake, as the approach of a group of people usually sends it slithering off in a panic.

The best way to avoid encountering the pit viper is to stay on marked trails and to make noise.

Rain

Rain, especially during violent storms, can render some trails, such as those on the Pitons du Carbet and Montagne Pelée, completely impenetrable. It is therefore better to hike these trails during the dry season. In any case, it is always wise to check the weather forecast before setting out.

Clothing

As a general rule, you should wear thin, light-coloured clothing. Your shoes should be thick and sturdy, yet light-weight, with good traction.

Bring a long-sleeved sweater for mountain trails, and don't forget your bathing suit if you're going to be walking along the coast or wading across a river. This, along with a raincoat, to keep you dry in case of rain, and a hat, to protect you from the sun, and you should be all set.

What to Bring

On each excursion, your backpack should contain the following objects: a canteen, a pocket knife, an antiseptic, bandages (both adhesive and non-adhesive), scissors, a snakebite kit, aspirin, sunblock, insect repellent and enough food for the trip.

 Swimming

The many beaches stretching along the coast and nestled inside little bays (*anses*) constitute one of Martinique's greatest natural treasures, or at least the one that attracts the most tourists.

There are the "classic" beaches of the southern Caribbean, or southwest, coast (Grande Anse des Salines, Sainte-Anne, Diamant, Anse Mitan), whose white sands are lapped by a turquoise sea and lined with coconut trees. But there are also the black-sand beaches of the northern Caribbean coast (Le Carbet, Anse Céron, Anse Couleuvre), which have a mysterious atmosphere all their own. Some visitors will enjoy roaming the untouched, isolated beaches of the southeast coast (Cap Chevalier, Anse Trabaud), where the choppy Atlantic is almost violent in places; others will prefer swimming farther north (Le François, Le Robert) among the *fonds blancs*, which are shallow, white sand bars protected by coral reefs, where the water is barely a metre deep. There are no nudist beaches in Martinique, but women may go topless if they wish, though it is definitely not common practice among islanders. Also, the Anse Meunier beach (see p 132) at the western tip of Grande Anse des Salines is a popular nudist spot amongst gay men.

In the "Parks and Beaches" section of every chapter in this guide, you will find a description of all regional beaches, be they small or large, equipped with facilities or not. You will also find a list of the facilities available at each beach. In addition, we have reproduced the water quality ratings accorded to the various swimming

OUTDOORS

A Fragile Ecosystem

Coral reefs are formed by minuscule organisms called coelenterate polyps, which are very sensitive to water pollution. The high level of nitrates in polluted water accelerate the growth of seaweed, which in turn takes over the coral, stops it from growing and literally smothers it. Diademas, a species of black sea urchin (whose long spikes can cause severe injuries), live on the coral and play a major role in controlling the amount of seaweed that grows there by eating what the fish cannot, unfortunately there are not enough of these urchins. An epidemic killed many of them in 1983, and as the waters became more and more polluted, seaweed proliferated, and the survival of a number of reefs was threatened. Scientific studies have since proved the importance of the diadema to the ecological balance, and the species has thus been restored on certain reefs. However, these little urchins cannot solve the problem on their own. Pollution control is essential in order to protect the coral reefs, upon which nearly 400,000 species depend for their survival.

areas by the Direction Départementale des Affaires Sanitaires et Sociales (DDASS):

- **A**   Good
- **B**   Average
- **C**   Occasionally Polluted
- **D**   Bad

Swimmers should never frequent those areas with a "D" rating (according to 1997 testing, there are none in Martinique) and should avoid those rated "C" for three days following any rainy period.

The ratings mentioned in this guide were based on 1,048 samples taken by the Laboratoire d'Hygiène de la Martinique between October 1, 1996 and September 30, 1997. Considering the rapid changes possible in such cases, this information is offered only as a general guide. For more information, contact the DDASS:

Direction Départementale des Affaires Sanitaires et Sociales: Boulevard Pasteur, 97263 Fort-de-France Cédex, ☏05.96.60.60.08.

 Scuba Diving

Martinique has everything an avid scuba diver could hope for – lots of interesting sites, diving clubs, an ideal water temperature (26 °C), abundant, colourful marine life and fascinating shipwrecks.

The Caribbean coast, being much calmer than the Atlantic, offers the greatest number of diving opportunities. There are remarkable sites in the south at Rocher du Diamant and near Anses-d'Arlet. The northern Caribbean coast has magnificent sites as well, the most spectacular being the harbour of Saint-Pierre, where several shipwrecks have lain since the tragic eruption of Montagne Pelée at the beginning of the century.

You must have a diving permit to take part in excursions in Martinique. For those who don't have one, the major hotels offer introductory courses in their swimming pools.

Frigatebird

Brown Pelican

Black-necked Stilt

Great Heron

Martinique Oriole

Sooty Tern

Cattle Egret

Zenaida Dove

Green Heron

Crested Hummingbird

Carib Grackle

Bananaquit

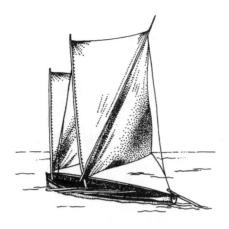

Yole ronde

 Snorkelling

Very little equipment is required for snorkelling – a mask, a snorkel and a pair of flippers. Because it's a sport anyone can take part in, snorkelling is a good way to discover the richness and beauty of the underwater world. You can enjoy this activity all around the island, wherever there are coral reefs close to the beach.

Scuba diving makes it possible to discover fascinating sights like coral reefs, schools of multi-coloured fish and amazing underwater plants. Don't forget that this ecosystem is fragile and deserves special attention. All divers must respect a few basic **safety guidelines** in order to protect these natural sites: do not touch anything (especially not urchins, as their long spikes can cause injury); do not take pieces of coral (it is much prettier in the water than out, where it becomes discoloured); do not disturb any living creatures; do not hunt; do not feed the fish; be careful not to disturb anything with

your flippers and, of course, do not litter. If you want a souvenir of your underwater experience, disposable underwater cameras are available.

 Fishing

Fans of deep-sea fishing can take part in excursions organized by clubs specializing in this sport, which leave from the biggest marinas (Pointe du Bout, Le Marin, Le François) and largest hotels on the island.

 Boating

Throughout the island, visitors are offered various programs of activities involving excursions at sea and rentals of all sorts of boats.

Accordingly, on the most popular beaches (Grande Anse, Sainte-Anne) and in the major sailing harbours, boat-rental outfits and yacht clubs offer the budding sailor an entire range of possibilities.

OUTDOORS

Gommiers and *Yoles Rondes*

Gommiers and *yoles rondes* (round skiffs) are two types of boats particular to Martinique. You are sure to spot one or the other during you stay here.

The more common of the two is the *gommier*, a fishing boat still found on a good many beaches on the island. It is recognizable by its bright colours and evocative name painted by the owner on the front of the boat. Traditionally, the Carib Indians carved these crafts out of the trunk of the white gum tree.

Gommier racing was once a popular pastime, but the need soon arose for a newer, swifter type of boat more suitable to regattas. Thus was born the round skiff, a sailing boat designed for 8 to 11 people and specifically for competition. The famous round skiff Tour de la Martinique takes place every year in August. This major sporting event is a spectacle of dozens of boats with large, brightly coloured sails trying hard to make it first across the finish line. Among the competitors, the team from the commune of Robert is the favourite.

Various water-oriented events are also held throughout the year, such as the *Semaine Nautique Internationale de Schœlcher* (February) and the famous *Tour de la Martinique* in *yoles rondes*, a kind of sailboat (August).

 Windsurfing

It is very easy to rent windsurfing equipment in the southern part of Martinique. The beaches of Sainte-Anne and Sainte-Luce are particular favourites among windsurfers.

 Tent and Trailer Camping

Unfortunately, Martinique's tourist infrastructure hasn't really been developed with campers in mind. There are however a few campgrounds in the following regions: Anse à l'Âne, Sainte-Anne, Vauclin and La Trinité.

During summer vacation (July and August), though, you can camp all along the most famous beaches of the south – Grande Anse des Salines, Grande Terre and Cap Chevalier. Many Martinican families go camping at this time, and while this might not suit visitors in search of peace and quiet, it does make it easier to get to know some of the island's inhabitants.

Prices are extremely low as a rule, but you must apply to the appropriate town hall for permission to camp in the area. In addition, there are several places on the island that rent trailers and camping equipment. For further details, see the "Outdoor Activities" section of the appropriate chapter.

 Bicycling

Bicyclists will be thrilled by all the winding roads on the island. The heat and the many hills to climb are bound to discourage some, however. You must be in good physical condition to enjoy this sport in the tropics, and especially in Martinique.

The *Tour Cycliste International de la Martinique* takes place every July.

Mountain Biking

The mountain bike craze has reached the French Antilles! It is therefore possible to rent mountain bikes at several places on the island, including Pointe du Bout, near Trois-Îlets (see p 102).

 Horseback Riding

Horse lovers be delighted to learn that there are several stables scattered across the island in the following regions: Trois-Îlets, Diamant, Sainte-Anne and the Fort-de-France area. Visitors are thus offered another way to explore the forests and untouched beaches of Martinique.

 Golf

There is only one golf course in Martinique, the Country Club de la Martinique, located on the southwest point near Trois-Îlets. It is commonly known as the "Golf de l'Impératrice", for part of it was laid out on land belonging to the family of Marie-Josèphe Rose Tascher de la Pagerie, later to become Empress Josephine.

Robert Trent Jones, the American landscape architect, designed this magnificent 18-hole course, whose reputation has spread beyond the borders of Martinique. It covers 63 hectares and is a tourist attraction in and of itself.

 Tennis

Most of the big hotels have tennis courts, some of which are equipped with floodlights. As a general rule, all equipment is supplied.

OUTDOORS

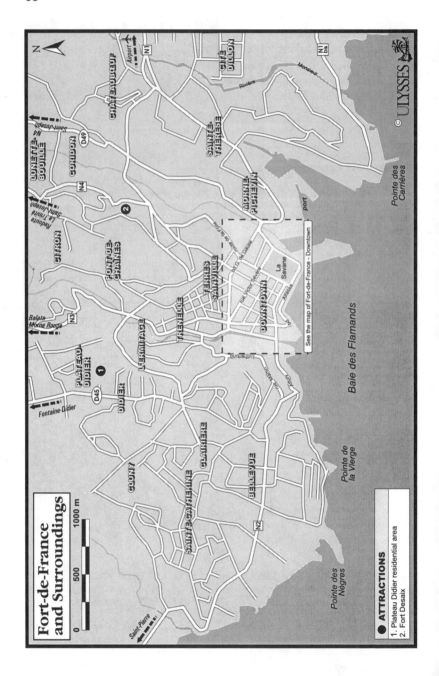

Fort-de-France
and Surroundings

0   500   1000 m

ATTRACTIONS

1. Plateau Didier residential area
2. Fort Desaix

© ULYSSES

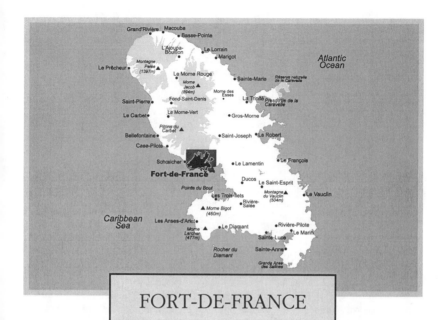

FORT-DE-FRANCE

Fort-de-France ★★ stands out on all scores as the most important city in Martinique. Not only the city with the largest population (100,000), it is also home to the island's main port through which all foreign ships pass. Fort-de-France, as the seat of the prefecture of Martinique and the centre of the island's administration, is home to the Regional and Economic Councils, major banks, consulates, the regional diocese, the Treasury, etc.

As recently as the last century, however, there was fierce competition between Fort-de-France and Saint-Pierre, which was the island's major port at the time and boasted a higher standard of living. At the beginning of the 20th century, there were 30,000 people living in Saint-Pierre and only 15,000 in Fort-de-France. Then, in 1902, Montagne Pelée erupted, destroying Saint-Pierre and putting an

abrupt end to the rivalry between the two cities.

Fort-de-France has had its own share of problems, however. The city's history has been marked by several natural disasters and military assaults. In 1674, the Dutch made a vain attempt to invade the city. The English were equally unsuccessful in 1759, 1762 and 1794, but finally succeeded in invading Fort-de-France and occupying Martinique in 1809. In 1839, an earthquake killed 500 residents, and in 1890, the entire city was destroyed by fire, only to be hit by a hurricane the following year.

The city's origins date back to the first days of French colonization. In 1638, Du Parquet ordered the construction of Fort Royal (now Fort Saint-Louis). In 1639, the first church was erected, and a community started to build up around it, thus marking the birth of the city of Fort-Royal. Establishing a colony in this area proved to be a difficult task, how-

Aimé Césaire

Of all the major figures in Martinican arts and politics, one individual stands head and shoulders above the rest: Aimé Césaire.

Mayor of Fort-de-France since 1945, founder of the *Parti Progressiste Martiniquais* (PPM) in 1958, deputy from 1946 to 1993, county councillor of Fort-de-France from 1946 to 1970 and president of the *Conseil Régional* from 1983 to 1988, Aimé Césaire has long been a political leader of remarkably wide-ranging influence.

However, Césaire is also a man of letters, a major poet who has greatly influenced French-speaking writers in the Antilles and Africa alike. His *Cahier d'un retour au pays natal* (*Return to My Native Land*) established him as a literary luminary. Rejecting the canons of white literature, he defends *"négritude"*, a term he invented to designate black culture as a whole.

In 1998, the poet-mayor of Fort-de-France celebrated his eighty-fifth birthday. Celebrations were held all over the island, and radio announcers called out, *"Bon anniversaire papa Césaire!"* ("Happy birthday, Papa Césaire!"). Despite Césaire's great stature and the reverence he inspires, Martinicans clearly view him as a good man who has maintained close ties with the people while at the same time becoming their leader. Perhaps that, after all, is the ultimate accomplishment of any great figure in society.

ever, for the land was swampy and infested with mosquitoes. Many of the first settlers were stricken with yellow fever, and had to put up with frequent flooding. These early colonists were not only supposed to cultivate the land they had been granted, but to drain it as well.

The true founder of Fort-de-France, however, was Charles de Courbon, Comte de Blénac. Governor General of the Windward Islands from 1677 to 1696, he laid out the city we know today.

In 1681, the title of capital fell to Fort-Royal when a decision was made to move the administrative headquarters there. Saint-Pierre thus lost its status as the administrative centre of the French Antilles. Its commercial development remained unhindered, however,

enabling it to compete with the new capital for over two centuries.

The city was known as Fort-Royal until 1802, when Napoleon ordered it renamed Fort-de-France. Fort Royal (the fortifications) became Fort Saint-Louis only in 1814.

Starting in 1902, the population of Fort-de-France increased rapidly after its rival city, Saint-Pierre, was destroyed by the volcanic eruption that same year. Its population reached 20,000 in 1920, 40,000 in 1936, 60,000 in 1952, 85,000 in 1961 and 100,000 in 1974.

Since 1945, the position of mayor has been filled by one of Martinique's most celebrated figures, the black poet Aimé Césaire, author of *Cahier d'un retour au pays natal* (Return to My Native Land)

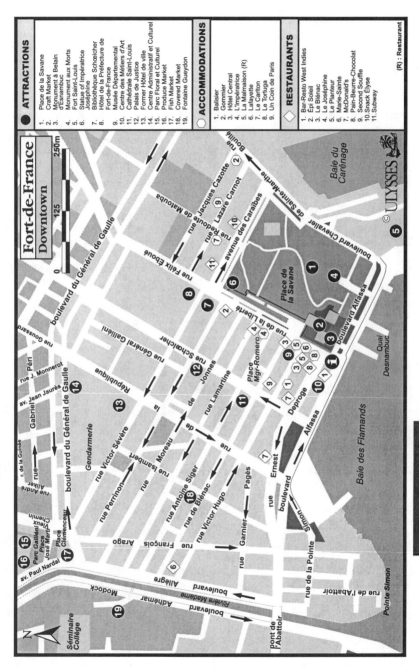

Fort-de-France Downtown

0   125   250m

© ULYSSES

● **ATTRACTIONS**

1. Place de la Savane
2. Craft Market
3. Monument à Belain d'Esnambuc
4. Monument aux Morts
5. Fort Saint-Louis
6. Statue of Impératrice Joséphine
7. Bibliothèque Schœlcher
8. Hôtel de la Préfecture de Fort-de-France
9. Musée Départemental
10. Centre des Métiers d'Art
11. Cathédrale Saint-Louis
12. Palais de Justice
13. Former Hôtel de ville
14. Centre Administratif et Culturel
15. Parc Floral et Culturel
16. Produce Market
17. Fish Market
18. Covered Market
19. Fontaine Gueydon

○ **ACCOMMODATIONS**

1. Balisier
2. Gommier
3. Hôtel Central
4. L'Impératrice
5. La Malmaison (R)
6. Lafayette
7. Le Carlton
8. Le Tortuga
9. Un Coin de Paris

◇ **RESTAURANTS**

1. Bar-Resto West Indies
2. Epi Soleil
3. Le Blénac
4. Le Joséphine
5. Le Planteur
6. Marie-Sainte
7. McDonald's
8. Pain-Beurre-Chocolat
9. Second Souffle
10. Snack Elyse
11. Subway

(R) : Restaurant

FORT-DE-FRANCE

and founder of the *Parti Progressiste Martiniquais*.

Today, Fort-de-France is expanding more and more, and residential areas are springing up in the hills surrounding the city. There are the working-class sections bordering the city centre, such as Saint-Thérèse and Trenelle. Fashionable neighbourhoods like Redoute, Didier and Balata lie higher up. Fort-de-France also extends so far to the west that it is no longer possible to distinguish where it stops and Schœlcher begins. The waterfront area in the east is also booming, due not only to the shipping industry, but also to cruise-ship tourism.

Arriving by sea on the ferry that departs from Pointe du Bout will enable you to appreciate Fort-de-France from its most flattering angle. Visitors enjoy a spectacular view of this bustling little city, nestled at the very farthest end of the magnificent Baie des Flamands and surrounded by hills, with peaks of some of the island's highest mountains silhouetted in the background. Once the ferry has docked, you may notice the city's limited number of monuments, which are also not quite as old as one might hope (very few date from before the fire of 1890). The big shopping streets are enjoyably lively, and residents bustle about, contradicting the traditional stereotypes of island nonchalance. You will also fall in love with Place de la Savane, a vast green space in the centre of downtown, where everyone comes to relax or see and be seen.

It takes a day to explore Fort-de-France. All of its monuments are located within a relatively limited area, which makes it easy to visit them on foot. The only reason you might need a car is to visit a few sights on the outskirts of town, which you can get to just as easily by taking a private or collective taxi. In fact, traffic is so congested in and around the city that it is much wiser, and much more pleasant, to take the ferry from Pointe du Bout and then explore the outskirts on foot.

FINDING YOUR WAY AROUND

By Car

To reach Fort-de-France from Lamentin Airport, take the *Route Nationale 5* (N5) to the N1, which goes into the city. Near the Dillon area, the N1 runs down towards the centre of the city, then comes to an end on Boulevard du Général-de-Gaulle.

Driving and parking are difficult downtown. We therefore recommend that you take the ferry from Pointe du Bout to Fort-de-France (see below).

Car Rentals

All of the international rental agencies in Martinique have prime locations in Fort-de-France:

Avis
4 Rue Ernest-Deproge
☎05.96.73.73.20 or 70.11.60

Budget
30 Rue Ernest-Deproge
☎05.96.70.22.75 or 63.69.00

Europcar
28 Rue Ernest-Deproge
☎05.96.73.33.13 or 42.42.42

Hertz
24 Rue Ernest-Deproge
☎05.96.60.64.64

By Taxi

It is easy to get a taxi in Fort-de-France. You will find several on Rue de la Liberté, which runs along the west side of Place de la Savane.

By Collective Taxi

The collective taxi depot is at Pointe Simon, on the waterfront. These taxis start running very early in the morning, but stop at 6pm. To give you an idea of the rates, it costs 17F to go to Trois-Îlets, 19F to go to Diamant, 31F to go to Sainte-Anne, 18F to go to Sainte-Pierre, and 40F to go to Grand-Rivière.

By Bus

Taking the bus is an inexpensive way to reach the outskirts of Fort-de-France. The main stations are on Boulevard du Général-de-Gaulle.

By Boat

Four ferries (for pedestrians only) make the trip between the Pointe du Bout marina and Quai Desnambuc in Fort-de-France. This service is operated by Somatour *(☎05.96.75.05.53)*. The rates are as follows:

Adults (one-way)	19F
Children (one-way)	10F
Adults (round-trip)	32F
Children (round-trip)	15F

There are frequent departures:

From Pointe du Bout to Fort-de-France: 6:10am, 7:15am, 8:30am, 9:30am, 10:30am, 11:30am, 12:45pm, 2:30pm, 3:30pm, 4:30pm, 5:30pm, 6:30pm, 7:30pm, 10:45pm, 11:45pm.

Visitors staying in the little hotels in Anse Mitan or even Anse à l'Âne need not go all the way to Pointe du Bout to catch a ferry, since a shuttle service is offered from the landing stages at both beaches. There are frequent departures and the fares are similar.

Ferries also ply between Fort-de-France and Guadeloupe, Dominica, Les Saintes and St. Lucia every day. The adult fares range from 305F to 450F (one-way). These ferries leave from the Quai Ouest in Fort-de-France, at the entrance to the dry dock. For departure times and exact prices, contact **L'Express des Îles** *(☎05.96.63.12.11, ⊶05.96.63.34.47)*.

 ## PRACTICAL INFORMATION

Tourist Information

Office Départemental du Tourisme de la Martinique: Boulevard Alfassa (on the waterfront), ☎05.96.63.79.60, ⊶05.96.73.66.93.

Municipal Tourist Office: 76 Rue Lazare-Carnot, ☎05.96.60.27.73, ⊶05.96.60.27.95.

Maison du Tourisme Vert: 9 Boulevard du Général-de-Gaulle, ☎05.96.73.67.92.

Union des Syndicats d'Initiative: 9 Boulevard du Général-de-Gaulle, ☎05.96.63.18.54 or 05.96.63.20.67, ⊶05.96.70.17061.

FORT-DE-FRANCE

Banks

Banque des Antilles Françaises: 34 Rue Lamartine, ☎05.96.60.72.72.

Banque Nationale de Paris: 72 Avenue des Caraïbes, ☎05.96.59.46.00.

Crédit Martiniquais: 17 Rue de la Liberté, ☎05.96.73.25.25.

Bred: Place Monseigneur-Romero, ☎05.96.63.77.63.

Currency Exchange

Change Point: Rue Victor Hugo (between Schœlcher and de la Liberté), ☎05.96.63.35.56; open from 8am to 6pm.

Change Caraïbes: Rue Ernest-Deproge, next to Air France, ☎05.96.60.28.40; open Mon to Fri 7:30am to 6pm, Sat 8am to 12:30pm.

Martinique Change: 137 Rue Victor Hugo, ☎05.96.63.80.33; open Mon to Fri 8:30am to 1pm and 2pm to 5:30pm, Sat 8:30am to 12:30pm.

Police Station

Gendarmerie: 120 Rue Victor-Sévère, ☎05.96.63.51.51

Town Hall

Mairie: ☎05.96.59.60.00, ≈05.96.60.91.69.

Post Office

At the corner of Rue de la Liberté and Blénac, ☎05.96.71.79.68.

Hospitals

Hôpital Clarac: Boulevard Pasteur, ☎05.96.59.25.90.

Hôpital de La Meynard: Route de Redoute, ☎05.96.55.20.00.

Pharmacies

Pharmacie Alain Bucher: Rue de la République, ☎05.96.71.30.04.

Pharmacie de la Cathédrale: 40 Rue Antoine-Siger, ☎05.96.70.20.69.

Pharmacie Glaudon: at the corner of de la Liberté and Antoine-Siger, ☎05.96.70.22.57.

Pharmacie J.F. Ponceau: 64 Avenue des Caraïbes.

Photo Processing

Photocolor: 62 Rue Ernest-Deproge, ☎05.96.60.47.40;

64 Avenue des Caraïbes, ☎05.96.60.28.82.

 EXPLORING

The vast majority of sights in Fort-de-France are clustered around Place de la Savane. We have outlined two walking tours which will enable you to discover the city centre. One covers the area immediately around Place de la Savane, the other, the streets nearby. In a third section, you'll find a list of interesting sights on the outskirts of the city.

If you wish, you may join a small group and take part in one of the four original walking tours designed by an organization called **Azimut** *(90F per person; 74 Route de la Folie; ☎05.96.60.16.59 or 05.96.70.07.00, ⚐05.96.63.05.46)*. One of these is a traditional tour of the major monuments, while the others introduce visitors to what's going on behind the scenes, unusual aspects of the city and lesser-known streets. All tours begin at the Belain d'Esnambuc monument on Place de la Savane.

Place de la Savane

As soon as you get off the ferry and look across Boulevard Alfassa, which runs along the waterfront, you will see a large green space consisting of 5 hectares of flower-fringed paths, majestic royal palms, benches to relax on, commemorative statues of a few prominent individuals and vendor's stalls where people are haggling over prices; this is the magnificent **Place de la Savane ★★★**.

Upon arriving in Fort-de-France, a lot of visitors head straight for the Savane, ready to bargain with vendors over beach towels, T-shirts, hats, dolls, paintings, and countless other articles at the **craft market** located in the west corner of the park.

Unfortunately, it is best to avoid Place de la Savane come nightfall, when it becomes a hangout for rather unsavoury characters.

Facing the sea in the same area, you'll find the bronze **statue of Belain d'Esnambuc**, which honors the "founder" of Martinique, who claimed

the island for France on September 15, 1635. Erected in 1955, it is the work of sculptor Marcel Armand Gaumont, whose other credits include decorating the steamship *Île de France* (1949).

If you head east along Boulevard Alfassa, taking in the sight of the sailboaps moored in the magnificent Baie des Flamands, you will soon reach the **Monument aux Morts**, a war memorial commemorating the Martinicans who gave their lives for France in the two World Wars and the conflicts in Algeria and Indochina.

Farther on, on the other side of Boulevard Chevalier-de-Sainte-Marthe, stands **Fort Saint-Louis ★** *(25F; guided tours Mon to Sat 10am, 11am, noon, 2pm and 3pm; ☎05.96.60.54.59)*. The present military structure stands on the site where Du Parquet and several colonists erected the first small wooden fort, Fort Royal, in 1638. A few years later, Governor De Baas ordered that the fort, which guarded the Baie des Flamands, be reinforced by adding a moat and high stone walls. It was completed in the Vauban style, as we know it today, around 1703.

Fort Royal, which became Fort Edward during the brief British occupations of 1762, 1794 and 1809, and then finally Fort Saint-Louis in 1814, has had a turbulent history. It was first used during the Dutch and English attacks in 1674 and 1759 respectively, and then, less successfully, to defend the city against a subsequent English attack in 1762. This defeat revealed the fort's weakness; surrounded by several hills, it was vulnerable to inland attacks. The construction of Fort Bourbon (see p 79), now Fort Desaix, in the hills of Fort-de-France, eliminated this flaw in the capital's defense system.

At the start of the century, Fort Saint-Louis was transformed into a zoo, but

FORT-DE-FRANCE

Bibliothèque Schœlcher

immediately after World War II, it became the staff headquarters of the Antilles-Guiana division of the French navy.

Back at the Savane, make sure to take a look at the white marble **statue of Empress Josephine**, which stands on the north side of the park. This monument serves as a reminder that Martinique, and more precisely Trois-Îlets, was the birthplace of Marie-Josèphe Rose Tascher de la Pagerie (1763-1814), wife of Napoleon Bonaparte. According to legend, the statue, a gift from Napoleon III, was originally erected on the exact spot where a cannon ball landed at the feet of the future empress in 1790. Sculpted by Vital Dubray (1813-1892), it was placed in the centre of the Savane in 1859. Josephine's left hand rests on a medal bearing Napoleon's image, while the bas-relief adorning the front of the base depicts her corona-

tion. In September 1991, the statue of the lovely Creole empress was decapitated, most probably by vandals, who thus subjected the monument to the fate Josephine herself narrowly escaped during the French Revolution. Just like the decision of the municipal government, headed by Aimé Césaire, to move the statue to the edge of the park in 1974, this incident reminds us that the legend of Josephine is one of a white Martinican, and that many people have never accepted Napoleon's decision to reintroduce slavery – upon her advice – in 1802.

Opposite the statue, on the other side of Rue de la Liberté, stands the **Bibliothèque Schœlcher** ★★★ *(free admission; Mon to Thu 8:30am to 5:30pm, Fri and Sat 8:30am to noon, ☎05.96.70.26.67)*, a building of irresistible charm. For many years, it was rumoured that this lovely edifice was built in Paris to house Martinique's pavillion at the 1889 World Fair, and was then dismantled and moved to its present location in 1893. In reality, however, the building was originally displayed in the Tuileries, near the Arc de Triomphe du Carrousel.

The library, which now contains more than 200,000 volumes, was named after Victor Schœlcher, the celebrated deputy who struggled to abolish slavery in the French colonies. Convinced of the importance of furthering education among the black population, he donated his personal collection of 10,000 books to the island in 1883 with the request that a public library be founded. Almost all of the volumes were destroyed in the fire of 1890, which fortunately did not prevent the plans for the library from going ahead. The handsome edifice was designed by Henri Picq, who was also the architect of the Cathédrale Saint-Louis (see below). Its style is somewhat difficult to define, however; some describe it as neo-Oriental, others as Roman-Byzantine, while the more cautious say baroque. In any case, the Bibliothèque Schœlcher, built at the same time as the Eiffel Tower, has become the symbol of Fort-de-France.

The **Hôtel de la Préfecture de Fort-de-France** stands on the other side of Rue Victor-Sévère. The U-shaped buildings are not only impressive in their own right, but are also laid out in a striking manner, forming a lovely ceremonial pathway. Built between 1925 and 1928, they were the first structures made of reinforced concrete to be erected in Martinique. The main building is modelled on the Petit Trianon at Versailles. Inside, you will find, among other things, a painting by Paul Mascart depicting workers cutting sugar cane (at the far end of the Salle Félix-Éboué), as well as a bust of Victor Schœlcher by Martinican artist Marie-Thérèse Lung-Fou, in the room that now bears

the celebrated abolitionist's name. Next door to the prefecture stands the **Pavillon Bougenot**, a stately yellow turn-of-the-century residence soon to become the Musée Départemental d'Art Contemporain.

Retracing your steps, continue your tour up **Rue de la Liberté**, which runs past a number of beautiful buildings housing hotels, bars, restaurants, shops, etc. You will soon reach the not-to-be-missed **Musée Départemental ★★★** *(adults 15F, children 5F; Mon to Fri 8:30am to 1pm and 2pm to 5pm, Sat 9am to noon, 9 Rue de la Liberté, ☎05.96.71.57.05)*. This museum, which focuses on the island's pre-Columbian history, informs visitors about the settlement of the Arawak and, later, Carib Indians on the island. More than 1,000 artifacts (pottery, figurines, engraved goblets, etc.) found during archaeological digs provide insights into Amerindian history in Martinique in the period between 4000 BC and 1660 AD. The building itself was previously the military supplies office, and dates back to 1898.

If you continue, you will reach the waterfront. The offices of Air France and the **Office Départemental du Tourisme** are both nearby.

Downtown

Right behind the departmental tourist office lies the **Centre des Métiers d'Art**, which offers a fairly comprehensive selection of local handicrafts (see p 86).

Walk a short distance back up Rue Schœlcher to **Cathédrale Saint-Louis ★**. Its lofty bell tower (59 m) with its metal framework is a landmark, recognizable from far away. The present church, designed by Henri Picq, dates

Cathédrale Saint-Louis

back only to 1895; it is in fact the seventh to be built on this site. The history of Fort-de-France's cathedral, however, can be traced back to the early days of colonization, and parallels the city's own turbulent past, for it has been destroyed and rebuilt time and again after various natural disasters and military assaults. The first church of Fort-Royal was erected near the wooden fort in 1639. It was moved to the present site in 1671; the present church stands on the original foundations. During the Dutch attack of 1674, the original chapel was burned. It was rebuilt in 1703, and then wiped out by a tidal wave in 1766. In 1839, an earthquake levelled it once more. It was devastated yet again by the fire of 1890, and the following year, a hurricane destroyed whatever had been left standing. The present church was inaugurated in 1895, but the earthquakes of 1946 and 1953 weakened the original bell tower so that it had to be demolished in 1971. The bell tower visi-

tors see today was erected in 1979, and the cathedral was restored in 1982.

Inside, the beautiful stained-glass windows depict the church's stormy history. Three governors have been interred in the cathedral's chancel: de Blénac, d'Éragny and d'Amblimont. Opposite the cathedral lies **Place Monseigneur-Romero**, a small square formerly known as **Place Labat**, which has recently been given a facelift.

Farther on, at the corner of Rue Moreau-de-Jonnes and Rue Schœlcher, you will see the **Palais de Justice ★**, or courthouse, also on the left side. In the centre of a square, surrounded by four neoclassic buildings, stands the **Victor Schœlcher Monument**, by Marquet de Vaselot, which dates from 1904; the Palais de Justice itself was not inaugurated until 1907. The monument shows Schœlcher accompanying the child of a recently freed slave along the path of education.

Continue walking until you reach Rue Victor-Sévère, then turn left on your way to the **former Hôtel de Ville ★**, or city hall, now the Théâtre Municipal. Even in the days when this building was still the city hall, the administrative offices shared their space with an Italian-style theatre! The building was constructed in 1901 on the exact spot where the first city hall had been built in 1848 and later destroyed by the fire of 1890 and the hurricane of the following year. When the city's administrative offices were moved in 1980, the building, which was entirely renovated in 1987, was given a new role. It is now used not only for theatrical productions, but also for occasional temporary art exhibits.

On April 29, 1908, a tragic event marked the building's history, when the city's black mayor, Antoine Siger, was shot and killed within its walls in the middle of his election campaign. Siger's body then lay in state on the table used by the city council.

Behind the Théâtre Municipal, you may well be surprised by the audacious, even aggressive architecture of the modern structure that now houses the mayor's office, the **Centre Administratif et Culturel**.

Continue walking to Place Clémenceau, at the very end of Rue Victor-Sévère, then turn right on your way to the entrance of the **Parc Floral et Culturel** (see "Parks and Beaches", p 80).

Your tour of downtown Fort-de-France ends with a visit to the city's various markets, which are always bustling: the **produce market**, the **fish market** and the **covered market** (see "Shopping", p 87).

Surroundings of Fort-de-France

Overlooking the right-hand side of the Rivière Madame is an eye-catching water tower, the **Fontaine Gueydon**, which is visible from the intersection of Boulevard Allègre and Rue Antoine-Sigier. It was built between 1854 and 1856 under the orders of Governor Louis-Henry de Gueydon to provide the city with drinking water. During the somewhat chaotic period following the abolition of slavery in 1848, Gueydon was assigned the task of putting people back to work and stabilizing public finances. He tackled his duty zealously, assigning mandatory jobs to the unemployed, then establishing a "passport" system, which enabled him to verify people's identities and make sure everyone was working – and paying taxes. Those who transgressed the law were immediately convicted. Gueydon was thus able to build the water tower

that bears his name at a very low cost, using labour provided by his own soldiers and those individuals found guilty of tax evasion.

Plateau Didier ★★

Be sure to take a stroll around Plateau Didier, which is probably the most beautiful residential area in the city. To get there, go over the Pont de l'Abattoir bridge that crosses the Rivière Madame at the end of Rue Ernest-Deproge, then take the D45 northwards. Gorgeous Louisiana-style colonial villas, gleaming white and surrounded by sumptuous gardens, line the road.

The road then winds along through lush vegetation and finally comes to an end at the **Fontaine Didier**, a thermal spring (33° C) whose waters contain carbonic acid and traces of iron. Back in 1853, Didier was the first person to use the water to treat people suffering from liver disorders and rheumatism. If you so desire, you can arrange a visit of the bottling plant, which opened in 1917 (☎05.96.64.07.88).

You can finish off your visit with a hike to the former Absalon spa (see p 80).

Fort Desaix

Route de la Redoute leads to Fort Desaix, originally known as Fort Bourbon. The 1762 English invasion exposed Fort Royal's vulnerability when attacked from inland, and the day after the signing of the Treaty of Paris, a decision was made to build this new Vauban-style fortress in the city's hills. It was completed in 1780.

During World War II, the gold from the Bank of France, which had been transported to Martinique on the cruiser

Émile-Bertin, was stored in Fort Desaix. Today the fort is the headquarters of the superior command of the Antilles-Guiana region, and houses the 33rd naval infantry regiment.

Finally, on Route de la Folie, the **Musée "Gen Lontan"** *(30F; Tue to Thu 9am to 1pm and 3:30pm to 5:30pm, Fri 9:30am to 1pm; 94 Route de la Folie, ☎05.96.63.88.62)* uses period clothing to illustrate the history of Martinique. It also exhibits a collection of Creole Christmas figurines.

PARKS AND BEACHES

Parc Floral et Culturel

These botanical gardens, located behind Place José-Marti (which is in fact more of a parking lot than a square) contain various species of tropical flowers. You can also visit the **Galerie de Géologie et de Botanique** *(adults 5F, children 1F; Tue to Fri 9am to 12:30pm and 2:30pm to 5:30pm, Sat 9am to 1pm and 3pm to 5pm, closed Sun and Mon; ☎05.96.70.68.41 or 05.96.63.65.51)* or take part in one of the many cultural events sponsored by the park (exhibits, concerts, etc.). Entry to the outside portion of the park is free.

Also within the Parc Floral et Culturel, is the **Exotarium** *(2F; Mon to Fri 9am to 4pm, closed Sat and Sun; ☎05.96.71.33.96)*, which is actually Fort-de-France's municipal aquarium.

Beaches

We do not recommend swimming at the beach at Fort Saint-Louis, which is right near the docks for ferries travelling between the Fort-de-France and Point du Bout, and is occasionally frequented by somewhat disreputable individuals. Martinicans themselves prefer Pointe du Bout, on the other side of the bay, or Anse Mitan and Anse à l'Âne (see p 95).

OUTDOOR ACTIVITIES

Hiking

Fontaine Didier - Absalon Trail

This trail starts at Fontaine Didier, at the very end of the D45, and follows the Rivière Dumauzé to the former Absalon spa.

It's a pleasant two-kilometre walk, which takes about an hour and a half, and is considered easy.

Horseback Riding

A stop at the La Gourmette stables *(☎05.96.64.20.16)*, located on the D45, can easily be added to our suggested tour of the area.

ACCOMMODATIONS

Place de la Savanne

Facing Place de la Savane on Rue de la Liberté, four attractive hotels compete for tourists' favour. The first one you'll come across, at the corner of Rue de la Liberté and Rue Ernest-Deproge, is **Le Tortuga** *(195-250F; ≡, pb; 3 Rue de la Liberté, 97200 Fort-de-France, ☎05.96.71.53.23, ⌐05.96.63.80.00)*, an inexpensive place with stark but well-kept rooms.

Ulysses' Favourites

Accommodations	**Restaurants**

Accommodations

For elegance:
L'Impératrice (p 82)

For sports buffs:
Squash Hotel (p 82)

For the architecture:
Valmenière (p 83)

For businesspeople:
Squash Hotel (p 82)
Valmenière (p 83)

Restaurants

For the finest dining:
La Mouïna (p 84)

For the romantic ambiance:
La Belle Époque (p 84)

For innovative cuisine:
Le Second Souffle (p 84)

For authentic Creole cuisine:
Marie-Sainte (p 84)

FORT-DE-FRANCE

Hôtel L'Impératrice

The **La Malmaison** *(300-330F; tv, ≡, pb, ℜ; 7 Rue de la Liberté, 97200 Fort-de-France;   ☎05.96.63.90.85, ⌐05.96.60.03.93)* hotel is located right next to the Musée Départemental. This is a friendly hotel where you'll always receive a warm welcome. The decor and size of the rooms vary; it's best to see them first before choosing one.

A short distance away lies the **Lafayette** *(400F; tv, ≡, pb; 5 Rue de la Liberté, 97200 Fort-de-France; ☎05.96.73.80.50, ⌐05.96.60.97.75)*, whose blue and white awnings are bound to catch your eye. It has 24 simple but spotless rooms.

🌴 Finally, a little further on, you'll find the magnificent **Impératrice** *(385-520F; tv, ≡, pb, ℜ; 15 Rue de la Liberté - 97200 Fort-de-France; ☎05.96.63.06.82, ⌐05.96.72.66.30)*. This is an extremely handsome hotel whose superb façade will remind you of a great ocean-liner. Inside, there are 24 comfortable rooms, as well as a pleasant restaurant called Le Joséphine.

Downtown

A number of small hotels lie tucked away on the charming little streets north of La Savane. These places cater mainly to budget-conscious travellers and locals.

Un Coin de Paris *(260F; tv, ≡, pb; 54 Rue Lazare-Carnot - 97200 Fort-de-France, ☎05.96.70.08.52, ⌐05.96.63.09.51)* is a wooden house whose faded appearance gives it an irresistible cachet.

A stone's throw away, **Le Carlton** *(250F; tv, ≡, pb; 9 Rue Redoute de Matouba - 97200 Fort-de-France, ☎05.96.60.78.67 or 05.96.60.19.85, ⌐05.96.60.19.88)* is housed in a lovely brown-and-tan building on the corner of Rue Redoute de Matouba. This rather commonplace and spartan establishment has nine rooms.

Finally, at the corner of Jacques-Cazotte and Bouillé stands the **Gommier** *(280-375F; tv, ≡, pb; 1-4 Rue Jacques-Cazotte - 97200 Fort-de-France, ☎05.96.71.88.55, ⌐05.96.73.06.96)*, a lovely pink and grey building equipped with balconies. Its spacious rooms offer a higher level of comfort than those of its neighbouring competitors.

A few more hotels lie scattered about here and there on the other streets downtown. As a general rule, they offer no-frills accommodation at affordable prices.

One of these is the **Hôtel Central** *(300-330F; tv, ≡, pb; 3 Rue Victor-Hugo - 97200 Fort-de-France, ☎05.96.70.02.12, ⌐05.96.63.80.00)*, which has tiny but nonetheless well-equipped rooms.

A pleasant place called the **Balisier** *(250F; tv, ≡, pb; 21 Rue Victor-Hugo - 97200 Fort-de-France, ☎/⌐05.96.71.46.54)* is also located on Rue Victor-Hugo. For greater peace and quiet, ask for a room at the back.

Surroundings of Fort-de-France

The little hotel **Victoria** *(350F; tv, pb, ≈, ≡, K; Route de Didier 97200 Fort-de-France,   ☎05.96.60.56.78, ⌐05.96.60.00.24)*, which has about 40 rooms and offers an unimpeded view of Fort-de-France and its lovely bay, is a good choice, considering its enchanting location (Route de Didier) and its proximity to the main city (less than 1 km).

You will find the city's most chic hotel, **Le Squash Hotel** *(745F; tv, ≡, pb, ≈, ℜ;*

3 Boulevard de la Marne - 97200 Fort-de-France, ☎*05.96.72.80.80,* ≈*05.96.63.00.74),* on the road to Schœlcher. This is a luxurious establishment, which has 108 rooms and offers a complete range of services to its clientele, frequented primarily by businesspeople. The hotel's health club is particularly well-equipped, with three squash courts, a weight-room, a sauna and a whirlpool.

 The most recently built hotel in Fort-de-France, the **Valmenière** *(640-690F; tv, ≡, pb, ≈; Avenue des Arawaks - 97200 Fort-de-France,* ☎*05.96.75.75.75, ≈05.96.75.69.70)* caters mainly to businesspeople. Its striking silhouette stands out on the left as you head east out of town, toward Lamentin Airport. Open since late 1994, it is a handsome glass building with suspended walkways and balconies, giving it a futuristic look. The Valmenière has 117 guest rooms, four conference rooms, a workout room and a swimming pool. A glass elevator will take you up to Le Dôme, a Creole restaurant on the 8th floor.

RESTAURANTS

Place de la Savanne

For a quick bite to eat, try **Pain-Beurre-Chocolat**, on the ground floor of the Tortuga hotel (see p 80), which offers a good selection of sandwiches. **L'Épi Soleil**, at the corner of De la Liberté and Perrinon, is a similar type of place.

The **Snack Élyse** *(20F)*, located near the Cinéma Espace Élysée on Avenue des Caraïbes, north of the Savane, is another economical option.

La Taverne Malmaison *(60F; closed Sun)*, on the ground floor of La Mal-

maison (see p 82), serves tasty, inexpensive food, including pizza, merguez sausages and steak.

The first restaurant facing the Savane that you will spot along Rue de la Liberté is **Le Planteur** *(150F; closed all day Saturday and Sun for lunch;* ☎*05.96.63.17.45)*. We recommend the *menu découverte*, which allows you to sample a variety of dishes, including *boudin* (blood pudding), *accras*, stuffed crab, chicken *colombo*, and *lambi* and *chatrou* fricassee. Since the restaurant is located on the second floor, it offers the added attraction of a panoramic view of Baie de Fort-de-France.

Le Joséphine *(250F; closed Sat; 15 Rue de la Liberté,* ☎*05.96.63.06.82)*, also located on the second floor of a hotel facing the Savane (the Impératrice, see p 82), serves delicious food in a romantic, typically Créole atmosphere. A 70F set menu is offered at lunchtime.

Downtown

Elsewhere downtown, there are a number of places where you can purchase your own food. You'll find several little grocery stores and fish-shops along **Rue Victor-Sévère**, near the **fish market**. Vegetables are also sold in many places on this street.

You can also try the **covered market**, at the corner of Blénac and Isambert, the **meat market** right behind it on Rue Antoine-Siger, and the **produce market** near the Parc Floral.

Finally, there is a **8 à huit** grocery store at the corner of Rue Victor-Hugo and Rue de la République and a **MATCH supermarket** on Rue Antoine-Siger.

FORT-DE-FRANCE

Those looking for cheap places to eat might not be disappointed to discover that Fort-de-France is being overrun by American fast-food giants. There are two **McDonald's**, located a block apart, which you can't miss, and a **Subway**.

The **Bar-Resto West Indies** *(70F; Rue Ernest-Deproge, ☎05.96.70.43.94)* (see also p 85), formerly known as Cocoloco, allows you to indulge in reasonably priced dishes, such as the 45F daily special (brochettes, chicken in coconut milk), in a lively ambiance.

🦐 However, if you are in the mood for something more authentic, head to **Marie-Sainte** *(90F; open only for lunch, closed Sun; 160 Rue Victor-Hugo, ☎05.96.63.82.24)*, a pleasant restaurant frequented by people who work in the neighbourhood. You will be served a generous portion of succulent homestyle Creole cooking. Rest assured, this is a very good place to eat, so don't be put off by the modest decor.

🦐 **Le Second Souffle** *(100F; closed on weekends; 27 Rue de Blénac, ☎05.96.63.44.11)*, located beside the cathedral, is not to be missed. This is a vegetarian restaurant whose chef clearly enjoys concocting a series of dishes based on the island's fruits and vegetables. The result is a menu made up of yam soufflés, breadfruit *parmentiers*, okra quiches, and the chef's own fruit cake. This is an address to remember! Credit cards are not accepted.

Closer to the Savane on the same street, you'll find **Le Blénac** *(150F; closed Sun evenings; 3 Rue de Blénac, ☎05.96.70.18.41)*, where you can eat very well without ruining your budget. Their tournedos, for example, are delicious. For dessert, try one of their home-made flans.

For a late supper, head to **La Case** *(190F; closed Sun; 108 Rue Ernest-Deproge, ☎05.96.63.04.00)*, a pleasant restaurant that serves meals until midnight. The menu lists Creole, French and Italian specialties. Friendly service and cozy decor.

Surroundings of Fort-de-France

Nowhere else will you find a better blend of Paris and the Antilles than at **Bistrot de la Marne** *(120-250F; Boulevard de la Marne; ☎05.96.72.80.80)*, the Squash Hotel's restaurant (see p 82). The interior is a perfect example of a traditional Parisian brasserie; while outside, the pool-side terrace is virtually enveloped by tropical vegetation. On the menu, you'll find various selections from the grill, a Creole paella and a lot of desserts.

La Fontane (see p 192).

When they met in the spring of 1991, François Mitterand and George Bush chose to dine at **La Mouïna** *(250F; closed on weekends; 127 Route de la Redoute, ☎05.96.79.34.57)*, a very pleasant restaurant located inside an equally pleasant colonial house in the hills of Fort-de-France. Their choice was a wise one. If you're looking for classic French cuisine, this is the place to come. The *escargots de Bourgogne*, veal kidneys and raspberry charlotte make a meal you won't soon forget.

🦐 What a beautiful place! We're talking about **La Belle Époque** *(250F; closed Sat for lunch and all day Sun; 97 Route de Didier, ☎05.96.64.41.19)*, a gourmet French restaurant in the chic neighbourhood of Didier. Its splendid dining room, adorned with finely carved, gleaming white furniture, opens onto a pretty Creole garden. A feast before the meal even begins and a romantic atmosphere.

  ENTERTAINMENT

Place de la Savanne

The bar at the **Impératrice** *(15 Rue de la Liberté)*, on Place de la Savane, is the perfect spot for an *apéritif*. In fact, sipping a glass of *ti-punch* at the Impératrice has become a sort of Fort-de-France tradition over the years. Why miss out?

One of the city's movie theatres, the **Espace Élysée** *(44 Rue des Caraïbes, ☎05.96.71.41.41)* is located on Rue des Caraïbes, on the north side of the park.

Downtown

On the waterfront, in the same building as the Centre des Métiers d'Art, you'll find **Bar-Resto West Indies** *(Mon to Sat 10pm to 3am, Sun from 6pm; Rue Ernest-Deproge, ☎05.96.63.63.77)*, a fun place to go for popular live music.

If you're looking for a really nice place to have a beer, try **Le Terminal** *(Mon to Fri 10:30pm to 2am, Sat and Sun 6pm to 2am; 104 Rue Ernest-Deproge, ☎05.96.63.03.48)*, which is right nearby, a few steps away from the collective taxi depot. You can sample some 60 beers and 35 whiskies.

Internet surfers, for their part, might want to check out the **Web Cyber Café** *(10am to 1am; 4 Rue de Blénac)*, where they can sip a beer or a planter's punch while browsing at one of two available terminals.

La Case (see p 84) will not only serve you dinner later than most other places in town, but also has a pleasant piano bar called **Le Jardin de la Case** *(108 Rue Ernest-Deproge)*, where you can draw out the evening until 2am.

If you're in the mood to make a spectacle of yourself, head to **Le Tuttifrutti** *(every day 6pm to 2am, Fri and Sat until dawn; 14 Rue François-Arago, ☎05.96.71.54.64)* for some karaoke.

Fort-de-France has a few theatres, the two largest being the **Théâtre Municipal**, in the former town hall, and the **Théâtre de la Soif Nouvelle**, on Place Clémenceau. The much awaited **Grand Centre Culturel de Fort-de-France**, on Boulevard du Général-de-Gaulle, was slated to open in the spring of 1998.

There are two movie theatres downtown, the **Ciné-Théâtre** *(65 Rue Victor-Sévère, ☎05.96.60.59.59)* and the **Cinéma Élysées** *(106 bis Rue Victor-Sévère, ☎05.96.59.35.34)*.

 SHOPPING

Shopping Streets

It won't take you long to notice that shopping is hectic in Fort-de-France. Several of the downtown streets welcome thousands of shoppers every day. Among these, **Victor-Hugo, Moreau-de-Jonnes, Antoine-Siger, Schœlcher** and **de la République streets** have the nicest shops. You'll see one famous name after the other – Chanel, Dior, Yves Saint-Laurent, Lacoste, Rolex, Mont Blanc...

Also worth noting are the **Galeries Lafayette** *(10 Rue Schœlcher, ☎05.96.71.38.66)*, located a stone's throw from the Cathédrale Saint-Louis.

FORT-DE-FRANCE

On the corner of Schœlcher and Perrinon is the **Librairie Antillaise** (☎05.96.60.61.60 or 50.66.44). This excellent bookstore has bit of everything, from travel guides on Martinique to beautiful picture books as well as the most recent works of Martinican authors. Fort-de-France actually has several bookstores. Among them, the **Librairie Générale Caraïbe** (109 Rue Victor-Hugo, ☎05.96.72.55.56), the **Librairie Alexandre** (54 Rue Lamartine) as well as the **Librairie Temps de Vivre** on the same street, close to Schœlcher. Not far on Rue Schœlcher is **La Cité du Livre**. Finally, also of note is the **Librairie de La Pensée** (87 Rue Moreau-de-Jonnes, ☎05.96.71.60.78).

If you're looking for hand-crafted jewellery, try the **Bijouterie Onyx** (☎05.96.73.65.05, 26 Rue Isambert). Gold forçat-style bracelets, necklaces and chains can be found at the **Gold Centres** (26 Rue Lamartine, 88 Rue Antoine-Siger or 44 Rue Victor-Hugo).

Fort-de-France also has its own outlet of the well-known chain of health food stores launched by the world-renowned nutrition expert **Michel Montignac** (77 Rue Blénac, ☎05.96.70.21.69).

Wine lovers will be delighted to discover the impressive selection of bottles at **La Cave à Vin** (118 Rue Victor-Hugo, ☎05.96.70.33.02). There is a little dining room at the back with a 59F lunch menu.

Souvenirs and Handicrafts

The **Centre des Métiers d'Art** (Rue Ernest Deproge), located on the waterfront, will provide you with an excellent overview of island handicrafts.

You'll find both treasures and trash in the souvenir shops lining **Ernest-Deproge** and **de la Liberté**. We recommend **Arts Caraïbes** (38 Rue Ernest-Deproge; ☎05.96.73.73.20) and the former **Carambole**, renamed **Paradise Island** (20 Rue Ernest-Deproge, ☎05.96.63.93.63), no doubt to make it more appealing to American tourists from the cruise ships that stop at nearby Pointe Simon, for carved wood, collectible dolls, and Creole jewellery; **La Case à Rhum** (5 Rue de la Liberté; ☎05.96.60.40.99), not only for rum, but also for honey, jam and candied fruits.

At **Artisanat Cas'inti** (73 Rue Blénac), a lovely shop located near the Cathédrale Saint-Louis, you will find beautiful reproductions of Arawak and Carib pottery, as well as lamps, vases and miniature Creole houses made of terra cotta.

For recordings of West Indian music, sheet music and instruments like drums, make your way to **Muzikol**, which is well-hidden at the corner of Rue Jacques-Cazotte and Rue de la Redoute de Matouba. Now there is another easier-to-find Muzikol branch at the Centre des Métiers d'Art, on Rue Ernest-Déproge.

The best bargains, however, are to be found at the **craft market on the Savane**. There is nothing more enjoyable than negotiating outdoors with the various craftspeople over their endless assortment of merchandise – T-shirts, dolls, head scarves, jewellery, etc. You are welcome to bargain, of course, and your "opponents" won't hesitate to butter you up with sweet talk. The game (for that's exactly what it is) is altogether irresistible.

There is another market exclusively for hand-made leather goods, located on Rue Moreau-de-Jonnes, at the corner of Rue de la République.

Markets

Make sure not to miss the exuberant energy, enticing edibles, extravagant vendors and kaleidoscopic nature of the city's markets.

Early in the morning, as soon as the fishermen return to shore, head over to the **marché aux poissons** (fish market), in Place Clémenceau on the banks of the Rivière Madame. You'll hardly believe your eyes when you see the brilliant colours of the tropical fish laid out in the stalls.

The **marché aux légumes** (produce market), located right nearby, next to the Parc Floral, is also a must. Here, too, the art of bargaining takes on epic dimensions.

Finally, there's the **marché couvert** (covered market), at the corner of Blénac and Isambert, a giant bazaar where you can buy just about everything under the sun – spices, flowers, medicinal herbs, handicrafts, etc.

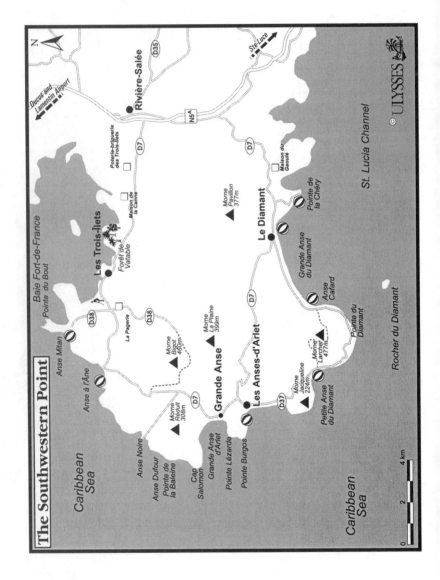

The Southwestern Point

N

Baie Fort-de-France
Pointe du Bout

Caribbean
Sea

Anse Mitan
Anse à l'Âne
Anse Noire
Anse Dufour
Pointe de
la Baleine
Cap
Salomon
Grande Anse
d'Arlet
Pointe Lézarde
Pointe Burgos

Ducos and
Lamentin Airport

Rivière-Salée

D35

Ste-Luce

Poterie-briquerie
des Trois-Îlets

Maison de
la Canne

Les Trois-Îlets

Forêt de
Vatable

La Pagerie

D38

D38

Morne
Bigot
460m

Morne
Réduit
308m

Morne
La Plaine
399m

D7

Grande Anse

Les Anses-d'Arlet

D7

D37

Morne
Jacqueline
224m

Petite Anse
du Diamant

Morne
Larcher
477m

Morne
Pavillon
377m

Le Diamant

D7

N5A

D7

Maison du
Gaoulé

Grande Anse
du Diamant

Anse
Cafard

Pointe du
Diamant

Pointe de
la Chéry

St. Lucia Channel

Rocher du Diamant

Caribbean
Sea

0   2   4 km

© ULYSSES

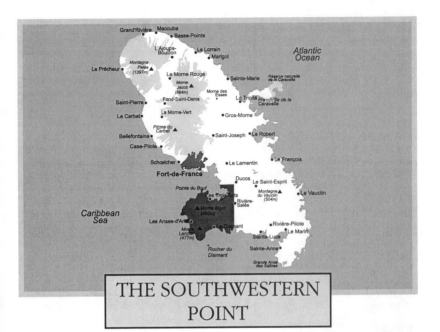

THE SOUTHWESTERN POINT

he southwest point, a large peninsula jutting out into the Caribbean Sea, whose westernmost part is marked by Cap Salomon, is Martinique's main tourist area. Its northern coast, lapped by the waters of the Baie de Fort-de-France, is directly across from the capital city, while its southern coast looks out on the St. Lucia Channel, where you'll see the famous Rocher du Diamant (Diamond Rock).

All along the coast, there are fine stretches of sand lined with various types of trees (coconut, almond, sea grapes, etc.). These beaches, some of which are among the most famous in the Caribbean, welcome visitors from all over the world (Grande Anse du Diamant, Grande Anse d'Arlet, Anse à l'Âne, Anse Mitan...). Further inland, however, the land becomes much more uneven, studded with strangely shaped hills (*mornes*), such as Morne Larcher

(477 m), which looks like a woman lying down; Morne Jacqueline (224 m), with its sharply pointed peak; and others, like Bigot (460 m), Réduit (308 m), La Plaine (399 m) and Pavillon (377 m).

The territory is divided into three districts. **Le Diamant**, in the south, has a long beach, which is pounded by an occasionally heavy surf; several luxury hotels on Pointe de la Chéry and the famous Rocher du Diamant, the symbol of Martinique. **Anses-d'Arlet**, on the west coast, is composed of several bays, which are frequented by fishermen using seines (large nets), and a beautiful family-oriented beach (Grande Anse). The **Trois-Îlets** district, in the north, presents itself as a kind of tourist paradise, with its upscale marina (Pointe du Bout), sumptuous hotels (the Méridien, the Bakoua, etc.), jam-packed beaches (Anse-Mitan, Anse à l'Âne), museums (Domaine de la Pagerie, Maison de la Canne, Parc des Floralies, etc.) and beautiful golf course.

The Southwest point has also been the site of several important historical events. The 1717 uprising of Creole sugar-plantation owners (the *Gaoulé*), for example, took place near Le Diamant. Then, in 1804, the English, aiming to conquer Martinique, took possession of Rocher du Diamant, fortified it and made it a veritable British Navy "vessel", so to speak. On top of these events, it was also in this region that Empress Josephine was born, in 1763, near the town of Trois-Îlets.

In short, the area has everything to please even the most demanding travellers. For that matter, its main industry, as you have probably already guessed, is tourism.

 FINDING YOUR WAY AROUND

By Car

From Fort-de-France, take boulevard Général-de-Gaulle to *Route Nationale* 1 (N1), towards Le Lamentin, and then head towards Sainte-Luce on the N5. You can then take either the exit for Trois-Îlets and Pointe du Bout, or the exit for Le Diamant, which is a little farther. The latter will start you on the clockwise tour of the area that is detailed in the following pages.

From Sainte-Anne, take *Route Départementale* 9 (D9) through the village of Le Marin, then get on the N5. The exit for Le Diamant is well marked.

Car Rentals

Diamant
Budget Diamant: ☎05.96.76.18.52.
Europcar International: Novotel Diamant, Pointe de la Chéry, ☎05.96.76.47.18

Pointe de la Chéry
Thrifty: ☎05.96.76.15.96, ≈05.96.76.15.97.

Pointe du Bout
Europcar   International: ☎05.96.66.04.29, ≈05.96.66.17.42
Avis: Hôtel Carayou Trois-Îlets, ☎05.96.66.04.27, ≈05.96.66.11.99.
Budget: ☎05.96.66.00.45
Discount: ☎05.96.66.05.34.
Dom Car Location: ☎05.96.66.11.63
Hertz: ☎05.96.60.06.59
Thrifty: ☎05.96.66.09.59; Hôtel La Pagerie, ☎05.96.66.16.79; Hôtel Novotel Carayou, ☎05.96.66.16.76.

Anse à l'Âne
Madicar: ☎05.96.68.31.65.
Suco: Anses-d'Andet, ☎05.96.68.62.09 or 05.96.68.63.38.

Collective Taxis

It requires a great deal of patience to explore an area by means of collective taxi. Nevertheless, to do so is something of an adventure, and, as such, has a certain appeal. Some people will no doubt let themselves be won over by these so-called "weed-killers". It costs between 14F and 20F to go from Fort-de-France to Trois-Îlets, Le Diamant, or Anses-d'Arlet.

By Boat

You can leave Fort-de-France on one of the ferryboats that shuttle passengers back and forth between the city's wa terfront and the Pointe du Bout marina (see schedule and rates, p 47). The trip, which takes about twenty minutes, is very pleasant and enables you to avoid getting stuck in traffic. Once off the ferry, it is easy to rent a car (as you can see above, there are a lot of rental agencies in Pointe du Bout). You may instead choose to explore the area by hitchhiking or by means of a collective taxi.

There are also ferryboats linking Fort-de-France with Anse Mitan and Anse à l'Âne.

| PRACTICAL INFORMATION |

Le Diamant

Tourist office: ☎05.96.76.14.36, ⇄05.96.76.25.62.

Police: ☎05.96.76.40.03.

Town hall: ☎05.96.76.40.11, ⇄05.96.76.25.62.

Gas station: Esso, on the way into town coming from the east.

Pharmacy: G. Charpentier, next to the cemetery, ☎05.96.76.42.70; A. Sainte-Rose, on the way into town, across from the hotel, Diamant les Bains.

Cleaners: near the post office, in the centre of town.

Anses-d'Arlet

Town hall: ☎05.96.68.62.02, ⇄05.96.68.68.38.

Pharmacy: M. Bernis and the Centre de Soins Infirmiers; open every day ☎05.96.68.73.10 or 68.63.60.

Laundromat: Grande Anse, ☎05.96.68.63.60.

Trois-Îlets

Tourist office: Place Gabriel-Hayot, ☎05.96.68.47.63, ⇄05.96.68.30.39.

Police: ☎05.96.68.31.06.

Town hall: ☎05.96.68.34.11, ⇄05.96.68.30.39.

Gas station: Shell, on the way out of town heading east, right after the traffic circle. Texaco, in Anse à l'Âne, near the Frantour hotel.

Foreign exchange: Martinique Change, Mon to Sat 8:30am to 1pm and 4pm to 6:30pm, ☎05.96.66.04.44 (fax service, photocopies, telephone cards).

Hospital: Avenue Impératrice Joséphine, ☎05.96.66.30.00.

Pharmacies: Pharmacie des Trois-Îlets, ☎05.96.68.30.52.
Pharmacie V. Etienne, Pointe du Bout, ☎05.96.66.00.75.

| EXPLORING |

After taking the Le Diamant exit off of *Route Nationale* 5 (N5), you'll turn onto the narrow, winding D7. Before long, you'll see the sea on your left, as well as the Novotel Hotel's little beach at the very end of Pointe de la Chéry.

Le Diamant ★★★

Maison du Gaoulé

It's very easy to miss the sign for the little road that leads to **Maison de O'Mullane**, also known as **Maison du**

Gaoulé ★, but make sure to stop at this historic sight, which some say was the scene of the first Martinican insurrection.

In 1717, the Governor General of the islands, Antoine d'Arcy, seigneur de La Varenne, was assigned the task of putting an end to the illegal sugar trade between the French islands and their neighbours. In May, he and his steward, Louis-Balthazar de Rincourat d'Hérouville, arrived in Martinique. They were invited to a large banquet at the Bourgeot estate, where, to their surprise, they were held captive by about a hundred furious colonists and then expelled from the island. In the following months, the commercial laws prescribed by France were gradually relaxed enough to satisfy the Martinican planters.

Maison de O'Mullane, now a historic monument, was built on the exact site of the Bourgeot plantation around 1740. The Creole plantation owners' revolt against the royalty in 1717 came to be known as the *Gaoulé*. No one is sure of this term's origins, though some claim it was the Carib word for "revolt." Today, you can visit the ruins of the stone house, which provide an interesting example of colonial architecture.

Pointe de la Chéry

If you continue along the D7, you'll soon reach a recently laid-out traffic circle. One of the roads branching off leads to the luxury hotel complexes (Novotel, Marine Hotel Diamant) on **Pointe de la Chéry**, also known as **Pointe du Marigot**. Take some time to stop and enjoy one of the area's little beaches or just drink in the gorgeous view of **Grande Anse du Diamant**, a superb white sand beach, and the famous **Rocher du Diamant**.

Rocher du Diamant ★★★

Rocher du Diamant, or Diamond Rock, which is indeed shaped like a huge diamond (180 m high, 1 200 m around); stands only 5 kilometres from the town of Le Diamant, which was named after it. This giant block of limestone, which has become a sort of symbol of Martinique around the world, has a unique history. In 1804, the English, led by Admiral Samuel Hood, seized and fortified the rock, they also built munitions depots, an unloading dock, a cistern and even a hospital there. They turned it into a British "warship", called the *HMS Diamond Rock*. Its "crew" of 107 men was charged with keeping the island under blockade by monitoring all sea traffic in the area. Governor Villaret-de-Joyeuse wasn't able to dislodge these men until June 1, 1805, when the French and Spanish fleet, led by Admiral Villeneuve, came to his assistance. The defeated British sailors fled to Barbados and were court-martialed for abandoning their "ship."

The Village of Le Diamant

As you enter the town limits of **Le Diamant**, you can continue on the D7, which becomes a pleasant road known as Route du Morne Blanc and leads straight to Anses-d'Arlet. If you do so, however, you will miss out on the lovely village of Le Diamant, its beautiful four-kilometre stretch of beach, and the gorgeous panoramic views you can take in as you skirt round Morne Larcher.

Inhabited by the Carib Indians as early as the 4th century, the site of the present-day village of Le Diamant, along with what is today the village of Anses-d'Arlet, was the second area on the island to be colonized in the 17th

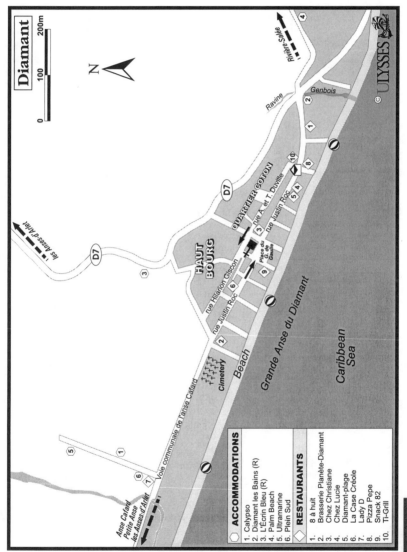

Diamant

0 100 200m

N

les Anses-d'Arlet

Anse Cafard
Petite Anse
les Anses-d'Arlet

Voie communale de l'anse Cafard

D7

HAUT
BOURG

QUARTIER COTON

D7

Ravine

Genbois

Rivière-Salée

rue Hilarion Gisson

rue Justin Roc

rue A. et T. Duville

rue Justin Roc

Place du
G. de Gaulle

Cimetery

Beach

Grande Anse du Diamant

Caribbean
Sea

ULYSSES

SOUTHWESTERN
POINT

⬡ **ACCOMMODATIONS**

1. Calypso
2. Diamant les Bains (R)
3. L'Écrin Bleu (R)
4. Palm Beach
5. Ultramarine
6. Plein Sud

◇ **RESTAURANTS**

1. 8 à huit
2. Brasserie Planète-Diamant
3. Chez Christiane
4. Chez Lucie
5. Diamant-plage
6. La Case Créole
7. Lady D
8. Pizza Pepe
9. Snack 82
10. Ti-Grill

century. A stone church was erected there in the year 1687.

The town stretches all along the main road, which runs through its centre, passing the post office, the town hall, and the **church**. This last building, listed as a historic monument, houses a basin carved out of a single piece of rock, which might very well be part of the original baptismal font (1687). Across the street, in the centre of **Place du Général de Gaulle**, there is a monument honouring those who gave their lives in the two World Wars. The public library, which sometimes arranges exhibits, is next door.

Just past the village, opposite Rocher du Diamant, lies the charming, colourful **Maison du Bagnard** (Convict's House), thus named because it was built in the early 1950s by one Médart Aribo, who had spent 15 years in prison in Guyana for murder before returning to Martinique. Upon his homecoming, he erected this little house, carving the numerous decorative elements himself. With the Rocher du Diamant in the background, it has figured on countless postcards and posters and in all sorts of books as the "symbolic image" of Martinique, thus becoming famous the world over.

Morne Larcher

The road then skirts round **Morne Larcher** (477 m), offering breathtaking panoramic views of the sea and Rocher du Diamant, now only 1,800 metres offshore. A marked path starting at Anse Cafard enables you to enjoy the very best this extraordinary viewing area has to offer (see p 100). On your way towards Anses-d'Arlet, you soon will pass through the modest little village of **Petite Anse**.

Anses-d'Arlet

The Village of Anses-d'Arlet ★★

The road winds up Morne Jacqueline, then starts a spectacular descent towards the village of **Anses-d'Arlet**, recognizable from a distance by the slender silhouette of the bell tower of its beautiful white **church**. The church itself faces a lovely white-sand beach and a large wooden landing stage, which juts out into the turquoise waters of the sea. In addition, an attractive new promenade, which runs along the entire length of the beach, is gradually becoming a local meeting place.

This fishing village, whose population is just over 3,000, was named after a Carib chief, Arlet, who negotiated a pact with Governor Duparquet in 1637, by which he agreed to cede all his land north of the island for settlement . The word "Anses" is written in the plural in reference to the village's location between two *anses* (coves), Petite Anse du Diamant to the south and Grande Anse d'Arlet to the north.

Grande Anse ★★

To leave the village, you must bear right soon after the church. You can then head back towards Le Diamant on Route du Morne Blanc, or continue on to the magnificent **beach at Grande Anse** ★★ (see p 98), which is a favourite among Martinican families. Vacation homes are springing up all over the area, which is becoming one of the most popular resorts on the island.

Anse Dufour and Anse Noire ★★

Continuing on the D7 towards Morne Bigot, be sure not to miss an astonishing geological oddity, the neighbouring beaches of Anse Dufour and Anse Noire. To get there, turn left about three kilometres after Grande Anse, and turn onto a small, discreetly marked road. This steep, narrow lane leads to the two beaches in question.

Anse Dufour, whose beautiful, golden beach is scattered with fishermen's huts and their boats, comes into view first. Park your car and continue on foot along a very short path leading to **Anse Noire**. This unusual and striking beach is covered in black sand, hence its name, and lined with tall coconut palms.

The coexistence of these two beaches, just metres apart, may be seen on the one hand as an interesting geological phenomenon and on the other as a juxtaposition of the two sides of Martinique – the south, with its magnificent beaches, and the north, with its more rugged landscape and dark volcanic soil.

Trois-Îlets ★★★

Anse à l'Âne

After crossing **Morne Bigot** (460 m; there is a hiking trail leading to the top; see p 101), the D7 will take you to **Anse à l'Âne**, another very popular beach, where, among other things, visitors can picnic and camp.

Pointe du Bout and Anse Mitan

Some three kilometres from Anse à l'Âne, you'll see a sign for the D38, which you must turn left onto in order to reach the heart of Martinique's tourist industry, **Pointe du Bout ★★★**. Here lies the greatest concentration of tourist establishments on the island – big luxury hotels, gourmet restaurants, a casino, discotheques and fashionable boutiques. Furthermore, Pointe du Bout is only about twenty minutes from Fort-de-France, thanks to the ferry (see schedule, p 47). The ferryboats pick up and drop off passengers at the marina, where a great number of yachts are moored as well.

In the spring of 1998, the **Village Créole**, a new apartment, shop and restaurant complex, was also under construction at Pointe du Bout.

Right nearby, the beach at **Anse Mitan ★★** welcomes both travelling and local families and is crowded with more modest establishments, such as pleasant inns, bungalows and small beach-side restaurants.

Domaine de la Pagerie ★★★

A little farther in the direction of Trois-Îlets, you will reach Domaine de la Pagerie, the birthplace of Marie-Josèphe Rose Tascher de la Pagerie (1763), who would later become Empress Josephine and wife of Napoleon Bonaparte. She spent her youth here, then left for France in 1779, upon marrying the son of the Marquis de Beauharnais, Alexandre de Beauharnais. In 1788, she returned to the estate with her two children, Eugène and Hortense, for two years, then went back to France. Her husband was executed a few years later, in 1794, during the upheavals of the French Revolution. Joséphine narrowly escaped the guillotine through Robespierre's downfall, and in 1796 finally married Napoleon Bonaparte, who crowned her empress. As she was no longer able to bear children, her

SOUTHWESTERN POINT

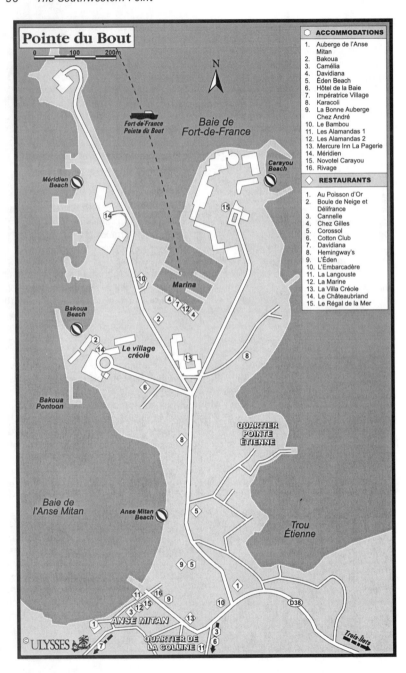

Pointe du Bout

0   100   200m

N

Baie de
Fort-de-France

Fort-de-France
Pointe du Bout

Méridien
Beach

Carayou
Beach

Marina

Bakoua
Beach

Le village
créole

Bakoua
Pontoon

QUARTIER
POINTE
ÉTIENNE

Baie de
l'Anse Mitan

Anse Mitan
Beach

Trou
Étienne

ANSE MITAN

D38

Trois-Îlets

© ULYSSES

QUARTIER DE
LA COLLINE

ACCOMMODATIONS

1. Auberge de l'Anse Mitan
2. Bakoua
3. Camélia
4. Davidiana
5. Éden Beach
6. Hôtel de la Baie
7. Impératrice Village
8. Karacoli
9. La Bonne Auberge Chez André
10. Le Bambou
11. Les Alamandas 1
12. Les Alamandas 2
13. Mercure Inn La Pagerie
14. Méridien
15. Novotel Carayou
16. Rivage

RESTAURANTS

1. Au Poisson d'Or
2. Boule de Neige et Délifrance
3. Cannelle
4. Chez Gilles
5. Corossol
6. Cotton Club
7. Davidiana
8. Hemingway's
9. L'Éden
10. L'Embarcadère
11. La Langouste
12. La Marine
13. La Villa Créole
14. Le Châteaubriand
15. Le Régal de la Mer

claim as empress was repudiated in 1809, and she retired to the Château de Malmaison, west of Paris, for the rest of her life. She died there of pneumonia in 1814.

Today, a small stone house is the home of the **Musée de la Pagerie ★★★** *(20F; Tue to Fri 9am to 5:30pm, Sat and Sun 9am to 1pm and 2:30pm to 5:30pm; ☎05.96.68.38.34 or 68.34.55)*, which pays homage to the lovely Creole empress. According to legend, a local black sorceress named Euphrémie David had predicted that Josephine would become "more than a queen". The museum displays an assortment of Josephine's belongings – furniture, letters signed by Napoleon, portraits, etc. As well as visiting the museum, you can stroll around the beautiful, lush estate, known in Josephine's time as Petite Guinée (little Guinea), where you can see the ruins of the main residence, the former sugar refinery and the cane mill.

The golf course at the **Country Club de la Martinique** *(☎05.96.68.32.81, ☎05.96.68.38.97)* stretches over 63 hectares of the former grounds of Domaine de la Pagerie. A magnificent 18-hole course, it was designed by the American expert, Robert Trent Jones. (See "Outdoor Activities" for more information on available facilities, p 102).

Right nearby, you can visit the **Parc des Floralies**, which hosted the 1979 International Flower Show (see p 100).

The Village of Trois-Îlets

This pretty little village, one of the most charming in Martinique, was named for the three tiny islands lying opposite it, Tébloux, Charles and Sixtain. The parish to which it belongs dates back as far as 1683, when it was known as "Cul-de-Sac-à-Vaches".

The present **church ★** was erected in 1724, and the parish was renamed Trois Îlets Bénits. It was in this church that Josephine's parents were married and she herself was baptized. Inside, you will find a reproduction of *The Assumption* by Murillo, a gift from Josephine's grandson, Napoleon III (third son of Louis Bonaparte, brother of Napoleon I, and Hortense de Beauharnois, daughter of Josephine from her first marriage). This modest but beautiful white church, the shady little square it looks onto, the zealously maintained public buildings and the attractive houses, whose façades are made of red brick from the nearby factory, create a perfectly charming atmosphere. All of these attributes, enhanced by the nearby hotels, restaurants and museums, come together to make Trois-Îlets the southern "tourist capital" of Martinique.

On the way out of town, you will come to a traffic circle; turn onto the road leading to Rivière-Salée.

Just a kilometre away, the **Forêt de Vatable**, with its picnic grounds and superb view of Fort-de-France, is worth a stop (see "Parks and Beaches," p 100).

A visit to the **Maison de la Canne ★** *(adults 15F; children 5F; Tue to Sun 9am to 5pm, closed Mon; ☎05.96.68.32.04)* at Pointe Vatable, as you leave the village, will help give you an idea of the important role sugar cane has played in Martinique's history and of the degree to which it has shaped islanders' lives, even inspiring native artists, novelists, musicians and filmmakers. You will discover how sugar cane, which was for a long time cultivated on sugar-producing estates run by pro-slavery owners, was the driving force behind Martinique's economy for over 300 years. Its economic role was not even diminished with the abolition of slavery, because the large central factories took over the work. Rum has helped to maintain the importance of sugar cane even today, despite the collapse of the international sugar market. The museum was founded in 1987 inside the former Vatable distillery with the aim of illustrating the richness of this part of the island's heritage. On display, there is a collection of instruments, models and pictures showing the techniques used in sugar-cane cultivation. **Maison de la Canne** is also indirectly a slavery museum, for it shows visitors what daily life was like for the people who worked on the plantations, and it explains the *Code Noir* (black code), which governed relations between masters and slaves.

A little further, a small, well-marked road on the left leads to the **poterie-briquetrie des Trois-Îlets ★** *(free admission; Mon to Fri 9am to 5:30pm, Sat 9am to 4pm; ☎05.96.68.03.44)*, where most of the bricks used to build houses and buildings on the island are produced. You can also see craftspeople making beautiful pottery vases, jars and carafes using the same methods as the Arawak and Carib Indians. As Martinique's oldest enterprise, dating back to the 18th century, this veritable institution now produces some 2,500 tons of different pieces each month. On one of the walls of the factory, you'll see a stone carved in 1783 with the words *"Ici le travail change la terre en or"* ("Here, work turns clay into gold").

A few hundred metres away, you'll see a huge, white satellite dish belonging to the *Centre de télécommunication spatiale*. This dish, which is 26 metres in diametre, maintains telephone links between Martinique and the rest of the world.

PARKS AND BEACHES

Le Diamant

Grande Anse du Diamant ★★★ (A)

The white sand beach that runs along the east side of Le Diamant is, at 4 km, the longest on the island. Its surroundings also make it without a doubt one of the most beautiful – the symbolic Rocher du Diamant in front, Morne Larcher at the end of the bay on the right, and countless palms, sea grape and almond trees behind. Unfortunately, the sea is a little rough making swimming dangerous in some spots. As caution is necessary, choose the part of the beach that stretches between the Diamant les Bains hotel and the cemetery if you want to go in the water. The rough water means, however, that the beach does not attract crowds, and has thus remained calm and untouched.

Anse Cafard (A)

The beach at Anse Cafard is in fact the westernmost part of Grande Anse du Diamant. It is a lovely beach which certainly does not deserve its name ("cafard" is cockroach in French). The view of Rocher du Diamant is most spectacular. It is also here, however, that the currents are strongest. There are two small restaurants on the beach.

Petite Anse (B)

This unassuming brown sand beach, where you'll see more fishing boats than pleasure craft, is not very well-known and is therefore virtually empty, which gives it a unique sort of charm. At the end of the little bay, on the right-hand side, you can see the pointed tip of Morne Jacqueline. Despite the peace of the place, there are two good restaurants just a stone's throw away from the beach (Au Dessous du Volcan and Aux Délices de la Mer).

Anses-d'Arlet

Beaches in the Village of Anses-d'Arlet (B)

Here, too, you'll have to share the beach with fishermen, which is hardly disagreeable. Small launches from Fort-de-France dock at the pier that juts out into the water. You'll also see several yachts moored offshore.

Grande Anse ★★ (B)

This is a real family beach. It's peaceful on weekdays and very busy on weekends and holidays, when it's invaded by families from Fort-de-France. There are several small, "temporary" fish restaurants on the beach as well.

The beach is somewhat wild to the south, then gradually becomes very wide and sandy on its way north, especially around the Ti-Sable restaurant (see p 112).

Facilities: Showers and toilets; a diving club; motor boat and scooter rentals.

Anse Dufour and Anse Noire ★★

These two completely different beaches lie right next to each other. One, of white sand, is a fishing base (Anse Dufour), while the other, with its black sand and row of coconut trees, remains unspoilt (Anse Noire). There is a restaurant near the beach at Anse

Dufour and another right on the sand at Anse Noire (see p 112).

Trois-Îlets

Anse à l'Âne ★ (C)

This beautiful, long, golden beach lined with tall coconut trees has been attracting more and more developers. It is now home to a few big hotels, notably the superb Frantour, and a great many fish and seafood restaurants.

The beach is quietest to the south, around the Frantour. In the middle, close to the pontoon, the beach is more populated and therefore the quality of the water is poorer. On the wilder northern part, beyond the little campground, you'll see shacks and fishing boats.

Facilities: Showers and toilets, camping, picnic tables, windsurfer rentals.

Anse Mitan ★ (A)

The water here is breathtakingly clear, and the flocks of little sailboats anchored at sea make the setting extremely attractive. With all that going for it, what could one possibly dislike about this beautiful white sand beach, which is located right near the celebrated Pointe du Bout? Certainly, it's crowded, but that, too, is appealing in some ways. The big pier welcomes ferryboats arriving from Fort-de-France.

Facilities: Showers and toilets, a public telephone, windsurfer and pedalboat rentals, restaurants, bars, picnic tables.

SOUTHWESTERN POINT

Flame Tree

Parc des Floralies ★

In 1979, the Trois-Îlets area hosted the second International Flower Show. Today, you can still visit the magnificent **Parc des Floralies** *(adults 10F, children 5F; Mon to Fri 8:30am to 5pm, Sat to Sun 9:30am to 1pm; ☎05.96.68.34.50 or 05.96.64.42.59)*, which was designed for the occasion at a cost of 2.5 million francs. In addition to displaying more than a hundred species of flowers, trees, and bushes in several attractive gardens, the park also has an open-air theatre, picnic areas, an aquarium and aviaries, which house a large number of exotic birds.

Forêt de Vatable

As you head east out of the village, take some time to visit the Forêt de Vatable, which has been wonderfully laid out, essentially for the schoolchildren of Martinique, by the *Office National des Forêts*. This is a pleasant recreation area with picnic areas where you can enjoy a nice meal. There is also a lovely view of Fort-de-France.

 OUTDOOR ACTIVITIES

 Hiking

Morne Larcher

The *Office National des Forêts* has marked a trail that starts at Anse Cafard and leads all the way up to a flat piece of land (414 m) near the summit of Morne Larcher (477 m), then back down towards Petite Anse. In addition to the breathtaking views it offers of Rocher du Diamant, the entire south coast of the island and the St. Lucia Channel, this trail also enables you to see a dry forest of *ti-baumes* and *bois d'Inde* (small evergreen trees).

The trail, which is straight and of average difficulty, is 3.5 kilometres long (one way) and should take you about 3 hours. Some sections are sloped, while others are covered with stones that become very slippery in rainy weather. It is best to tackle this trail early in the morning, as the afternoon heat can be unbearable, increasing the risk of sunstroke. Make sure to take along plenty of water.

Morne Bigot

Between Grande Anse and Anse à l'Âne, a short distance past the little road leading to Anse Dufour and Anse Noire, there is another road, on the right this time, which leads to a short trail up Morne Bigot (460 m). You can also reach this trail from the north, by way of the D38, which you can pick up at the intersection of the roads to Pointe du Bout and the village of Trois-Îlets.

This trail takes two hours and is relatively easy; it affords a remarkable view of the Baie de Fort-de-France and the Pitons du Carbet to the north, as well as Morne Larcher and Rocher du Diamant to the south.

 Scuba Diving

There are several diving sites worth mentioning in the region. First of all, in the area around **Rocher du Diamant**, there is a series of underwater faults, caves and tunnels. East of the rock, you'll also find a coral plateau crowded with fish. The Novotel Hotel organizes daily excursions for the Sub Diamond Rock diving club, with all equipment provided (*☎05.96.76.25.80*). A neighbouring hotel, the Marine, also has a diving club (*☎05.96.76.46.00, ext. 1600*), as does Okeanos (*☎05.96.76.21.76*) of the Calypso hotel.

At **Pointe Burgos and Pointe Lézarde**, north of Anses-d'Arlet, you can see a coral cliff and a rich varietyof marine life.

Cap Salomon, a little further north, is famous for its abundant, colourful flora.

Equally unforgettable is **Pointe de la Baleine**, with its crystal-clear waters, or

Anse Dufour, whose rocky plateau is teeming with flora and fauna.

The beach at **Grande Anse d'Arlet** has a diving club named Plongée Passion (*☎05.96.68.72.50 or 05.96.68.71.78*).

In **Anse Mitan**, the club at the Bambou hotel, Lychée Plongée (*☎05.96.66.05.26*), arranges "baptisms", night dives and underwater photo trips. The Balaou club (*☎05.96.66.07.61*) near Auberge de L'Anse Mitan also organizes such excursions.

At the **Pointe du Bout** marina, you can climb aboard the 14 metres boat *Planète Bleue*, which heads out to sea twice a day *(from 9am to noon and 3pm to 6pm)*. A dive costs about 200F per person, and all necessary equipment is available on the boat. For information and reservations, call or fax ☎05.96.66.06.22, ⇝05.96.66.00.50.

At Pointe du Bout, Espace Plongée (*☎05.96.66.01.79 or 05.96.66.14.34*) offers daily excursions at 9am and 2pm.

 Fishing

The company Scheherazade (*☎05.96.66.08.34*), at the Pointe du Bout marina, organizes full and half-day deep-sea fishing trips. It costs 480F per person to go out from 6am to noon, and 700F if you want to stay out until 6pm.

 Pleasure Boating and Cruises

There are countless excursions to take part in and many different kinds of boats to rent in this area. Here are a few examples:

SOUTHWESTERN POINT

On the beach at **Grande Anse**, an outfit by the name of Localizé *(☎05.96.68.64.78, ⇌05.96.68.68.88)* invites you to spend a half-day, full day or more aboard a luxurious yacht.

Le Mantou *(150F; ☎05.96.68.39.19)*, which departs from the **Pointe du Bout** marina or the village of **Trois-Îlets**, takes you to the Trois-Îlets and Rivière-Salée mangrove swamp to explore its exceptional fauna. Departures every day except Sunday, at 9:30am and 2:30pm. Travel time: 2 hours, 30 minutes.

At the **Pointe du Bout** marina, you'll have no trouble renting a catamaran, a motorboat or a sailboat, with or without a crew *(Star Voyages Antilles, ☎05.96.66.00.72; 3S Organisation, ☎05.96.66.07.07, ⇌05.96.66.14.08; Loca-Boats, ☎05.96.66.07.57, ⇌05.96.66.07.49)*.

 Tent and Trailer Camping

There's only one campground in the area, the Nid Tropical, right on the beach at **Anse à l'Âne** (see description p 106).

 Horseback Riding

You can rent horses for a pleasant trail-ride at the following places: Club La Cavale *(☎05.96.76.22.94)* in **Pointe de la Chéry**; Ranch Jack *(☎05.96.68.37.69)*, in the Galocha district in **Anses-d'Arlet**, and Black Horse *(☎05.96.66.00.04)* near Domaine de la Pagerie in **Trois-Îlets**. Rates run about 150F per person for a two-hour ride.

 Golf

The Country Club de la Martinique *(☎05.96.68.32.81, ⇌05.96.68.38.97)*, near the village of **Trois-Îlets**, has an internationally renowned 18-hole golf course designed by American Robert Trent Jones and stretches over 63 hectares. Additional facilities include a restaurant, a bar, a pro-shop and two tennis courts. All necessary equipment may be rented on the premises. A round of golf costs about 270F during high season, excluding golf cart (250F) and clubs (100F).

 Mountain Biking

Enthusiasts of this sport will be happy to learn that they can rent mountain bikes from VT TILT *(☎05.96.66.01.01)*, located in the Trou Étienne parking lot (Hertz) at **Pointe du Bout**, a little before the Pagerie Hotel (rates per hour or half-day).

 ACCOMMODATIONS

Le Diamant

Pointe de la Chéry

A small road about two kilometres east of the village of Le Diamant leads to Pointe de la Chéry, where you'll find four different hotels. The first one you'll see is the **Marine Hotel Mercure** *(615-1158F; ≋, pb, ≈, ℜ, K; Pointe de la Chéry - 97223 Diamant, ☎05.96.76.46.00, ⇌05.96.76.25.99)*, a large, luxurious complex with 150 fully equipped apartments, all with a view of the famous Rocher du Diamant. While there is no beach, the hotel does

Ulysses' Favourites

Charming hotels:
   Karacoli (Pointe du Bout, p 108)

For the welcome:
   Diamant les Bains (Diamant, p 104)
   Chambres d'Hôtes Diamant Noir (Diamant, p 105)
   Auberge de l'Anse Mitan (Anse Mitan, p 107)

For luxury:
   Novotel Diamant Coralia (Diamant, p 103)
   Novotel Carayou (Pointe du Bout, p 108)
   Bakoua (Pointe du Bout, p 108)
   Méridien (Pointe du Bout, p 109)

For the view:
   L'Écrin Bleu (Diamant, p 104)
   Villa Félicité (Diamant, p 105)
   Panoramic (Anse à l'Âne, p 106)

For the lively ambiance:
   Le Bambou (Anse Mitan, p 108)

For the tropical garden:
   Frantour Trois-Îlets (Anse à l'Âne, p 106)

have an enormous swimming pool with slides. Guests have long since found a way of compensating for the missing beach by heading over to the Novotel's beaches, although the walk is fairly long.

Next come two small bungalow villages, the first being **Diamant Bleu** *(393F; ≡, pb, ≈, K; Pointe de la Chéry - 97223 Diamant, ☎05.96.76.42.15, ⇌05.96.76.40.67)*, which houses 24 studios in wooden cottages spread about a lovely garden.

The second is the **Relais Caraïbes** *(650F to 1,200F; tv, ≡, pb, ≈, ℜ; Pointe de la Chéry - 97223 Diamant, ☎05.96.76.44.65, ⇌05.96.76.21.20)*, a slightly posher complex with 12 snug bungalows and 3 comfy rooms.

The place that stands out, however, is the **Novotel Diamant Coralia** *(895-1,985F, bkfst incl.; tv, ≡, pb, ≈, ℜ; Pointe de la Chéry - 97223 Diamant, ☎05.96.76.42.42, ⇌05.96.76.22.87)*, one of the best hotels on the island. It is located at the very tip of the peninsula, looking out on Rocher du Diamant. Inside, the rooms are extremely comfortable, both spacious and nicely decorated, with a soft blend of pink rattan furniture and walls and doors turquoise and white-painted. A large swimming pool, straddled by a little bridge, is the hotel's meeting place. Guests also have access to three private beaches. And even though the Novotel has 180 rooms spread over four three-floor pavilions, its best qual-

SOUTHWESTERN POINT

ity is its tranquility, which makes it an excellent place to spend a vacation.

The Village of Le Diamant and Area

One place especially worth mentioning in this area is a *gîte* owned by **M. Paul Sidalise-Montaise (no. 027, ⏷)** *(1,395F per week; located below the owner's vacation home; Dizac - 97223 Diamant).*

On the road to Anses-d'Arlet, above the village of Le Diamant, lies a small hotel worth checking out, the **Écrin Bleu** *(380-594F; ≡, pb, ≈, ℛ; Route des Anses-d'Arlet - 97223 Diamant, ☎05.96.76.41.92, ⌐05.96.76.41.90),* whose spectacular view of the bay and Rocher du Diamant, weight-room, attractive swimming pool and proximity to the area's only discotheque will make you forget about being far from the shore.

Located right on the outskirts of the village, the quiet and secluded **Palm Beach** *(480F; ≡, pb, ≈; Ravine Jean Bois – 97223 Diamant, ☎05.96.76.47.84)* boasts eight pleasant rooms with views of the Rocher du Diamant.

Don't miss the **Plein Sud** *(490-870F; tv, ≡, pb, ≈, K; 97223 Diamant, ☎05.96.76.26.06, ⌐05.96.76.26.07),* a recent hotel complex made up of two three-story buildings and located on the D7 west of the village, which runs along this area's coastline. It has a small shopping arcade on the ground floor, where you'll find a grocer's, as well as a banking machine. The ocean is just across the road from this modern complex run by *Pierre et Vacances.*

 The **Diamant les Bains** *(380-480F; tv, ≡, pb, ≈, ℛ, ℝ; 97223 Diamant, ☎05.96.76.40.14, ⌐05.96.76.27.00),*

has 24 rooms and bungalows and enjoys what is without a doubt one of the best locations in the region, at the edge of the village, right on the beach. Don't be put off by its immediate surroundings (the neighbouring gas station and grocery store); this hotel is an oasis of peace, even in the heart of such a busy area. What's more, the staff is as pleasant as can be. To top it all off, the restaurant has an excellent reputation, which is rightfully deserved (see p 110).

The **Hôtel Ultramarine** *(510-1060F; tv, ≡, pb, ≈, K; Quartier Dizac - 97223 Diamant, ☎05.96.76.46.46, ⌐05.96.76.20.43)* consists of two three-story buildings containing a total of 77 apartments. It is slightly set back from the ocean (past the Calypso hotel), a drawback counterbalanced by the tranquility of its magnificent garden and the cool water of its large swimming pool.

The **Calypso** *(640-990F; tv, ≡, pb, K, ≈; Quartier Dizac, 97223 Diamant, ☎05.96.76.40.81, ⌐05.96.76.40.84),* which opened in January, 1993, has fully equipped studios and apartments in a breathtaking setting. Set back a little from the road that runs along the coast, in the hills, the hotel is partially surrounded by a cliff. There's a small bar near the pool where you can relax and take in the truly extraordinary surroundings.

Anse Cafard

There are two *gîtes* at Anse Cafard, one belonging to **M. Roland Boclé (no. 016, ⏷)** *(1,930F per week; independent unit on the main floor of a pretty villa; Anse Cafard - 97223 Diamant);* the other to **M. Jean-Yves Adele (no. 023, ⏷)** *(2,055F per week; independent unit; Anse Cafard - 97223 Diamant).*

🐚 Everyone in the area knows about the **Chambres d'Hôtes Diamant Noir**, known better as **Chez Élène** *(312-395F; ⊗, pb, ℝ; Anse Cafard - Dizac, 97223 Diamant ☎05.96.76.41.25, ⇌05.96.76.28.89, www.sasi.fr/diamnoir)*. The two names refer to the same thing – a sort of local institution, which has been lodging tourists for over 20 years. Five lovely rooms with private baths are available in the main villa. Guests can get to know one another in the large common kitchen, or around the grill in the beautiful garden, where you'll be delighted to find a large number of fruit trees. A second three-story Creole house, located 60 metres from the sea on the Anse Cafard beach, now comprises four more lovely rooms on two floors. When making your reservation, therefore, be sure to specify whether you'd like a room by the garden or by the sea. Special rates for honeymooners as well as for groups of six people or more. Present your Ulysse Travel Guide MARTINIQUE and get a 10% discount.

Résidence Les Océanides *(350F; ≡, pb, K; Anse Cafard - 97223 Diamant, ☎05.96.76.48.25, ⇌05.96.76.49.34)* offers about ten fully equipped studios, though lacking in decor and charm. Its pleasant wooded surroundings and bargain prices make up for these shortcomings, however.

The eight wooden bungalows of the **Anse Bleu Le Paladien** *(555F; tv, ≡, ≈, K; Anse Cafard - 97223 Diamant, ☎05.96.76.21.91, ⇌05.96.76.47.50)* make up a kind of miniature village, set back just a little from the main road at Anse Cafard.

Opposite the famous Rocher du Diamant, on the edge of Anse Cafard's pleasant beach, which is in fact the westernmost part of the long beach at Grande Anse du Diamant, lies the **Village du Diamant** *(670F; ≡, pb, ≈, ℝ, K; Dizac - 97223 Diamant, ☎05.96.76.41.89, ⇌05.96.76.25.21)*, a series of three-story buildings and bungalows painted blue, red and white. In all, there are 59 rooms, each with a balcony, centred around an attractive swimming pool.

Anses-d'Arlet

The Village of Anses-d'Arlet

There are very few places to stay in and around the village of Anses-d'Arlet. One that stands out, however, is **Villa Félicité** *(tv, ≡, K; Rue du Calvaire - 97217 Anses-d'Arlet)*, a beautiful, newly built Creole house with two studios (2,600F a week) and a couple of two-room apartments that can accommodate up to five people each (4,500F a week). Weekly rentals only. Rates go down for longer stays. Located in the hills a little south of the village, the establishment affords magnificent vistas of the sea. The upstairs rooms are graced with a large wrap-around veranda. Reservations are made through Tournor in metropolitan France *(☎03.20.47.03.51, ⇌03.20.67.04.30)*.

There is also a charming eight-room hotel right next to the church, in the heart of the village – the **Madinakay'** *(350F; tv, ≡, pb, K, ℝ; 97217 Anses-d'Arlet, ☎05.96.68.70.76, ⇌05.96.68.70.56)*. The kind owner, for his part, will put fresh fruit and flowers in your room to give you the warmest welcome possible. The decor is modest and sober; the location, extraordinarily calm; the hosts, touchingly kind; and the beach, just across the street. What more could you ask for?

Grande Anse

La Sucrerie *(1,900F per week; pb, K; Grande Anse - 97217 Anses-d'Arlet, ☎05.96.68.66.66, ⇌05.96.68.72.99)* rents out spanking new studios opposite the Complexe Communal des Sports des Anses-d'Arlet. The place is slightly out of the way, but nevertheless within walking distance of Grande Anse beach.

Another option is the **Tamarin Plage** *(360F; ℜ; Grande Anse - 97217 Anses-d'Arlet, ☎05.96.68.71.30)*, which is hardly luxurious, but has the advantage of facing onto the beach.

Trois-Îlets

Anse à l'Âne

There are several noteworthy *gîtes* in the area, all in pretty houses. The owners are as follows: **Mme Giovanny Bracciano (no. 021,** ¶¶) *(1,855F per week; below the owner's house; Anse à l'Âne - 97229 Trois-Îlets)* and **M. Gérard Frédonie (no. 87-88,** ¶¶) *(2,415 per week; below the owner's house; Anse à l'Âne - 97229 Trois-Îlets)*.

In the hills, the tourist apartments of a little complex with the pretty name **Anthurium-Acalypna-Flamboyant** *(1,500-3,800F per week; Anse à l'Âne, 97229 Trois-Îlets, ☎05.96.68.38.06 or 05.96.68.36.03, ⇌05.96.68.42.96)* are a bit far from the beach, but offer peaceful, verdant surroundings and a lovely view.

You can pitch your tent right on the beach at **Nid Tropical** (90F), a small campground on Anse à l'Âne. Though the site is not exactly beautiful, the location and the rates are excellent. A few apartments are also available *(250-300F; ≡, K; Anse à l'Âne - 97229,*

Trois-Îlets, ☎*05.96.68.31.30,* ⇌*05.96.68.47.43).*

You might be surprised to discover a cluster of little wooden houses on the beach at Anse à l'Âne, not far from the landing stage; this is **Le Courbaril** *(190-260F; pb, K; Anse à l'Âne - 97229 Trois-Îlets, ☎05.96.68.32.30, ⇌05.96.68.32.21)*. The units, all crowded together, each contain a studio for two or an apartment for four.

Near Anse à l'Âne, alongside the main road, lies a group of houses with orangey roofs and pink walls. Some of these belong to the **Hotel Arawaks** *(450-500F; ≡, ≈, K; Anse à l'Âne, 97229 Trois-Îlets, ☎05.96.68.40.23, ⇌05.96.68.31.50)*, which has about a dozen rooms in all, while the others belong to the **Maharadja Village** *(380F; tv, ≈, K; Anse à l'Âne - 97229 Trois-Îlets, ☎05.96.68.36.70, ⇌05.96.68.37.51)*, which has 26. It is in fact difficult to tell the two neighbouring places apart.

If there is one hotel in Martinique that lives up to its name, it's the **Panoramic** *(690F; tv, ≡, pb, ≈, K; Anse à l'Âne - 97229 Trois-Îlets, ☎05.96.68.34.34, ⇌05.96.50.01.95)*, located in the hills. Its 36 rooms, all with balconies, offer an unimpeded view of the beach and village of Anse à l'Âne, as well as, on clear days, part of the Baie de Fort-de-France in the background. The hotel's grounds are lush and abounding with flowers.

Your senses will inevitably be aroused by the luxuriant vegetation in the superb garden that lies at the centre of the **Frantour Trois-Îlets** *(800-1,200F, bkfst incl.; tv, ≡, pb, ≈, ℜ; Anse à l'Âne, 97229 Trois-Îlets, ☎05.96.68.31.67, ⇌05.96.68.37.65)*. Guests of this deluxe hotel complex also enjoy direct access to the beach at Anse à l'Âne (unfortunately, not the nicest part). Each one of the Frantour's 77 rooms has a balcony or, better yet, a small private garden.

Anse Mitan

For good, reasonably priced accommodations in this hugely popular place, there's the **Rivage** *(350-480F; ≡, ≈, K, ℜ; Anse Mitan - 97229 Trois-Îlets, ☎05.96.66.00.53, ⇝05.96.66.06.56)*, located only a step away from the beach, just like the **Bonne Auberge Chez André** *(400F bkfst incl.; ≡, ⊗, pb, ℜ; Anse Mitan - 97229 Trois-Îlets, ☎05.96.66.01.55, ⇝05.96.66.04.50)*. The best thing about the latter is its attractive restaurant (see p 113). The friendly owners allow you to take your pick of 32 decent rooms, all equipped with air conditioning or a ceiling fan, and all at the same price - just 50 metres away from the beach and pier!

Another modest place is the **Hôtel de la Baie** *(320-380F; ≡, pb, K; Anse Mitan - 97229 Trois-Îlets, ☎05.96.66.06.66, ⇝05.96.63.00.70)*, hidden away on the hill. It has about a dozen studios for two to four people each.

Les Alamandas 2 *(893-1,040F; tv, ≡, pb, ≈, ℜ, K; Anse Mitan - 97229 Trois-Îlets, ☎05.96.66.03.66, ⇝05.96.66.08.57)*, also right near the beach and the pier, is good value for the money. A small hotel complex, it has about thirty soberly decorated but comfortable rooms, all with balconies and some with a view of the sea. A few are also equipped with a kitchenette. With its view of the sea and pleasant terrace restaurant Cannelle (see p 113), this pretty pink and white hotel is extremely appealing.

Its little brother, **Les Alamandas 1** *(624F; tv, ≡, pb, K; Anse Mitan - 97229 Trois-Îlets, ☎05.96.66.06.06,* ⇝05.96.66.07.01) lies on the hillside and offers equipped studios.

Visible from the beach, the blue and white silhouette of the **Camélia** *(580-685F; tv, ≡, pb, ≈; Anse Mitan - 97229 Trois-Îlets, ☎05.96.66.05.85, ⇝05.96.66.11.12)*, located in the hills of Anse Mitan, will captivate you as soon as you lay eyes on it. Twenty-two of its 49 rooms are equipped with kitchenettes.

If you've been dreaming of finding a nice, old, French-style inn in Martinique, rest assured that one exists – the **Auberge de l'Anse Mitan** *(420F; ≡, K; Anse Mitan - 97229 Trois-Îlets, ☎05.96.66.01.12, ⇝05.96.66.01.05)*. A huge colonial house facing the sea, it was converted into an inn over 60 years ago. In short, it's a lovely old place with many regular guests.

Just before the Auberge de l'Anse Mitan, there is a small sign indicating the dirt road where you turn left to get to the **Impératrice Village** *(740F; tv, ≡, pb, ≈, K; Anse Mitan - 97229 Trois-Îlets, ☎05.96.66.08.09, ⇝05.96.66.07.10)*, a pretty hotel complex set back a bit from the road in an extremely peaceful setting. There are 50 studio apartments available, separated in groups of three or four in attractive bungalows with orange-coloured roofs, similar in style to Creole houses. Though you'll feel removed here, the Anse Mitan beach is less than a ten-minute walk away.

Located alongside the Anse Mitan beach, the **Éden Beach** *(500-690F; tv, K, ≡, pb; Anse Mitan, 97229 Trois-Îlets, ☎05.96.66.01.19, ⇝05.96.66.04.66)* offers its guests two choices: the "Éden option" includes 16 rooms and 9 bungalows by the garden; the "beach option", 13 rooms and 2 suites with a view of the sea. The entrance hall is not only lovely, but also contains a pool table. To top it all off, the place has both a restaurant (see p 113) and a bar.

At the Éden's neighbour, an Anse Mitan classic called **Le Bambou** *(840F; tv, ≡, pb, ≈, ℜ; Anse Mitan - 97229 Trois-Îlets,   ☎05.96.66.01.39, ⇝05.96.66.05.05)*, a paved pathway winds through a pretty garden studded with strange-looking little double cottages. With its attractive pool, direct access to the beach and large dining room open on two sides, this place might remind you of a family campground. There is live music every night at dinnertime, and guests pour onto the dance floor to kick their heels up to tunes like *Célimène*, *Donne-moi un Tibo* and *Il Tape sur les Bambous*. A few studios are also available in a three-story building on the property.

Pointe du Bout

The famous Pointe du Bout and its equally famous sailing harbour are shared by three grand hotels and a few other more modest ones.

The most inexpensive hotel in this prestigious area is the **Davidiana** *(350F; ≡, pb, ℜ; Pointe du Bout, 97229 Trois Îlets,   ☎05.96.66.00.54, ⇝05.96.66.00.70)*, which is nonetheless located right in front of the marina. It has 14 no-frills rooms.

To the right of La Pagerie (see below), there is a road leading up to the **Karacoli** *(375-535F; ≡, pb, ≈, K; Pointe du Bout - 97229 Trois-Îlets, ☎05.96.66.02..67, ⇝05.96.66.02.41)*, which is a bargain as far as accommodations in Pointe du Bout are concerned. As soon as you go through the door and walk into its lovely garden,

you will know that you've arrived at a truly charming spot. The rattan furniture adorning the entrance hall and the pretty terrace, the tiny swimming pool, the little bar... all of these features are on a human scale, tastefully laid out in a way that will quickly make you forget the flashiness that puts many people off when they visit Pointe du Bout. This appealing place has 18 attractively decorated rooms, each equipped with a kitchenette.

Mercure Inn La Pagerie *(640-1,150F; tv, ≡, pb, ≈, K; Pointe du Bout - 97229 Trois-Îlets,   ☎05.96.66.05.30, ⇝05.96.66.00.99)* and its ground-floor shopping arcade, lie straight ahead of you as you arrive at the point. This hotel suffers little by comparison with its wealthier neighbours (see below), even though they have their own beaches and it does not. Considering its location, its rates are excellent. Besides, everything it lacks (beach, discotheque, casino) is right nearby – at the neighbouring hotels.

A few minutes' walk away, you'll find **Le Novotel Carayou** *(945-2,060F; tv, ≡, pb, ≈, ℜ; Pointe du Bout - 97229 Trois-Îlets,   ☎05.96.66.04.04, ⇝05.96.66.00.57)*, on your right as you arrive at the point, located at the end of a path lined with trees and flowers. This 200-room hotel is equipped with all the comforts you could possibly desire, including a private beach, a discotheque and a large swimming pool. The rooms are big, sunny and tastefully decorated.

On the other side of the point, you'll find the elegant **Bakoua** *(1,010-2,830F; tv, ≡, pb, ≈, ℜ; Pointe du Bout - 97229 Trois-Îlets,   ☎05.96.66.02.02, ⇝05.96.66.00.41)*, which is built around a superb swimming pool shaped like a giant shell. Recently renovated, the Bakoua has definitely regained its former splendour.

But the most stylish place of all is without a doubt the **Méridien** *(1,000-2,900F; tv, ≡, pb, ≈, ℛ; Pointe du Bout - 97229 Trois-Îlets, ☎05.96.66.00.00, ⌐05.96.66.00.74)*, a magnificent 300-room hotel located right on a beautiful, fine-sand beach. It caters, as you might already have guessed, to a wealthy clientele, as well as to conventions. The Méridien also has one of the island's two casinos.

RESTAURANTS

Le Diamant

The Village of Le Diamant

First of all, for those intending to prepare their own meals, there is an **8 à huit grocery store** conveniently located at the east edge of town, near the Esso station and the Diamant les Bains hotel.

Also, if you're wild about fresh *boudin* (blood pudding), a woman sells mouthwatering *boudin* and *accras* in front of the church every Sunday morning after mass.The area is crowded with expensive restaurants, but visitors looking for a good, reasonably-priced place to eat should try **Lady D** *(50F; 97223 Diamant)*, the snack bar in the Plein Sud Hotel (see p 104). The menu features simple dishes, such as *brochettes*, grilled meats, savory and sweet crêpes, sandwiches and pizzas you can enjoy on a small outside terrace.

Pizza Pepe *(50F; closed Mon; Rue Principale)*, located in the centre of the village, on the main road, is another good, inexpensive place to eat. A few tables and chairs on a terrace overlooking the sea, three or four flowerpots,

and you've got a restaurant. But people don't come here for the friendly service or the decor (especially not the decor!); they come for the tasty pizza and delicious omelettes, which, thanks to the minimalist decor, can be had for next to nothing.

Snack 82 and its beachfront terrace can still be found on Place du Général de Gaulle, behind what was formerly Diam's restaurant, victim of a fire. The place offers an 80F set menu at lunch time.

At the very heart of the village of Le Diamant, right on the beach, you'll find two quaint restaurants side by side, in friendly competition, **Chez Lucie** *(100F; closed Wed; Rue Justin-Roc, ☎05.96.76.40.10)* and **Diamant-Plage les Pieds dans l'Eau** *(100F; closed Mon; Rue Justin-Roc, ☎05.96.76.40.48)*. These simple, unpretentious restaurants serve a wide variety of good food. The sea acts as the decor, and the sound of the waves sets the mood. Go to Chez Lucie for their *soupe z'habitants* and shark *touffé*, and to the Diamant-Plage for their delicious rock lobster, crayfish and chicken fricassees and tasty fish soup.

 If you're not careful, you'll go right past **Chez Christiane** *(100F; closed Mon; ☎05.96.76.49.55)*, a mistake you'll regret for the rest of your life. You have to know how to find it, on the main street, right next to the town hall. Above all, don't let yourself be put off by the somewhat unattractive room in front. The restaurant is hidden in the back, inside a charming room with reed walls. And the food! It's absolutely succulent. Make sure to try the *estouffade de raie au gingembre* (braised ray with ginger) and the shrimp fricassee in Caribbean sauce.

Ulysses' Favourites

For the finest dining:
Diamant les Bains (Diamant, p 110)
Ti-Sable (Grande Anse, p 112)
La Villa Créole (Anse Mitan, p 114)

For authentic Creole cuisine:
Chez Christiane (Diamant, p 109)
Anse Noire (Anse Noire, p 112)

For the terrace:
Flamboyant des Isles (Anses-d'Arlet, p 111)

For the welcome:
La Bonne Auberge Chez André (Anse Mitan, p 113)

The restaurant in the **Écrin Bleu** *(100F; Route des Anses-d'Arlet, ☎05.96.76.41.92)*, a hotel located on the inland road to Anses-d'Arlet, above the village of Le Diamant, is worth a detour. The terrace, which is open on all sides, but at the same time warmly inviting, offers a striking view of the bay, and you'll find a charming little bar at the far end. As for the food, the tagliatelle with salmon is delicious, and so is the *filets de vivaneau sauce américaine* (red snapper in white wine and tomato sauce) and the salmon *au noilly*.

Not far from Place de l'Église, in the heart of the town of Diamant, you'll find a bar/restaurant called **La Case Créole** *(100F; ☎05.96.76.10.14)*. The menu consists of Creole classics like crayfish fricassee, a seafood platter and coconut blanc-mange.

Just past the entrance to the village, on the main street at the corner of Rue A. et T. Duville, is the unmistakably quaint and colourful Creole house harbouring the **Ti-Grill** *(100F; Rue Justin-Roc)*. As its name suggests, this restaurant spe-cializes in grilled fish and steaks. Friendly ambiance.

🏊 The restaurant in the **Diamant les Bains Hotel** *(150F; closed Wed; ☎05.96.76.40.14)*, as you enter the village, has acquired an excellent reputation over the years, and with good reason. After crossing the hotel's handsome lobby, you will be offered a seat on an attractive green and white terrace with a view of the swimming pool, the exquisite garden around it and, a little farther beyond, the sea. Moreover, the food measures up to the gorgeous setting in which it is served. Just to name a few dishes, the fish soup, *potage cultivateur,* curried fillet of red snapper and fillet of beef with vegetables are all delicious.

Right next to the cemetery on the small market town's main street, the large, two-floor **Brasserie Planète Diamant** *(175F; Rue Justin-Roc, ☎05.96.76.49.82)* features French and Creole specialties. Good selection of beer on tap. Live music on weekends. Set menu at 75F.

Anse Cafard

Paillote Bleue *(100F; closed Thu; ☎05.96.76.21.91)* serves delicious food grilled over a wood fire. You can order, for example, a rib steak for 85F, a T-bone for 95F or skewered merguez sausages for 65F. Or, treat yourself to a grilled rock lobster for 160F.

Petite Anse

One of the area's institutions, which you'll hear about from all the locals, is **Au Dessous du Volcan**, also known as **Chez Hans** *(150F; 7pm to 11pm, closed Thu; ☎05.96.68.69.52)*. The restaurant is known for its rib steaks (80F), garlic shrimps' tails (100 F) and grilled fish (75F), as well as its delicious desserts. Right next door, you'll see **Aux Délices de la Mer** *(100F; ☎05.96.68.69.69)*, which also does good business with its 85F set menu, which includes shark *touffé* and chicken fricassee. You can enjoy your meal on their large, attractive terrace.

Anses-d'Arlet

The Village of Anses-d'Arlet

There are a few canteens that serve lunch on the beach. You can sit at a table shaded by large trees right on the waterfront and partake of cod or lobster *accras* (fritters), merguez sausages, grilled chicken or fish. **Le Balaou** *(60F)* and **Chez Alex** *(60F)* are two charming beach eateries worth mentioning.

At south end of the boardwalk, **Chez Roger et Rose Hélène** *(65F; ☎05.96.68.62.43)* serves up succulent cod and lobster *accras* (40F), which you can savour in a marquee of sorts. Also on the menu are grilled meats and brochettes.

Flamboyant des Isles *(100F; closed Sun evening and Tue; ☎05.96.68.67.75)*, located just before the village of Anses-d'Arlet on the road from Le Diamant, is a delicious find. The decor alone will please even the most demanding tastes: inside, black furniture with red tablecloths; outside, an extraordinary terrace overhanging the sea and offering gorgeous panoramic views of the bay and the little village. True to its name, the place is surrounded by superb flamboyants, trees whose red and yellow flowers set Martinique ablaze from June to October. The restaurant serves what's known as *nouvelle cuisine Créole*: *burgos du Flamboyant* (a variety of snail), *balaous des Caraïbes* (a small white fish served breaded or boiled) and *Saint-Pierre farci aux oursins ou aux lambis* (sea bream stuffed with sea urchins or *lambis*). And as if all that weren't enough, the prices are reasonable! The Sunday lunch buffet, for example, is a real bargain at 50F a person.

On the way out of the village, heading toward Grande Anse, you will come upon **Le Fatzo** *(140F; open from 7pm only)*, in a large, beautiful, blue-shuttered white house. The menu here features such commendable dishes as the economical *poulet créole* (Creole chicken; 70F), the promising *magret de canard à l'ananas* (breast of duck with pineapple; 90F) and the intriguing dish of *écrevisses sauce antillaise* (freshwater crayfish with Antillean sauce; 95F).

Grande Anse

There are all sorts of places to eat on the family beach at Grande-Anse – stalls selling fresh fruit, vegetables and fish, unpretentious beach restaurants and slightly more sophisticated places as well.

If you're looking for food to prepare yourself, you need only follow the little road that runs alongside the beach. You'll have no trouble finding places to purchase fruit and fish, as well as a little grocery store, the **Épicerie Deloy** (☎05.96.68.62.68).

Budget-conscious visitors can also opt for a modest beach restaurant like **À l'Ombre des Cocotiers**, **Bid Joul** (☎05.96.68.65.28), which has a beautiful bamboo decor, or its neighbour **Les Délices des Anses** (85F; 68.68.33).

The **Quai Sud** (85F; closed Mon; ☎05.96.68.62.44), for its part, serves caramel pork (yum!) and stewed *lambis*. At the "coco-bar", which is shaped like a *gommier*, you can sip a drink just steps away from the ocean, right near Ti-Sable (see below).

Ti-Sable (150-200F; closed Mon; ☎05.96.68.62.44), located at the north end of the beach, is the best restaurant in the area. Here, you can savour delicious cuisine inside a superb colonial house or on a no-less superb terrace, which is very spacious and looks out onto a very attractive part of the beach. A large Creole buffet featuring spit-roasted meat, grilled fish and chicken Trinidad is served on Sunday evenings. This barbecue-style feast costs 165F per person, including wine and service. The restaurant also has chaise-longues for guests who want to work on their tan.

Anse Dufour and Anse Noire

A little restaurant named **Sable d'Or** (65F; closed Tues; ☎05.96.68.62.97) overlooks Anse Dufour's golden beach, offering a beautiful view of the sea and delicious grilled fish in a completely unpretentious atmosphere.

Nevertheless, if you feel like trying truly innovative cuisine, head over to the neighbouring black sand beach, to **Anse Noire** (65-120F; opens at noon, closed Mon; ☎05.96.68.62.82), where you can sit at a long table in a big hut and enjoy delicious fresh fish. It's worth your while to eat a meal here, if only to have the time to soak up the unique surroundings.

Trois-Îlets

Anse à l'Âne

Right on the beach at Anse à l'Âne, with your feet in the sand, you can treat yourself to a quick fix at **Épi Soleil** (35F; every day 11:30am to 3pm and 6:30pm to 9pm; ☎05.96.68.31.30), the snackroom of Nid Tropical (see p 106). Hamburgers and *croque-mon-sieur* (toasted ham and cheese sandwiches) are less than 20F, fried merguez sausages are 35F, and there's a slightly more elaborate menu for 100F.

Chez Jojo (75F; ☎05.96.68.37.43), located near the landing stage, is a pleasant enough place, just like its next-door neighbour, **Pignon sur Mer** (75F; closed Sun evenings and Mon; ☎05.96.68.38.37), which serves chicken brochettes, fried fish and *langouste*.

Le Calalou (☎05.96.68.31.67), the restaurant in the Frantour hotel (see p 106), serves an 85F fish brochette at lunchtime and a 165F half-rock-lobster at dinner. Live music every night.

On the road, opposite the entrance of the Frantour, **Ti-Calebasse** (180F; closed Sun evenings; ☎05.96.63.38.77) is worth considering. In its lovely, flower-decked dining room, you can start your meal off slowly with a succulent fish soup. Next, you will succumb to the charms of the *gratin de christophines* with rock lobster or sea urchin. The coconut flan will put a sweet finishing touch on it all. Talk about a lovely evening! Live music on Friday nights.

Anse Mitan

For an inexpensive meal in Anse Mitan, try the **Corossol** *(30-90F; ☎05.96.66.02.07)*, located on the road to Pointe du Bout. The menu lists buckwheat crepes and a variety of salads.

Those on a tight budget who prefer to prepare their own meals will find what they need on the road from Anse Mitan to Pointe du Bout. The **Jardin Créole** *(☎05.96.66.06.78)* sells fruit and vegetables, while **Bora Bora** is a grocery, butcher shop and delicatessen rolled into one.

Hemingway's *(85F; closed Sun; ☎05.96.66.14.24)* is a most interesting newcomer in the area. Like several other restaurants at Anse Mitan, it boasts a seaside terrace. Its pub-like interior, however, differentiates it from its counterparts. Here, you serve yourself at a hot-and-cold buffet. Lunch menu 65F; 85F dinner menu.

Just a step away from the pier at Anse Mitan, there's a nice little restaurant worth sampling, **La Langouste** *(100F; ☎05.96.66.04.99)*. Seated on an attractive, shady terrace, you can savour fish grilled over a wood fire, chicken *colombo*, a rib steak or the *assiette antillaise*, which includes *accras*, blood pudding and raw vegetables. You can't miss La Langouste, which is strategically located over the beach, near the landing quay.

Another good choice at Anse Mitan is **Restaurant Cannelle** *(150F;* ☎*05.96.66.03.66)*, which is set back somewhat, but nevertheless offers a lovely view of the boats moored in the bay. We especially recommend the *magret de canard à l'ananas* (duck cutlet with pineapple) and the fricasseed crayfish. The tasteful, sober decor, made up of attractive rose-patterned rattan furniture, will put you right at ease. In the Alamandas hotel (see p 107)

One of Anse Mitan's nicest restaurants is still, however, **La Bonne Auberge** *(150F; ☎05.96.66.01.55)*. With its long bar and dark wood furniture, this place is truly charming. You can choose the 150 F menu including the *assiete antillaise* (blood pudding, *accras* and raw vegetables), grilled rock lobster and banana flambé; or the *assiette créole* (blood pudding, stuffed crab, *accras* and raw vegetables).

L'Éden *(200F; ☎05.96.66.01.19)*, the restaurant in the Éden Beach hotel (see p 107), has an attractive terrace looking right out onto the beach. The menu lists dishes like fish and meat *à la créole*, *Saint-Jacques poêlés au jus de passion* and duck stuffed with *lambis*.

Opposite La Langouste (see p 113), **Le Régal de la Mer** *(200F; ☎05.96.66.11.44)* is just the place for those who wish to treat themselves to prime rib of beef (210F for two people) or grilled lobster. Between noon and 2:30pm, the *assiette fraîcheur*, composed of melon and watermelon slices (35F), is also offered. Set menus go for 120F and 250F.

Waitresses wearing traditional dress will welcome you at **Au Poisson d'Or** *(250F; closed Mon; ☎05.96.66.01.80)*, located opposite one of the two entrances of the Bambou on the road to Pointe du Bout. No setting could be more typically Caribbean, what with

SOUTHWESTERN POINT

the walls and ceiling made of reeds, flowers on the tables, plants everywhere and trees all around. The menu consists of grilled meats and Creole specialties.

🐚 Finally, we couldn't possibly leave out **La Villa Créole** *(250F; closed Sun all day and Mon for lunch, ☎05.96.66.05.53)*, a local institution situated on the street leading to the beach. Seated on a terrace looking out onto a lovely garden, where a small stage and a dance floor have been set up, you are sure to go into raptures over the pure poetry of the menu. If you're not convinced, here's an example: *pavé de saumon caraïbe au foie gras sur coulis d'écrevisses* (Caribbean salmon with foie gras on crayfish coulis). So what do you think? Very often, the owner himself takes the stage with his guitar. For obvious reasons, this place is very popular, so reservations are a must.

Pointe du Bout

Even at stylish Pointe du Bout, you can have a quick bite to eat without spending a lot of money. To do so, head over to **L'Embarcadère** *(15-40F)*, right beside the pier where passengers board the ferryboat to Fort-de-France. Of course, the food is simple – salads (40F), hamburgers (15F) and fish brochettes (38F).

There is also a **Délifrance** (croissants, pastries, breads and sandwiches) and an ice cream shop called **Boule de Neige**, which serves breakfast as well.

If you're looking for something a little more elaborate around the sailing harbour, try **La Marine** *(100F; ☎05.96.66.02.32)*. The restaurant's three big rooms are airy and warmly inviting at the same time, decorated mainly with wood. You'll have a hard time choosing between the steak tartare (75F), the grilled fillet with pepper (85F), the seafood risotto and the *lambis* fricassee (70F). If you're really hungry, treat yourself to the *plateau du pêcheur*, or fisherman's platter (390F), which includes rock lobster, shrimp, stuffed crab, *gambas* (giant shrimp) and fried squid. There is also a selection of pizzas for 38F to 50F.

Another place worth mentioning at the marina is **Davidiana** *(100F; ☎05.96.66.09.44)*, which serves French and Creole cuisine on an attractive terrace stylishly decorated with white rattan furniture. The *requin poêlé au beurre blanc* (pan-fried shark in a light butter sauce) and the grilled red mullet should help restore your strength before you continue your tour of Martinique. The restaurant is part of the hotel of the same name (see p 108).

Another establishment overlooking the marina, right next door to Davidiana, **Chez Gilles** *(120F; ☎05.96.66.12.87)* offers pizza, pasta, *galettes* (buckwheat pancakes), crepes and salads. You can also come by for a drink at the friendly bar.

Upon arriving at Pointe du Bout, you will see **Cotton Club** *(250F; closed Mon; ☎05.96.66.03.09)*, formerly Amphore, on the left, right by the entrance of the Bakoua (see p 108). Here, in the coziest of atmospheres, you can dine on a rock lobster fished right out of the tank, then grilled or cooked in a court-bouillon. After enjoying a delicious meal in this intimate setting, you can hop over to the Cotton Club (see p 116), located in the same building, to finish off your evening.

As a general rule, the big hotels in this area have good restaurants; most, however, are quite expensive. For example, at **Le Châteaubriand** *(280F; ☎05.96.66.02.02)* in the Bakoua, you can enjoy dinner and dancing. The menu features mouthwatering dishes like *cœur de filet de bœuf en chevreuil sauce poivrade*. On Fridays, there is a huge Creole buffet and entertainment provided by the Grands Ballets de la Martinique.

The Village of Trois-Îlets

In the village, you will find everything you need to make your own meals. Try the charming **market** *(Wed to Sun from 7:30am on)* on the central square.

Immediately to the left of the church, you will find the grocery store **Chez Zozime**. There is a **bakery** *(☎05.96.68.32.24)* on the other side of the church, facing the cemetery.

Finally, heading out of the village, on the way to Rivière-Salée, you will see a **butcher shop**, located shortly before the traffic circle.

  ENTERTAINMENT

Le Diamant

There is a good discotheque, **Le Neptune** *(open daily, except Mon, from 10pm; ☎05.96.76.25.47)*, at Morne Lacroix. To get there, take the D7 up to the village of Le Diamant.

The **Brasserie Planète-Diamant** *(☎05.96.76.49.82)*, located right next to the cemetery, is livened up by bands on Friday, Saturday and Sunday nights. Good selection of beer on tap.

Region of Anses-d'Arlet

In the heart of the village of Anses-d'Arlet, near the church, there is a small movie theatre called **Atlas**.

Trois-Îlets

Anse à l'Âne

On the Anse à l'Âne beach, a fabulous zouk band lets loose every Friday night at the bar-restaurant **Chez Jojo** *(☎05.96.68.37.43)*.

Anse Mitan

At the **Bambou**, a hotel reminiscent of a family campground (see p 108), there is live music every night at dinnertime. The whole family can have a ball on the big dance floors.

At the **Baracuda** *(☎05.96.66.07.88)*, located right on the beach, loudspeakers blare out popular music every night. This is a fun place to revel the night away under the stars. It also offers a good selection of lagers and dark beer.

Pointe du Bout

The Trois-Îlets area has one of the liveliest nightlives in Martinique. First of all, it is home to one of the island's two casinos, the **Casino du Méridien** *(70F, identification required; ☎05.96.66.00.30)*, where you can gamble away to your heart's content until the wee hours of the morning. Games include blackjack and roulette, from 9pm to 3am, while the slot machines operate from noon to 3am. Shorts are only permitted until 7pm; more formal dress is required in the evening. The **La Baraka** discotheque

SOUTHWESTERN POINT

rounds off the Meridien's nightlife facilities.

The restaurant **Cotton Club** (see p 114), located near the entrance of the Bakoua hotel, is paired with a pleasant bar *(every day 11pm to 3am)*, which has an impressive selection of whisky and aged rum. Karaoke nights.

You can enjoy dinner and dancing at the restaurant **Le Châteaubriand** (see p 115), in the Bakoua. On Friday night, entertainment is provided by the Grands Ballets de la Martinique.

 SHOPPING

Le Diamant

Heading toward Le Diamant from the east, you will come across a **ceramic studio** between Pointe Chéry and the village.

In the town itself, you will find a variety of souvenirs in two shops: **Papaye** and **Cœur Caraïbes**.

There is also a **craft market**, set up every day on Place du Général-de-Gaulle, opposite the church.

Finally, there is a small shopping arcade on the first floor of the **Plein Sud Hotel**, as you head west out of the village of Le Diamant.

Anses-d'Arlet

Behind the church in the village of Anses-d'Arlet, the **Suco** shop *(☎05.96.68.62.09 or 05.96.68.63.38)* prides itself on having everything under one roof – and for every purpose: you can purchase newspapers, magazines, souvenirs, handicrafts and even... rent a car.

Trois-Îlets

Anse Mitan

On the road leading to Pointe du Bout, opposite one of the entrances of the Bambou hotel, you can't miss the shop **Carib-Curious** *(every day 7:30am to 7:30pm)*, which is virtually bursting at the seams with T-shirts, beach towels, jewellery, madras and other popular souvenirs.

Pointe du Bout

Pointe du Bout is swarming with little shops, each one more stylish and expensive than the last.

There are all kinds of boutiques for women's clothing and souvenir shops, such as **Philleas Fogg**, as well as a small art gallery and a bookstore.

At the **Boutique Lafleur**, facing the marina, you will find lovely, colourful women's clothing inspired by traditional Martinican dress.

If you like posters and postcards, you'll be thrilled by the selection at **L'Hypocampe**.

You can stock up on flowers at the **Jardins de l'Ajoupa**, in the parking lot, or across the street at **McIntosh**.

Finally, the **Librairie La Page** is more of a newsstand than a bookstore, but you can dig up a few volumes here.

The Village of Trois-Îlets

Numerous artisans gather at the square opposite the church, next to the village market, to offer passers-by hand-painted T-shirts, reproductions of gumtrees and round skiffs, etc.

Right nearby, opposite the market, the **tourist office** displays local arts and crafts.

The **poterie-briqueterie des Trois-Îlets** *(Mon to Fri 9am to 5:30pm, Sat 9am to 4pm;* ☎*05.96.68.03.44)*, three kilometres east of the village, is where you'll find the most interesting things to buy. You can watch crafts-men making gorgeous vases, pots, jars and other objects with the same tech-niques used by the ancient Arawak and Carib Indians.

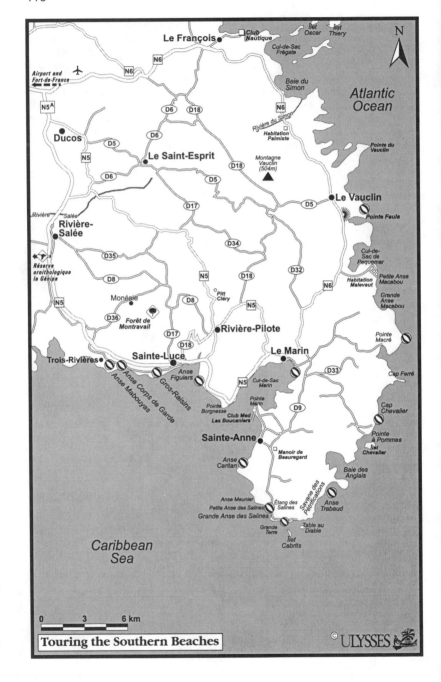

Touring the Southern Beaches

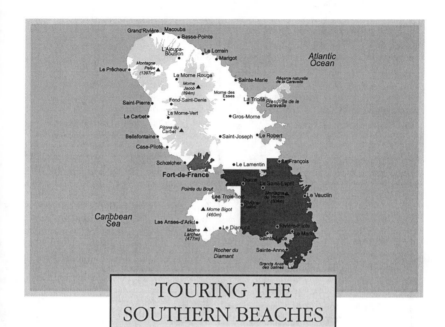

TOURING THE
SOUTHERN BEACHES

The beach at Grande Anse des Salines, with its immaculate white sand and incredibly clear turquoise water, is internationally renowned. Club Med Les Boucaniers (The Buccaneers), which is also known the world over, has long been established a little to the north, at Pointe Marin, near Sainte-Anne. Moreover, the lovely beaches in the Sainte-Luce area have been enticing more and more people to build vacation homes there. And lastly, on the Atlantic coast, the jagged shoreline has promoted the development of countless little beaches, most still untouched, which will amaze even the most jaded visitors. The area around Le François, farther up the coast, was the Creoles' vacation "domain", where they indulged in the tradition of sipping *ti-punch* on the *fonds blancs*, high, white sandbanks sheltered by reefs, where the water is no more than one-metre deep.

Clearly, the southern part of Martinique is a sort of giant playground, a great place to enjoy the sun and sea, a place that will make you forget all your cares. The tour outlined in this chapter will help you discover this land of enchantment.

 FINDING YOUR
WAY AROUND

By Car

From Fort-de-France, take Boulevard du Général de Gaulle to *Route Nationale* 1 (N1) in the direction of Le Lamentin, then take the N5 towards Sainte-Luce. At Marin, the *Route Départementale* 9 (D9) will take you towards Sainte-Anne and Grande Anse des Salines, while the N6 heads up to Le Vauclin and Le François, bringing our tour of the region to an end.

From the Trois-Îlets area, take the D7 towards Rivière-Salée, then head south on the N5 to begin the tour of the region.

If you're starting from the Diamant area, head east on the D7, then south on the N5.

Car Rentals

Ducos
Pop's Car: ☎05.96.56.06.22 or 05.96.56.08.45.

Le François
Pop's Car: 2, Rue François-Anago, ☎05.96.54.59.91.

Sainte-Anne
Avis: Hôtel Anchorage, Domaine de Belfond, ☎05.96.76.70.74, ≈05.96.76.88.94;
Rent Eco: ☎05.96.76.76.65;
Thrifty: Club-Med, ☎05.96.76.80.82;
Domaine de Belfond, ☎05.96.76.81.83.

Le Marin
Ozier Lafontaine: Carrefour Diaka, ☎05.96.74.82.49 or 05.96.76.79.66;
Rent Eco: ☎05.96.74.89.90;
Thrifty: Boulevard Allègre, ☎05.96.74.71.77 or 05.96.74.79.77.

Sainte-Luce
Rent Eco: Hôtel Brise Marine, ☎05.96.62.46.94, ≈05.96.62.57.17.

By Scooter

The scooter, a very popular means of transportation in the Sainte-Luce and Sainte-Anne areas, makes it possible to travel along the coastal roads all the way to Grande Anse des Salines, the southernmost part of the island.

Scooter Rentals

Sainte-Luce
Sainte-Luce Locations: 6 Rue Schœlcher, ☎05.96.62.49.66.

Sainte-Anne
Sud Loisirs: near the entrance to Club Med, ☎05.96.76.81.82.

Collective Taxis

Again, you may explore the region by means of collective taxis. This does, however, require patience. You should also be willing to hitchhike, as you might ultimately have to do so to speed things up a little.

PRACTICAL INFORMATION

Ducos

Police: ☎05.96.56.13.12.

Town hall: ☎05.96.56.13.01, ≈05.96.56.18.17.

Pharmacies:
Pharmacie Marie Magdeleine Julien, ☎05.96.56.13.36.
Pharmacie Louison Reinette, Place Éloi-Virginie, ☎05.96.56.18.88.

Saint-Ésprit

Tourist office: ☎05.96.56.59.88, ≈05.96.56.59.88.

Police: ☎05.96.56.61.10.

Town hall: ☎05.96.56.61.02, ≈05.96.56.53.83.

Pharmacies:
Pharmacie de la Poste, 19 Rue Cap Pierre Rose, ☎05.96.56.56.65;
Pharmacie de l'Église, Rue Gueydon, ☎05.96.56.61.13.

Rivière-Salée

Police: ☎05.96.68.03.53.

Town hall: ☎05.96.68.01.90, ⇌05.96.68.21.71.

Gas station: Esso and Shell, in the centre of town.

Pharmacies:
Pharmacie Adrien Altius, Rue Principale, ☎05.96.68.02.66;
Pharmacie Thérèse Yung Hing, Rue Félix-Éboué, ☎05.96.68.00.45;
Pharmacie JC Marie Nelly, Rue Joinville, St-Prix, ☎05.96.68.14.77.

Laundromat: Laverie Saléenne, in the centre of town, ☎05.96.68.00.98.

Saint-Luce

Tourist office: Place de la Mairie, ☎05.96.62.57.85, ⇌05.96.62.30.15.

Police: ☎05.96.62.55.00.

Town hall: ☎05.96.62.50.01, ⇌05.96.62.30.15.

Pharmacies:
Pharmacie Michel-Édouard Londe, Place de la Mairie, ☎05.96.62.50.25;
Pharmacie Venant, Rue Schœlcher, ☎05.96.62.40.99.

Laundromat: Gros Raisins, ☎05.96.62.59.21.

Rivière-Pilote

Police: ☎05.96.62.60.08.

Town hall: ☎05.96.62.60.03, ⇌05.96.62.73.65.

Pharmacy: Pharmacie Danielle Binet, Place du 22 Mai, ☎05.96.62.60.10.

Laundromat: Rue Victor-Hugo, ☎05.96.62.70.28.

Le Marin

Tourist office: 3 Place Joffre, ☎05.96.74.63.21, ⇌05.96.74.72.96.

Police: ☎05.96.74.90.04.

Town hall: ☎05.96.74.90.02, ⇌05.96.74.96.60.

Pharmacies:
Pharmacie Lucien Ductor, Rue Duquesnay, ☎05.96.74.90.26.
Pharmacie Alain Laventure, Rue Schœlcher, ☎05.96.74.92.41.

Laundromat: Quai La Agnès, ☎05.96.74.89.63.

Sainte-Anne

Tourist office: ☎05.96.76.73.45 or ⇌05.96.76.70.37.

Town hall: ☎05.96.76.73.06, ⇌05.96.76.76.95

Gas station: on the road between the D9 and the municipal campground

Pharmacy:
Pharmacie du Panorama, on the shoreline road, in front of the cemetery, ☎05.96.76.98.94.

Laundromat: Domaine de Belfond, ☎05.96.76.84.42 .

Le Vauclin

Tourist office: Rue de la République, ☎05.96.74.40.38 or 05.96.74.40.40, ⇌05.96.74.54.94.

Police: ☎05.96.74.40.02.

Town hall: ☎05.96.74.40.40, ⇌05.96.74.44.11.

Pharmacy: Pharmacie Marie-Louise Fonrose, Rue Victor Hugo, ☎05.96.74.41.45.

Laudromat: Pressing, on the way into town, ☎05.96.74.53.85.

Le François

Tourist office: Boulevard Soleil-Levant, ☎05.96.54.67.50, ⇌05.96.54.53.27.

Police: ☎05.96.54.30.03.

Town hall: ☎05.96.54.30.02, ⇌05.96.54.76.76.

Hospital: (rural) ☎05.96.54.38.77 or 05.96.54.30.49.

Gas station: on the way out of town heading to Robert, on the left.

Pharmacies:
Pharmacie Centrale M. Laurencine, 35 Rue Homère Clément, ☎05.96.54.33.86;
Pharmacie de la Place, near the church, ☎05.96.54.32.45;
Pharmacie Victor Élana, 151 Rue de la Liberté, ☎05.96.54.42.50.

Laundromat: 10 Rue de la Liberté, ☎05.96.54.71.44.

EXPLORING

Ducos

Ducos, the first town on our itinerary, has over 12,000 inhabitants and is located in a primarily agricultural area, which produces sugar cane, bananas and vegetables. The town was officially named Ducos on September 4, 1855, in honour of Navy Minister Théodore Ducos, who in his time played an important role in establishing France's authority in New Caledonia and the Lesser Antilles. Before, the place had been known as "Trou au Chat" (The Cat's Hole), in reference to the first Frenchman to settle in the area in the early days of colonization, whose name was Lechat (the cat).

Destroyed by a hurricane in 1891, the **Église Notre-Dame-de-la-Nativité** was rebuilt by Henri Picq, the architect of many buildings in Martinique, including the Cathédrale Saint-Louis (see p 77) and the Bibliothèque Schœlcher (see p 76) in Fort-de-France.

The *"Château Aubéry" (on the N6, in the direction of Le François)* is also located within the *commune* of Ducos, at the edge of Le Lamentin. This neo-classical building, designed by Italian architects Volpi and Balesco, was erected between 1928 and 1931 for Eugène Aubéry, the administrator of a central sugar refinery. After Aubéry's death in 1942, the remarkable "château" was forsaken by his family, and then purchased by the *département* in 1954. It was used as a training college for teachers from 1957 to 1973, and then sold to the *commune* of Ducos in 1987. Now vacant, it is used only rarely, as a setting for cultural activities.

Saint-Ésprit

In the 18th century, the village of Saint-Esprit belonged to the *commune* of Rivière-Salée, and was known as Les Coulisses. This strange name was a reference to the system of slides (*coulisses*) used to transport sugar cane to the foot of the hills in the region. The village became a *commune* in 1837, and was renamed Saint-Esprit, but the river running through it is still called Rivière des Coulisses.

Before heading south, you can make a detour to Saint-Esprit. Although most people simply pass through this isolated farming village, you might want to stop for a few minutes to visit the little **Musée des Arts et Traditions Populaires** *(25 F; Tue to Sat 9am to 1pm and 3pm to 5pm, Sun 9:30am to noon, closed Mon; ☎05.96.56.76.51)*, established in 1987. The exhibit consists mainly of farming implements and handicrafts, while the building itself is a former college dating back to 1913.

The pretty **town hall**, an historic monument dating from 1924, is also worth a look.

Finally, Saint-Esprit's **church** bell has a remarkable history. Originally from a Cossack village in the Caucasus, it was sent here in 1855 by Abbé Favreau, a parish priest who had become chaplain of a task force in Crimea, as a gift to his cherished former parishioners. Cast in Stravopol in 1849, the bell is known as **La Sébastopol**.

Rivière-Salée

Get back on the N5, which is fast and flat in this area, and continue to Rivière-Salée (Salty River), a district with about 9,000 inhabitants which has the great distinction of being the gateway to the **Réserve Ornithologique de Génipa**, a bird sanctuary (see "Parks and Beaches," p 131).

A river does run through Rivière-Salée, and its water is indeed salty, due to the motion of the tides. In addition, it was in this area that the first steam mill, imported from France, was installed around 1820. The Meaupoux property, which was the site of this grand première, has been known ever since as "Vapeur" (Steam).

Rivière-Salée is actually two villages, each with its own distinct character. Both grew up around central sugar refineries, one of which closed down in 1970 (Petit-Bourg) and the other in 1973 (Rivière-Salée or Grand-Bourg).

Writer Joseph Zobel is a native of Petit-Bourg, and when his novel *Rue Cases-Nègres* was adapted for the screen by Euzhan Palcy, the **Petit-Bourg refinery** (not open to visitors) was brought back to life while the film was being shot.

Rivière-Salée's local fair is held on Midsummer Day (June 24). Traditionally, a big land-crab hunt, carried out at nightfall, is organized for the occasion in the neighbouring mangrove swamp.

Sainte-Luce ★★

Trois-Rivières and the Vacation Areas

After Rivière-Salée, continue on the N5 for another five kilometres and then take the exit for **Trois-Rivières**, where you can visit a small **rum distillery** *(Mon to Fri 9am to 5:30pm, Sat 9am to noon; ☎05.96.62.51.78)*. It was on the grounds of the present distillery that Louis XIV's superintendent of finance was able to build a veritable château in 1635, using the fortune he had fraudulently amassed in the course of performing his duties. Jean-Baptiste Colbert denounced him to the king, who consequently ordered the demolition of the scoundrel's luxurious retreat.

Monésie

Farther along the road leading to the Trois-Rivières distillery, a series of signposts will guide you to the **Art et Nature studio** *(Mon to Fri 10am to 1pm and 2:30pm to 6pm; ☎05.96.62.59.19)*, where a charming artist couple produces one-of-a-kind paintings. These works are made exclusively from over 130 varieties of sand (!) collected throughout Martinique, from which 230 earth colours are derived. The two artists explain their technique and demonstrate their know-how to visitors.

Next drive along the coast on a small road leading to the village of Sainte-Luce for the chance to stop at one of the area's three beautiful white-sand beaches, **Anse Mabouyas ★**, **Anse Corps de Garde ★★** or **Gros Raisins ★★**.

The Village of Sainte-Luce

Enter the **village of Sainte-Luce**. Inhabitants of the village and its surroundings (5,500 inhab.) survive mainly on fishing and tourism. The region is in fact a steadily developing tourist area, so much so that the population literally doubles during summer vacation. Residents of the countryside around the village also raise livestock (cattle, sheep and goats).

Historically, the region of Sainte-Luce has been through some extremely difficult times. First, in 1693, the English invaded the village and set fire to it,

forcing a large portion of the population to flee to the neighbouring hills. Then in 1817, a hurricane devastated the village once again. Today, with its little white church and the countless gum trees planted by local fishermen, Sainte-Luce is a tranquil village enlivened every summer by the arrival of vacationers. Its proximity to Fort-de-France (less than 20 min on a fast, modern road) and beautiful neighbouring beaches, have been attracting more and more visitors, some of whom build vacation homes in the hills, while others take advantage of the area's many and varied accommodations (inns, hotels, etc.).

Before leaving Sainte-Luce, be sure to make a short detour to the **Forêt de Montravail ★**, where you can see rocks carved by the Arawak Indians. To get there, head north on the D17 (see "Parks and Beaches", p 131).

Rivière-Pilote ★★

Immediately after Sainte-Luce, head inland on the D18 towards Rivière-Pilote, a remarkably lively village, especially around the covered market and recently renovated church. It was named after a Carib chief nicknamed Pilote, who, like Arlet, agreed to side with the French invaders.

In 1870, the day after the Third Republic was declared, Rivière-Pilote was the scene of the *"Insurrection du Sud"* (southern insurrection) following the sentencing of a black man named Léopold Lubin. This public uprising was marked, among other things, by the assassination of Assistant Judge Louis Codé and the pillaging of the Mauny property. Furthermore, once the revolt was put down, 12 of the insurgents were sent before the firing squad.

Today, the village's 12,500 or so inhabitants depend on the cultivation of sugar cane, bananas and vegetables, livestock raising and fishing for a living.

There are two famous sites a little north of Rivière-Pilote, both of which may be reached by taking the road that winds through the tropical forest. The first is **Pitt Cléry** ★ *(50F; fights Sun and Wed between 2:30 and 6pm; ☎05.96.62.81.92)*, the most popular place on the island to see cockfights and battles between mongooses and snakes.

The second is the nearby **Distillerie La Mauny** *(free tour and samples; Mon to Fri 9am to 5:30pm, Sat 9am to 1pm; ☎05.96.62.62.08)*, Martinique's most famous rum distillery, which is worth a visit. In 1749, Joseph Ferdinand Poulain, Compte de Mauny (in Normandy), gave the La Mauny estate its present name. Today, La Mauny rum controls 50% of the island's domestic market and is setting sales records in Europe (1,000,000 bottles a year), where it is distributed by Barton & Guestier.

After turning back towards Rivière-Pilote, you will notice some towering **erratics**, on the outskirts of the village. An erratic is a rock formation that has been carried far from its original location by a glacier.

The **Parc de l'Escoet** *(☎05.96.62.60.11)* is worth a visit. It is a modest little private zoo, that houses a few local animals, such as mongooses and a collection of naturalized birds.

Heading back to the N5, take the first exit on the right, which will take you to the small family beach at **Anse Figuier** ★★ (see p 132), which the district of Rivière-Pilote has recently developed. Once there, you can also visit the **Écomusée de Martinique** ★★ *(20F; Tue to Sun 9am to 5pm, closed Mon; ☎05.96.62.79.14, ⌐05.96.62.73.77)*, located inside a former distillery. The two-floor museum explains the significant periods of Martinique's history, covering the pre-Colombian Arawak and Carib civilizations, the colonial era, the proslavery system and the plantation economy. To round off your visit, stop in at the museum's handicraft shop.

Le Marin

Back on the N5, you will soon drive alongside Pointe Borgnesse, where you can take in a **remarkable view of the Cul-de-Sac-du-Marin** ★★, the long, narrow bay alongside which Le Marin, now an important administrative centre, is nestled. Many motorists, enchanted by the scene, pull over to the side of the road here. Just opposite, you will see the white, red-roofed buildings of Club Med Les Boucaniers.

You will then enter the village of **Le Marin** itself, which is one of the island's two sub-prefectures. Turn right to **Église Saint-Étienne**, dating from the 18th century. Its lovely Jesuit-style façade is enchanting, while the remarkable ornamentation and marble statues inside are not to be missed. These were originally intended to grace the cathedral of Lima, Peru, but when the boat that was transporting them was caught in a storm, the captain, according to legend, swore to give away his precious cargo if he and his crew were saved. The boat then ran aground at Le Marin, all its passengers safe and sound.

On the square facing the church, stands a monument honouring Dr. Osmann Duquesnay, a native of the village. Duquesnay was mayor of Le

Église Saint-Étienne (Le Marin)

Marin, then deputy and mayor of Fort-de-France before enlisting voluntarily for the war in 1914 – at the age of 70.

Le Marin was also the birthplace of Admiral Auguste-Delvrier Despointes, who, around 1853, claimed New Caledonia for France.

Because of its strategic location, Le Marin was coveted by the English and as a result endured repeated attacks in 1672, 1693, 1759, 1792, 1808 and even in 1884, during the Mexican War. As if that weren't enough, the village was devastated by a hurricane in 1891, and again in 1903.

In addition to its sailing harbour, Le Marin has a pleasant **waterfront**, which is nice to walk along.

Sainte-Anne ★★★

A short distance after the village of Le Marin, turn right on the D9, which leads to Sainte-Anne and the southern beaches. When you reach the outskirts of Sainte-Anne, you'll see two side roads leading to the centre of the village. The first goes directly to the entrance of the **public beach** and the campground, as well as to **Club Med Les Boucaniers** *(guided tours available, including sports, for 250-400F per day)*. Afterwards, bear left, and you'll head into the centre of the village on a pleasant road that runs alongside the coast, offering a beautiful view of the beach and Pointe Marin below. If, on the other hand, you take the second road before turning right towards Sainte-Anne, you will see the soft-hued pavilions of the luxury hotel complex, Le Hameau de Beauregard, not to be confused with the famous **Manoir Beauregard**, an historic hotel, which, is known for its superb collection of antique furniture. Ravaged by a major fire at the end of the 1990s, it has since been completely renovated and is slowly regaining its lustre of yesteryear.

Sainte-Anne, which has about 4,000 residents, is Martinique's southernmost district. Its main industries are fishing,

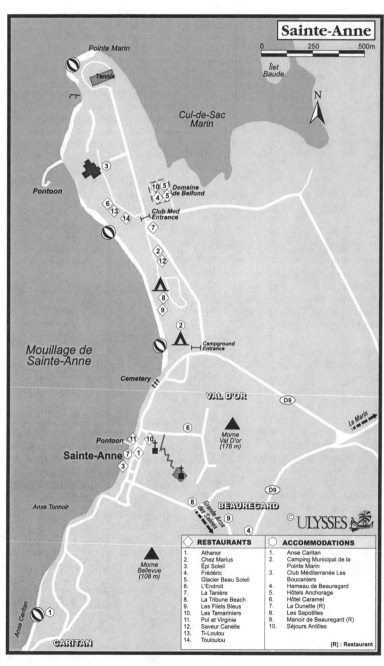

Sainte-Anne

0   250   500m

Pointe Marin

Îlet
Baude

Tennis

Cul-de-Sac
Marin

N

Pontoon

Domaine
de Belfond

Club Med
Entrance

Mouillage de
Sainte-Anne

Campground
Entrance

Cemetery

VAL D'OR

D9

Le Marin

Pontoon

Morne
Val D'or
(176 m)

Sainte-Anne

D9

Anse Tonnoir

BEAUREGARD

Grande Anse
des Salines

©ULYSSES

Morne
Bellevue
(108 m)

Anse Caritan

CARITAN

◇ RESTAURANTS	◯ ACCOMMODATIONS
1. Athanor	1. Anse Caritan
2. Chez Marius	2. Camping Municipal de la
3. Épi Soleil	Pointe Marin
4. Frédéric	3. Club Méditerranée Les
5. Glacier Beau Soleil	Boucaniers
6. L'Endroit	4. Hameau de Beauregard
7. La Tanière	5. Hôtels Anchorage
8. La Tribune Beach	6. Hôtel Caramel
9. Les Filets Bleus	7. La Dunette (R)
10. Les Tamariniers	8. Les Sapotilles
11. Poï et Virginie	9. Manoir de Beauregard (R)
12. Saveur Canelle	10. Séjours Antilles
13. Ti-Loulou	
14. Touloulou	(R) : Restaurant

steer-, sheep- and goat-breeding and, most importantly, tourism. The village is absolutely charming, with its flower-filled **cemetery**, its little seaside square, where the **church** and **town hall** are located, its shops, restaurants and **craft market**.

On the other side of the village, there is another beautiful beach, which is great for families, **Anse Caritan**.

Les Salines ★★★ and the Beaches of the Southeast Coast ★★

Back on the D9, you will head towards what some call "the most beautiful beach in the Caribbean" or, better yet, the "pearl of the Antilles" – **Grande Anse des Salines** (see p 132), the best known and most heavenly beach on the island, stretching over more than a kilometre of pure white sand.

Near these idyllic surroundings lies the spectacular lunar landscape of the **Savane des Pétrifications ★★**. This barren area, which you can only reach on foot, was at one time the site of a forest that had been petrified by lava. Though not a single piece of petrified wood remains today, it is still worth a visit, as its desolate landscape is unique in Martinique.

From Grande Anse des Salines, you can walk to several small beaches, some still untouched, which are scattered here and there over a distance of 20 kilometres and lapped by the waters of the Atlantic Ocean. You will walk alongside the **Étang des Salines**, the largest pond on the island, before reaching **Grande Terre** beach; the lovely beach of **Anse Trabaud ★★**; **Baie des Anglais**; **Cap Chevalier ★★**; **Cap Ferré** and **Pointe Macré**, among others. Small, often unpaved roads lead to most of these places, making them accessible by car, as well (see p 133).

Le Vauclin

Once you have finished exploring the Sainte-Anne area, you have little choice but to head back to Le Marin. From there, take the N6, which heads north towards Le Vauclin, passing through mahogany and banana plantations on its way. About 4 km from the village, a small road on the right side passes by the ruins of an old mill and the main residence of the **Malevaut Estate** on its way to the beaches of **Petite Anse Macabou** and **Grande Anse Macabou** (see p 133).

Farther on, just before the village, there is a roadside viewing area where you can stop to gaze upon the Atlantic Ocean, the village of Le Vauclin and the area's pastures.

Le Vauclin has 7,500 inhabitants, most of whom rely on fishing for their income. Secondary activities include retailing, the cultivation of fruits and vegetables (eggplant, melon, potato, etc.) and cattle-, sheep- and goat-breeding.

At the very beginning of the 18th century, the Compte de Vauclin settled in the southern part of Martinique, where he became a prominent landowner and cultivated tobacco and sugar cane. The town that gradually grew up near his land was soon known as Le Vauclin. The area, which had long been inhabited by Carib Indians, was one of the first to be colonized by the French. It is interesting to note that recent excavations have revealed traces of both Carib and Arawak settlements around the volcano, and more specifically, in the Paquemar area.

The village itself has little to offer in terms of tourist attractions, aside, perhaps, from the sight of its many fishermen coming in from the sea at the end of the morning, or the remarkable stained-glass window over the entrance of its large modern **church**. You should nevertheless take the time to go to the top of **Montagne Vauclin** (504 m), the highest point in southern Martinique. To do so, take the D5 towards Saint-Esprit, then follow the signs for "Coulée d'Or." The footpath that leads up the mountain is the same route taken by pilgrims every September on their way to the little chapel at the top.

South of the village, the delightful **Pointe Faula** (see p 133) beach, with its easily reached white-sand sea beds, is a real gem.

Le François ★★

Between Le Vauclin and Le François, the road runs alongside a jagged coastline, where you'll see numerous points jutting out into the ocean. A lot of Creoles (*békés*) built their vacation homes in the area, thereby turning it into a sort of resort for white islanders, just like the Le Robert area further north. Near the Rivière Simon lies the estate called **Habitation Palmiste**, the birthplace of General Brière de l'Isle, one of the conquerors of the Sudan and Tonkin.

Make sure to visit **Au Village** *(every day, 8:30am to 6pm; ☎05.96.54.95.58)*, also located between the two villages. It is a partial recreation of an early 20th century village, featuring peasant shacks made mainly with bamboo. A handful of people in period costume add life to the site, which also provides information on a number of crops, such as coffee and cotton.

Le François is the island's fourth largest district in terms of population (17,000 inhab.). It was named after the handful of French settlers who arrived in the area around 1620, before the colonial era had even started.

Upon visiting this lively village, you might be surprised by the positively futuristic lines of the **Église Saint-Michel-du-François**, which has the most daring architecture of any religious building on the island. It was designed by Martinican architect Marc Alie as a replacement for the former church, which was completely destroyed by fire in 1973. Saint-Michel-du-François is actually the sixth church to be built on this site since Père Labat founded the parish. It looks out onto pretty **Place Charles-de-Gaulle**, which is graced with a magnificent World War I memorial.

Right nearby, the colonial-style **town hall** offsets its neighbour's futuristic architecture, considered by many to be too extreme.

Le François also has an attractive **sailing harbour**, from which you can take a boat to the area's *fonds blancs* ★★, such as the **baignoire de Joséphine** (Josephine's Bath). A *fond blanc* is a high, white sandbank protected by coral reefs, where the water is no more than one-metre deep. You can enjoy the typically Creole custom of standing on the *fonds blancs*, up to your waist in water, sipping a glass of punch and chatting. The pure white sand and extraordinarily clear water, married with the distinctive taste of the punch that results from this unique atmosphere, make the experience of this custom altogether unforgettable.

Albert Mongin, for one, organizes this type of excursion *(adults 185F, children aged 7-15 1/2 price, children under 7 50F; leaving from the marina at 9am; ☎05.96.54.70.23)*. The outing lasts all

Habitation Clément

day and includes music, activities, *accras*, a stop at the Baignoire de Joséphine, lunch on **Îlet Oscar**, *ti-punchs* and *planteurs* (planter's punch). Another option is to make arrange-ments with the fishermen in Le François, who will gladly take you to the *fonds blancs* aboard their little boats.

Le François is also known for its ex-cellent team of *yoleurs*, as those who race *yoles rondes* (small sailboats pecu-liar to Martinique) are known. If a *yole ronde* race happens to be taking place while you are in the area, make sure not to miss it.

Le Domaine de l'Acajou ★★★

A short distance outside the city, on the road from Saint-Esprit, lie the **Domaine de l'Acajou** *(40 F)*, which is better known as the **Habitation Clément** ★★★ that houses the

Distillerie Clément *(free samples; every day 9am to 6pm;* ☎*05.96.54.62.07)*, founded in 1917 by Dr. Homère Clé-ment, deputy and mayor of Le François. Until 1988, the most famous Martinican rums were made here and at La Mauny (see p 125). The rum is now made at the distillery in Simon, five kilometres from Le François, before Le Vauclin; the place is now solely used for stocking and aging rum. Vieux Clément is a special favourite amoung connoisseurs, and 1952 and 1970 were legendary years for it. There is a beautifully restored 18th century resi-dence on the grounds. Visitors are also shown two films, one on the history of rum in Martinique and the other on François Mittérand's and Georges Bush's meeting here during the Gulf War in 1991.

This 16-hectare park contains the master's house, which is listed as a historic monument and is decorated with magnificent 18th- and 19th-century furniture from the *Compagnie des Indes Occidentales et Orientales*. Also on the grounds are the outbuildings (kitchen, stables), the house of the plantation manager or *géreur* (where the tour begins and where you can sample the rum) and the distillery filled with aging barrels. The park is a magnificent site in itself with its 300 plant species classified by the Office National des Forêts.

Back in the village, you can complete your tour by heading west on the N6.

  PARKS AND
BEACHES

Rivière-Salée

Réserve Ornithologique de Génipa

The bird sanctuary occupies a large mangrove swamp, which runs along the Baie de Génipa and may be reached through the village of Rivière-Salée. During the rainy season, it is the home of many different species of migratory birds, including teals and wood pigeons. The swamp is also the scene of the big land-crab hunt that takes place every year on June 24 as part of the local fair. You should naturally arm yourself with a good insect repellent if you decide to explore the area.

Sainte-Luce

Anse Mabouyas ★ (A)

Anse Mabouyas is the first in a series of pretty white sand beaches that you can reach by taking a small path that runs parallel to the main road between Trois-Rivières and the village of Sainte-Luce. The short beach, which is still a relatively well-kept secret, looks out onto clear, calm water.

Anse Corps de Garde ★★ (A)

You can't miss the parking area of the fully equipped beach on Anse Corps de Garde, a little further on. This is a very popular place, especially on weekends and during summer vacation.

Facilities: Showers and toilets; parking; areas for soccer and volleyball; beachside restaurants.

Gros Raisins ★★ (A)

Though more and more people discover it every day, the Gros Raisins beach is long enough to accommodate the crowd fairly well. Here, too, you'll find calm water and beautiful white sand.

Forêt de Montravail ★

The *Office National des Forêts* has developed this site for public use. Picnic areas and almost a dozen paths are scattered about with signs explaining the different plant species in the area. The forest also provides access to a private property where, as recently as 1970, an economist named Jean Crusol discovered a collection of stones engraved by Arawak Indians – the only glyphs to be found on the island to date. You'll see, for example, 11 figurines decorating a 2-by-1.4 metre boulder, a mask carved right into the edge of a big stone, and a table made out of a flat rock. It is, however, important to remember that the site is on private property, so you may only visit it with the owner's permission, and apparently he is not always in the mood to receive guests.

In addition, an organization named Journée Verte (☎05.96.62.54.23) arranges walks through the forest, which start at the village of Sainte-Luce at 9:30am every day except Sunday, and include stops at Pitt Cléry and Morne Gommier.

Rivière-Pilote

Anse Figuier ★★ (A)

This beautiful white-sand beach was recently outfitted with facilities for the use of local families. There is sign at the entrance reminding visitors that all forms of nudity are prohibited, thus emphasizing the family-oriented nature of the place. In addition to the beach itself, you can also visit the Écomusée de Martinique (see p 125).

Facilities: Showers and toilets, parking, playgrounds; beach-side restaurant.

Sainte-Anne

Plage Municipale de Sainte-Anne ★★★ (A)

The Sainte-Anne public beach, which is in fact the continuation of the renowned Club Med beach at Pointe Marin, is quite simply magnificent. White sand, coconut trees, clear, calm, shallow water and a pleasant little village right nearby; all these ingredients make this beach one of the nicest on the island. Theoretically, you are supposed to pay a small entry fee *(15F per car)* for the beach, but the regulars avoid doing so by parking on the street near the Club Med entrance, then gaining access to the beach through an opening in the gate next to the restaurant Touloulou. The municipality laid out a paid parking lot on this popular spot, but there are still many "free" places, mostly across from the car renters.

Facilities: Showers and toilets; paid parking; public telephones, first-aid station, campground; playgrounds; windsurfer, catamaran and pedalboat rentals; water-skiing; diving club; numerous restaurants.

Grande Anse des Salines ★★★ (A)

Imagine the perfect beach: fine, white sand; shallow, warm, turquoise water; a row of coconut trees bending toward the sea... This is a perfect description of Grande Anse des Salines, the most beautiful, and most popular, beach in Martinique. Be careful, though, because along with the coconut trees, there are a lot of *mancenilliers* (see p 42), which produce a highly poisonous milky sap, and are usually marked with a red line of paint by the *Office National des Forêts*.

Facilities: Showers and toilets; camping allowed on weekends, holidays and during summer vacation; picnic tables; food stands and one restaurant.

Grande-Terre ★★

Grande-Terre is often viewed as the continuation of its more famous westward neighbour, Grande Anse des Salines. The beach faces Îlet Cabrits and the **Table au Diable** (Devil's Table), a large, flat rock that forms a little island. This is where the waters of the Caribbean meet those of the Atlantic. Here, too, you should look out for the manchineel trees.

Facilities: Picnic tables; camping allowed on weekends, holidays and during summer vacation.

Petite Anse des Salines and Anse Meunier

At the westernmost tip of Grande Anse des Salines, a short path leads to a few other beautiful, quiet and rather secluded beaches. You will first reach Petite Anse des Salines, then Anse Meunier. The latter is popular with gay-male nudists.

Facilities: none, but Grande Anse des Salines is right nearby.

Anse Trabaud ★★ (A)
and Baie des Anglais

The beach at Anse Trabaud, though relatively easy to get to, is not nearly as busy as the one at Grande Anse des Salines. It has the same white sand and clear water, but is not equipped with any facilities.

On the other side of **Pointe Braham**, tucked away in the Baie des Anglais, lies another pretty little beach. From this point on, you'll notice that the beaches have been left in a more natural state, and are virtually empty. The wind blows harder here, and the surf is heavier.

To get to Anse Trabaud, you can either walk from Grande Anse des Salines, or pay 15F to drive along a private dirt road which is fairly well indicated on the D9, near the village of Sainte-Anne.

Cap Chevalier ★★ (A)

There are several small, untouched beaches worth discovering around Cap Chevalier, including **Anse Michel**, **Anse aux Bois** and **Pointe aux Pommes**. This area is especially good for windsurfing. You can also go for an outing on **Îlet Chevalier**, which is just in front of the beach. To get there, climb aboard the Taxi Cap (☎05.96.76.93.10), near the restaurant Chez Gracieuse (see p 147). To reach the area by car, go left on the D33 shortly after Le Marin on your way to Sainte-Anne. On your right, you'll

see a sign for the extremely narrow little road that leads to the Cap Chevalier beaches.

Facilities: a few restaurants; sailboard rentals at Anse Michel.

Cap Ferré and Pointe Macré (A)

If you choose instead to continue on the D33, you'll wind up on a dirt road leading to **Cul-de-sac Ferré**, which is squeezed in between Cap Ferré and Pointe Macré (also accessible via a road to the north), and is the site of yet another beautiful white sand beach. A path leads northwards to the pristine beach on **Anse Grosse Roche ★★**.

Facilities: Weekend snack bar.

Le Vauclin

Anses Macabou (A-B)

About four kilometres south of the village of Le Vauclin, there is a small road that leads to the Macabou district, as well as to Petite Anse Macabou and Grande Anse Macabou. Surprisingly, the water is calm at the former and considerably rougher at the latter.

Facilities: Camping at Ranch de Macabou; restaurant.

Pointe Faula (A)

Pointe Faula's little beach, located less than a kilometre south of the village of Le Vauclin, is relatively uncrowded in spite of its undeniable beauty. Its shallow water and pure white sand, which has the same composition as the famous *fonds blancs* of Le François and Le Robert, make it an especially good spot for families. What also sets this place apart are the white sandy sea-beds which extend right to the shore, so you can walk far out to sea in barely one metre of water. The only way to reach Pointe Faula from the village is to take the coastal road.

Facilities: Showers and toilets; picnic tables, restaurants.

 OUTDOOR ACTIVITIES

 Hiking

In **Le Marin**, Les Splendeurs Marinoises *(☎05.96.74.67.85)* organizes hiking excursions on a stretch of the Trace des Caps (see below), namely between Cap Macré and Cap Chevalier. Box lunch included. Departure at 8am, return around 4pm.

La Trace des Caps

The *Office National des Forêts* has marked a long trail known as La Trace des Caps, which enables you to explore the island's southern coast from Anse Caritan, near Sainte-Anne, all the way to Petite Anse Macabou, south of Le Vauclin on the Atlantic coast. Because the trail is so long, it has been divided into the following five sections: from Anse Caritan to Grande Anse des Salines (5 km, 2 hours); from Grande Anse des Salines to Anse Trabaud (5 km, 2 hours); from the Baie des Anglais to Cap Chevalier (6.5 km, 3 hours); from Cap Chevalier to Cap Macré (7 km, 3 hours); and from Cap Macré to Petite Anse Macabou (5 km, 2.5 hours). These trails are considered easy. Sunstroke and manchineel trees are the only things you'll have to worry about.

Montagne du Vauclin

This path, which you can reach from the D5 as you leave the village of Le Vauclin, leads to the highest point in southern Martinique (504 m). It is in fact the same trail taken by dozens of pilgrims every September. From the top, there is a breathtaking view of the Atlantic coast all the way to the Presqu'île de la Caravelle. You will also discover a cave about 50 metres deep, dug entirely by an old hermit who claimed he was trying to link the mountain to the road to Saint-Esprit.

 Scuba Diving

Several scuba diving excursions are available in the area. In **Sainte-Anne**, for example, some leave from the Anse Caritan Hotel *(☎05.96.76.81.31)*, and others directly from the public beach *(Centre de Plongée Kalinago, ☎05.96.76.92.98)*.

 Fishing

Those interested in going deep-sea fishing can call Caraïbe Yachting *(☎05.96.74.95.76 or 05.96.74.79.78, ☎05.96.74.95.60)* at the sailing harbour in **Le Marin**. Rates run about 400F per person.

 Pleasure Boating and Cruises

There are two large sailing harbours in the region covered in the tour of the southern beaches, one belonging to **Le Marin**, on the Caribbean coast, the other to **Le François**, on the Atlantic coast. At both, you can take part in a variety of planned excursions or rent a boat of your own.

At the **Le Marin** marina, you can call on the services of ATM Yachts (☎05.96.74.98.17 or 05.96.74.87.88, ≈05.96.74.88.12), who will rent you one of their 110 yachts and catamarans, with or without crew. The company also runs a spare parts store and makes sails. Caraïbe Yachting (☎05.96.74.95.76 or 05.96.74.79.78, ≈05.96.74.95.60), also in Le Marin, handles sailboat rentals. You can also rent a catamaran from Catana Antilles (☎05.96.74.88.87, ≈05.96.74.70.09).

At the village of Sainte-Anne's landing quay, you will see a strange-looking vessel, the **Aquascope Zemis** *(120F; daily departures at 9:30am, 11am, 2pm and 3:30pm; excursions last 1 hour 15 min;* ☎*05.96.76.83.71)*, a sort of semi-submarine that lets you explore underwater sights without getting so much as your little toe wet.

At the **Le François** marina, you can rent a motor boat from Star Voyage (☎05.96.54.68.03).

Furthermore, the region offers a variety of options for those who wish to join an organized boating excursion. There are expeditions to the white sandy sea beds departing from the **Le François** marina. Some of the outfits offering this activity are Albert Mongin (☎05.96.54.70.23) and River Cat (☎05.96.74.96.79). Vedette Évasion Les Fonds Blancs *(*☎*05.96.54.96.26 or 05.96.54.96.87)* also offers these excursions, but from Baie du Simon, between Le Vauclin and Le François.

You can also go on a sea-kayaking expedition with Caraïbe Coast Kayak (☎05.96.76.76.02) to white sandy sea beds and mangrove swamps. Departures from **Cap Chevalier**.

Aquabulle *(*☎*05.96.74.69.69)*, offers glass-bottom boat trips leaving from **Le Marin**. They cost around 130F to 160F for a 90-minute to 2-hour journey, swimming optional.

 Windsurfing

Windsurfing is extremely popular in the area, and it is relatively easy to rent the necessary equipment. In **Sainte-Luce**, go to Antilles Loisirs *(*☎*05.96.62.44.19)*, and in **Sainte-Anne**, to Hobby Cat *(*☎*05.96.76.90.77 or 05.96.74.89.00)*. Also worth mentioning is Alizé Fun Dillon *(*☎*05.96.74.71.58)*, at Anse Michel in **Cap Chevalier**.

 Tent and Trailer Camping

There are a few noteworthy campgrounds in the area. If you're interested in a place with hot showers, try the campground at Pointe Marin *(*☎*05.96.76.72.79)*, near the public beach in **Sainte-Anne**, or Ranch Macabou, a little south of **Le Vauclin**.

Camping is also permitted in the area around **Grande Anse des Salines** and **Cap Chevalier** on weekends and holidays and during summer vacation (see descriptions of these areas in the "Accommodations" section).

As far as equipment is concerned, you can rent tents and other gear on site at the **Sainte-Anne** campground and at Tropicamp de Gros Raisins *(*☎*05.96.62.59.00)* in **Sainte-Luce**. If you're interested in renting a camper, call West-Indies Tours *(*☎*05.96.54.50.71)* in **Le François**.

 Horseback Riding

There is a horseback-riding club in **Rivière-Salée**: the Centre Équestre de Thoraille *(*☎*05.96.68.18.66)*.

Flying Excursions

In **Saint-Luce**, Alizé Air Services *(☎05.96.62.24.25, ⌨05.96.62.56.39)* lets you explore Martinique from the skies in a seaplane. Departures from **Saint-Anne** or **Salines**.

ACCOMMODATIONS

Saint-Luce

In the Village

The Sainte-Luce area is becoming more and more popular with tourists, and has several *gîtes ruraux* to choose from. You can stay at the *gîte* of **Raymond René (no. 56** ¦¦¦) *(2470F a week; Deville district, 97228 Sainte-Luce)* or at the one of **Jeanne Capoul (no. 146,** ¦¦¦) *(3270F a week; Lot Les Moubins no. 131 - 97228 Sainte-Luce)*.

Gros Raisins

In Gros Raisins, just before Sainte-Luce on the little road that runs alongside the sea and passes through the Trois-Rivières and Désert areas, there is an entire series of residences where you can rent fully equipped studios and apartments. Considering the strategic location, just a short distance from the southwest point's many attractions and the magnificent southern beaches, renting here can prove to be an inexpensive option for those wishing to stay in the area. One of the nicest residences is a lovely white house named **Les Deux Cocotiers** *(2,500F per week; ≡, pb, K, ℝ; B59 Gros Raisins - 97228 Sainte-Luce, ☎05.96.62.41.50, ⌨05.96.62.50.85)*. The friendly owners have transformed the first floor rooms

into four pleasant studio apartments, and there is a pretty little beach just behind the house. There are also televisions available for 150F a week. Remember, however, that the apartments may only be rented on a weekly basis.

There are many similar places in the area, including one right next door, **La Résidence Douce Vague** *(pb, ≡, K; Gros Raisins - 97228 Sainte-Luce, ☎05.96.62.47.47, ⌨05.96.62.49.75)*, which offers comparable rates.

The biggest of the group, however, is the **Brise Marine** *(3,340F per week for a studio apartment, 4,700F per week for an apartment; ≡, ⊗, pb, K, ℝ; Gros Raisins - 97228 Sainte-Luce, ☎05.96.62.46.94, ⌨05.96.62.57.17)*, which has five two-person studios and seven apartments that can comfortably accommodate up to five people. It looks right onto the beach, and is surrounded by a magnificent garden with armchairs and chaise-longues where guests can relax. They also rent cars.

This area also has its share of *gîtes ruraux*, all duly registered, such as the **Résidence Saint-Antoine (nos. 082 to 086,** ¦¦¦) *(1,400F per week; 5 units in the same building; Gros Raisins - 97228 Sainte-Luce)* and the one belonging to **M. Stéphane Saint-Paul (no. 105,** ¦¦¦) *(2,700F per week; on the second floor of a villa; Lotissement Gros Raisins B14 - 97228 Sainte-Luce)*.

Take note that the **Village Vacances Familles de Saint-Luce**, also located in the Gros Raisins district, was under renovation when we passed through (March 1998) and was consequently closed for the time being.

Tropicamp *(184 Les Moubins, Gros Raisins - 97228 Sainte-Luce, ☎05.96.62.59.00, ⌨05.96.62.59.29)* offers family holiday packages including

Ulysses' Favourites

Accommodations

Charming hotels:
> La Frégate Bleue (Le François, p 141)
> Les Îlets de l'Impératrice (Le François, p 142)

For the welcome:
> Les Deux Cocotiers (Sainte-Luce, p 136)
> Le Brise Marine (Sainte-Luce, p 136)

For the tropical garden:
> Les Amandiers (Sainte-Luce, p 138)

For history buffs:
> Résidence Hôtelière La Girafe (Le Marin, p 139)
> Manoir de Beauregard (Sainte-Anne, p 140)

For water sports enthusiasts:
> La Riviera (Le François, p 141)
> Club Méditerranée Les Boucaniers (Sainte-Anne, p 140)

For the view:
> La Frégate Bleue (Le François, p 141)

airfare, rental car and fully equipped camping facilities. Apartments and villas can also be rented through this organization.

The **Résidence Grand Large** *(378F; tv, ≡, pb, K; 97228 Sainte-Luce, ☎05.96.62.54.42, ≈05.96.62.54.32)* stands in the midst of a pretty garden near the beach. It offers studios for two and apartments for four, all fully equipped. Mountain bikes, scooters and sailboards are also available for rent here.

A little farther on your left, you will see a big, pink gabled house with balconies, which has been converted into an inn, **La Petite Auberge** *(420F bkfst incl., 620F 1/2 b; ≡, ≈, ℜ, ℝ, ⊘; 97228 Sainte-Luce, ☎05.96.62.59.70,* ≈*05.96.62.42.99)*. Though imposing at first sight, this typically Martinican house has only a dozen rooms, which means that visitors receive personalized attention. The inn looks out on the sea.

Outside the Village

Another option in the area is the **Résidence Deville** *(290-530F; tv, ≡, pb, K; Quartier Deville - 97228 Saint-Luce, ☎05.96.62.50.64,* ≈*05.96.62.58.78)*, located in the hills of Saint-Luce, reached via the Rivière-Pilote-bound D18. The hotel boasts eight fully equipped suites as well as a dozen rooms, the whole set up in a magnificent Creole house.

Right across from the Les Amandiers complex (see below) is the brand-new

Caribia *(710F; ≡, pb, K, ≈; 97228 Sainte-Luce, ☎05.96.62.20.62, ≈05.96.62.59.62)*, a Best-Western holiday village comprising some 76 suites equipped with kitchenettes. The whole is nestled between the N5 and a small road leading to the Saint-Luce area beaches. To enjoy some measure of peace and quiet, try to get a room in one of the front buildings, as the ones in the rear are only a stone's throw from the highway. A pleasant bar, adjacent to a small swimming pool, and a tennis court round off the establishment's facilities.

The most fashionable hotel complex in the area is named **Le Mercure Inn Les Amandiers** *(880-1,150 F; tv, ≡, pb, ≈, ℜ; 97228 Sainte-Luce; ☎05.96.62.32.32, ≈05.96.62.33.40)*. It's a cluster of four salmon-pink, blue and green two-story buildings containing a total of 117 rooms. The enchanting surroundings are enhanced by a magnificent swimming pool nestled in a beautiful tropical garden; a tennis court and direct access to a white-sand beach. If you want to get a good night's sleep, request a room in the front, near the reception area. Otherwise you'll face the back, which overlooks the swimming pool and the large hut containing the bar and restaurant, and have to put up with all the noise from the activities held there in the evening. The rooms are large and attractively fitted out with wicker furniture.

Tourism has been attracting a growing number of property developers to this area, as evidenced by the complexes still under construction during our visit (March 1998). One of these, the **Amyris**, will be the Amandiers' next-door neighbour and boast 110 rooms. Moreover, a few kilometres closer to the village, a second large-scale establishment is soon to be added to the hotel stretch around Saint-Luce.

Quartier Montravail

Located in the hills of Sainte-Anne, Forêt Montravail provides a unique setting for nature lovers who wish to stay in the area, and the local *gîtes* are perfectly suited to the surroundings. Here is someone you can contact: **M. Gabin Salomon (no. 036, ¦¦)** *(1,705 per week; located below the owner's residence; Quartier Montravail, 97228 Sainte-Luce)*.

Rivière-Pilote

A small sign on the N5 indicates the exit for **Roy Christophe** *(250-385 F; ≡, K, ℜ; Anse Figuier - 97211 Rivière-Pilote, ☎05.96.62.76.17, ≈05.96.62.76.17)*, a 20 room hotel located in the hills. The hotel overhangs the beach at Anse Figuier, whose facilities are managed by the town of Rivière-Pilote.

In the same area, a very steep road leads up to **Le Paradis de l'Anse** *(330-380F; tv, ≡, K; Anse Figuier - 97211 Rivière Pilote, ☎05.96.62.90.60, ≈05.96.62.38.90)*, a lovely little house clinging to the side of a hill. Besides its splendid view, the place has equipped bungalows, studios and apartments.

Le Marin

The **Auberge du Marin** *(200F to 250F; tv, ≡, pb, ℜ; 21 Rue Osman-Duquesnay - 97290 Le Marin, ☎05.96.74.83.88, ≈05.96.74.76.47)* is a convenient place on account of its location, in the very heart of Le Marin. The inn has but five rooms of rudimentary comfort, however.

SOUTHERN BEACHES

Near the marina, just behind the market, you'll find the **Résidence Hôtelière La Girafe** *(400-550 F; tv, ≈, pb, K, ℜ; 13 Rue Émile-Zola - 97290 Le Marin,* ☎*05.96.74.82.83,* ⇒*05.96.74.90.51)*, a charming old 18th-century townhouse. The main floor boasts a magnificent dining room with attractive stone walls. This may be your best option in the Le Marin area.

In addition, you always have the option of staying in a *gîte*. A few of the especially noteworthy ones belong to **M. Ernest Jeannot (nos. 075-076,** ⏐⏐**)** *(1,600 F per week; on the first floor of the owner's residence; 30 Rue Osman Duquesnay - 97290 Le Marin)*, **M. Alex Louis-Joseph (nos. 193 and 194** ⏐⏐⏐**)** *(1,900 F per week; independent units; Quartier Pérou, 97290 Le Marin)* and **M. Gabriel Louis-Joseph (nos. 091-093** ⏐⏐⏐**)** *(1,470-1,995F per week; below the owner's residence; Quartier Pérou - 97290 Le Marin)*.

There are a few other places worth mentioning in the vicinity of Le Marin. Among these is the **Albarena Hôtel** *(390F to 750F; tv, ≈, pb, K, ≈; Quartier Le Huvet - 97290 Le Marin,* ☎*05.96.76.75.75,* ⇒*05.96.76.97.13)*, a pleasant establishment nestled on a hilltop three kilometres from the village. The hotel has some 30 studios that sleep four, which come equipped with kitchenettes, mezzanines, and terrace out back.

Also of note is the **Habitation Lafontaine** *(520F to 635F; tv, ≈, pb, ≈, K, ⊘; 97290 Le Marin,* ☎*05.96.74.82.49,* ⇒*05.96.74.96.09)*, which consists of five houses, each comprising 10 studios and as many apartments. Set up in a lovely hillside tropical garden, only 200 metres from the Le Marin marina, this small complex also has a tennis court.

Sainte-Anne

The most economical option in the area is without a doubt Point Marin's **municipal campground** *(50F per day with your own gear; B.P. 8 - 97227 Ste-Anne,* ☎*05.96.76.72.79,* ⇒*05.96.76.97.82)*, which runs along Sainte-Anne's magnificent public beach. The atmosphere is entirely family-oriented (there is even a day-care centre). The campground offers playgrounds, bathrooms, a number of restaurants and direct access to the beach. Tents, trailers and camping gear are available for rent as well *(1,140F per week)*.

Another budget hotel in the area, the **Hôtel Caramel** *(350F; tv, pb, K; Derrière Morne - 97227 Saint-Anne,* ☎*05.96.76.77.03,* ⇒*05.96.76.74.81)*, only 50 metres from the village centre, has eight studios (for two people) and two apartments (for four people).

There are also a few *gîtes* where you can stay without spending a fortune, including those belonging to **M. Jean Prales (no. 20,** ⏐⏐**)** *(2,600F; independent unit; Derrière-Morne - 97227 Sainte-Anne)*, **Mme Rémy Psyché (no. 032,** ⏐⏐**)** *(2,015 per week; adjoining the owner's residence; Quartier Poirier - 97227 Sainte-Anne)* and **M. Armand Belmo (nos. 066-067,** ⏐⏐**)** *(1,880F per week; two units in a separate house; Derrière-Morne - 97227 Sainte-Anne)*, just to mention a few.

On the road heading south out of Sainte-Anne, toward Les Salines, you'll find **Les Sapotilles** *(*☎*05.96.76.79.38,* ⇒*05.96.63.15.22)*, where you can rent one of several little blue bungalows surrounded by flowers.

Back in Domaine de Belfond, **Séjours Antilles** *(1,800-2,800F per week; pb, K; Domaine de Belfond - 97227*

Sainte-Anne, ☎05.96.76.74.31, ⚏05.96.76.93.22), rents bungalows, studio apartments and villas that can comfortably accommodate up to eight people.

 In the same area, you'll find the **Anchorage** (520-925F; ≡, ≈, ℛ, K; Domaine de Belfond, 97227 Sainte-Anne, ☎05.96.76.92.32, ⚏05.96.76.91.40), a vast, very unusual ensemble of five hotels containing a total of 186 studio apartments and duplexes. The result is a calm, very pleasant "neighbourhood" offering its "residents" both a miniature golf course and a tennis court.

 In the heart of the village, there is a pleasant 18-room hotel named **La Dunette** (600-700F; tv, ≡, pb, ℛ; 97227 Sainte-Anne, ☎05.96.76.73.90, ⚏05.96.76.76.05). Some of the rooms command a view of the sea, and are simple, but bathed in sunlight. Guests can relax among the flowers in the superb garden out back. It is also worth mentioning that La Dunette serves some of the best food in the area (see p 145).

The **Anse Caritan** (700-1,050F, bkfst incl.; ≡, pb, ≈, K, ℛ; 97227 Sainte-Anne; ☎05.96.76.74.12, ⚏05.96.76.72.59) lies past the village of Sainte-Anne. In addition to the standard facilities available at similar luxury hotel complexes, this place also has its own discotheque. Child care service is provided as well.

 As you head out of the village of Sainte-Anne, you're sure to see the **Hameau de Beauregard** (430-890F; tv, ≡, pb, ≈, ℛ, K; 97227 Sainte-Anne, ☎05.96.76.75.75, ⚏05.96.76.97.13), a large vacation village composed of blue, pink and white buildings that seem to have suddenly sprung up in the middle of nowhere. Taken as a whole,

though, the place is pleasant enough, once you've gotten over your initial surprise. There are 90 luxury apartments surrounding a large swimming pool.

 Right nearby, the venerable **Manoir de Beauregard** (900-1,100F; tv, ≡, pb, ≈; 97227 Sainte-Anne, ☎05.96.76.73.40, ⚏05.96.76.93.24) seems determined to survive till doomsday. Ravaged by fire in the early 1980s, it has risen from its ashes in all its former splendour and the main building, dating from the 18th century, has been fully restored. The interior is once again adorned with woodwork and mahogany furniture, giving this superb hotel back all its charm and character.

And, of course, no description of the area would be complete without the **Club Med Les Boucaniers** (all-inclusive club package; ≡, pb, ℛ; Pointe Marin - 97227 Sainte-Anne, ☎05.96.76.72.72, ⚏05.96.76.72.02), one of the most reputed branches of the famous international network. In addition to week-long vacation packages, which include all activities, there are also two weekend packages: 1,300F per person, which last from 7pm Friday to midnight Sunday; or 900F per person, which last from 10am on Saturday to midnight Sunday. This offer is of course only valid as long as there are places left open by guests purchasing week-long packages. Among the many activities available, there is scuba-diving, water skiing, windsurfing and tennis. Take note, however, that children under twelve are not admitted, as this Club Med, unlike Club Med family villages, does not have facilities designed expressly for them.

Les Salines and the Southeast Beaches

Keep in mind that you can camp free of charge along some of these beaches, including the famous Grande Anse des Salines, on weekends and holidays, as well as during summer vacation.

Furthermore, **Mireille** *(1,400-2,200F per week; pb, K; ☎05.96.76.72.31, ⌐05.96.76.99.18)* rents out bungalows on the road to Cap Chevalier and its magnificent, unspoiled beaches. There is a small grocery store on the premises, where you can purchase what you need to prepare your own meals.

Le Vauclin

The **Ranch Macabou** campground, located a little south of Le Vauclin, near Petite Anse Macabou, is only open during school vacation. The place is nevertheless of only limited interest.

In the centre of the village of Le Vauclin, there is a simple hotel named **Chez Julot** *(280F; ≡; Rue Gabriel Péri - 97280 Le Vauclin, ☎05.96.74.40.93)*, which also has a good little restaurant (see p 147).

Finally, you can rent a small room at the **Flamboyant Bay** *(200F; ℜ; ☎05.96.74.53.50. ⌐05.96.74.22.72)*, a little hotel-restaurant located on Pointe Athanase. To get there, head south out of Le Vauclin, in the direction of Pointe Faula, on the road that follows the coast.

Le François

There are several *gîtes* in the Le François area. Especially recommended are those belonging to **M. Jules Lucien (nos. 97 and 98,** ⫴**)** *(1430 per week; Quartier Chopotte - 97240 le François)* and **Mme Sylvette Octavius (nos. 198, 246 and 247)** *(1,545-2,155F per week; Quartier Magdelonette - 97240 Le François)*.

You can't miss the beautiful white building, opposite and just above the Le François marina, which houses the brand-new **Hôtel Les Fonds Blancs** *(380F; ≡, ℜ; Presqu'île du François - 97240 Le François, ☎/⌐05.96.54.20.68)*.

The remarkable **Les Brisants** *(380F, bkfst incl., 520F 1/2 b; ≡, ℜ; 97240 Le François, ☎05.96.54.32.57, ⌐05.96.54.69.13)* hotel is set back from the road less than five kilometres south of the village of Le François, when coming from Vauclin. This place is not striking for its size – it has only five rooms. What makes Les Brisants remarkable, especially considering that it is in a relatively new house, is its wonderfully friendly atmosphere.

On the road linking the village to the sailing harbour, you will pass a charming seaside hotel, **La Riviera** *(480F; tv, ≡, ℜ; Route du Club Nautique - 97240 Le François, ☎05.96.54.68.54, ⌐05.96.54.30.43)*, which has 14 very comfortable rooms and facilities for a variety of water sports. This is a good spot to keep in mind.

To reach **La Frégate Bleue** *(1,000F to 1,200F brkfst incl.; tv, ≡, pb, ≈, K; Quartier Frégate - 97240 Le François, ☎05.96.54.54.56, ⌐05.96.54.78.48)* you'll have to take a rather long and bumpy road, but once there, you are almost in paradise. The exquisitely peaceful site alone is worth the trip. The magnificent Creole house overlooking the ocean has five upstairs rooms that offer breathtaking vistas of Îlets Oscar and Thierry and the white sandy sea beds of the famous Baignoire de

Joséphine. Each room is fitted out with superb mahogany furnishings, and two of them boast a mezzanine that can accommodate two extra people. A member of the Relais du Silence international chain, the establishment also has two bungalows without views and a recently added two-floor house (6,500F a week). The owners, Yveline and Charles, offer a fixed-price meal on Thursday evenings, just to get acquainted with their guests. An exceptional place! On the N6, between Le Vauclin and Le François.

The most outstanding hotel in the region, however, is **Les Îlets de l'Impératrice** *(800F bkfst incl., 1,400 ½b, 1,750 fb; pb, ℜ; 97240 Le François, ☎05.96.47.75.40 or 05.96.65.82.30, ⌐05.96.53.50.58)*, where you can stay in one of two authentic Creole houses set in the peaceful surroundings of the little islands (Oscar and Thierry) off the coast of Le François. One house has five rooms, the other six. Rates include transportation by boat from Le François. What is lined up for you once you arrive? Sun, turquoise water, *fonds blancs* and water sports. If you can afford it, your stay in this one-of-a-kind hotel will be unforgettable.

 RESTAURANTS

Rivière-Salée

There is a **Champion supermarket** *(Mon to Sat 8am to 8pm, Sun 8am to 1pm; ☎05.96.68.50.50)* on the way into Rivière-Salée, as well as a market in the centre of the village.

For a quick bite to eat, another option is the snack bar **Chez Malou**, also located in the heart of the village.

Sainte-Luce

In the Village

A must for the absolutely delicious *accras*, or fritters, **Palmier Chez Suzette** is a tiny kiosk located near the free health centre.

At **Épi Soleil** *(50F; ☎05.96.62.30.33)*, on a small shoreline street in the village, you can eat well and spend little. This pleasant place has become a local favourite, so much so for that matter, that the front terrace extends all the way to the other side of the street, where tables have been set up beneath a big tent, right next to the fishing boats. Besides the customary sandwiches and Viennese bread and buns, the place serves grilled meats (roast chicken, brochettes, steaks) on an outdoor barbecue Friday and Saturday nights.

Pizza lovers, for their part, can stop in at the **Pizzeria Slaac** *(55F; Tue to Sat, lunch and dinner; Sun and Mon, dinner only; 55 Rue Schœlcher, ☎05.96.62.37.37 or 05.96.62.37.38)*, which, when it all comes down to it, is really more of a take-out counter than a restaurant. A few tables are available to customers at the front, however. Two dozen varieties of pizza are cheerfully prepared here, as are sandwiches and sweet and savoury crepes.

La Casa Pepe *(75F; Rue Schœlcher, ☎05.96.62.28.72)* has a split personality. The front room, which opens onto the street, houses an ordinary restaurant. In the back room, which faces the seafront, a young crowd gathers at a laid-back bar (see p 148). The restaurant's formula is a winning combination. There are three buffets from which you can eat to your heart's

Ulysses' Favourites

For the finest dining:
  La Corniche (Sainte-Luce, p 144)
  Manoir de Beauregard (Sainte-Anne, p 145)
  Poï et Virginie (Sainte-Anne, p 145)

For the warm welcome:
  Kaï Armande (Sainte-Luce, p 143)

For the view:
  Le Point de Vue (Le Marin, p 144)

content. The cold buffet consists of salads, cold cuts, fruit, etc; the hot buffet boasts a truly gargantuan paella, pork stew (for hearty appetites), ginger chicken and *colombos*. Finally, you can top off your lavish meal with something from the dessert table. One buffet costs 45F; two 65F; all three, 75F. Economical and lively.

La Terrasse Chez Aglaé *(90F, ☎05.96.62.50.09)*, in the centre of the village, is an unpretentious place that serves good, traditional homestyle cooking. As an added attraction, the terrace mentioned in the name is located on two sides of the second floor, offering lovely views of the sea and the village. The decor, for its part, remains rather minimalist and the service unpretentious. On the menu, the smoked shark stands out.

La Vague du Sud *(100F; closed Wed; Rue Schœlcher, ☎05.96.62.59.46)* can be reached via Rue Schœlcher or the seafront. This lovely upstairs restaurant boasts a sizeable dining room surrounding a large bar and opening out onto the ocean, but the real draw is the seafood. Myriad paintings and other artwork add to the decor. Set menu available for 75 F.

Set up in a small, intimate and charming room overlooking the seafront, the **Kaï Armande** restaurant *(100F; closed Tue; ☎05.96.62.52.67)* is a place worth considering. The cream-coloured walls as well as the beautiful doors and dark-wooden furniture confer a warmth to the place that is further complemented by the kindness of the hosts. Numerous paintings further add to the decor – the place also doubles as an art gallery. On the menu, the lobster with three sauces proves perfectly delectable. Leave some room for the *glace coco nègre* (chocolate-covered coconut ice cream) desert. Set menu available for 68F.

Just before entering the village of Saint-Luce from Gros Raisins, you will see the large transparent tent on the right housing **Le Coup de Canon** *(125F; closed Wed; Place de la Vierge, ☎05.96.62.36.32)*. The always smiling and attentive owner personally welcomes guests who, despite the lack of decor or ambiance, will get their money's worth. Indeed, it is the food here that makes the place what it is, the chef preparing delectably simple dishes that will pleasantly surprise you every time. The rib steak with Canon sauce is particularly noteworthy. The mixed grill, a succulent dish comprising chicken, lamb and merguez sausage, is also a good choice. Finally, the coconut flan rounds off the meal on a sweet note.

Gros-Raisins

The restaurant in **La Petite Auberge** *(160F, lunch menu 99F; closed Mon for lunch;* ☎*05.96.62.59.70)*, in Gros Raisins, serves good country-style cooking in a very friendly atmosphere. Meals are served on the lovely, large, white-painted front terrace, with views of the lovely garden swimming pool and the ocean in the distance. The specialities of the house include the grilled lobster, the salmon plate and the *bavette à l'échalote* (undercut with shallots). The seafood platter alone *(285 F)* can satisfy even the heartiest appetite.

Trois-Rivières

Near the Trois-Rivières district, there are signs inviting motorists to follow the road to Monésie all the way up to a very good hotel and restaurant named **La Corniche** *(250F; closed Sun evening and Mon;* ☎*05.96.62.47.48)*. The ascent can seem endless, but is definitely worth it. This gourmet restaurant, which serves equally delicious Creole and French food, is an extraordinary find. Try the fillet of sea bream with "belle doudou" sauce, or the quail stuffed with passion fruit. In addition, the terrace commands a unique view of the area's *mornes* and, off in the distance, the sea and Rocher du Diamant. On Saturday evenings, there is a pianist.

Rivière-Pilote

The village of Rivière-Pilote has a pleasant **covered market** where you can enjoy stocking up on assorted produce.

Le Marin

You can't miss the **Supermarché Annette** on your way into town. Beside it, you'll also find a small **fish market**.

In the same place, you can have a quick, inexpensive bite to eat at **L'Épi Soleil** snack bar.

At the marina, there is a **Délifrance** counter where you can get a good sandwich.

On the beach, below the church, is the pleasant **La Paillotte** *(110F;* ☎*05.96.74.75.03)*, also known as Le Cayali. The waterfront restaurant serves salads, grilled fish, chicken, escalope and rib steak. Set menu for 90F and 65F snack menu.

The **Mango Bay** *(145F;* ☎*05.96.74.60.89)* is located alongside the marina. Seated at a long wooden table, you can treat yourself to grilled lobster or pizza while contemplating the comings and goings of the boats. Set menu available for 95F. You can also opt for the snack menu (omelettes, mussels, etc.), which costs from 30F to 45F.

Just before you reach Le Marin, on your way from Sainte-Luce, follow the signs for Morne Gommier to reach **Point de Vue** *(150F; closed Sun pm and Mon;* ☎*05.96.74.74.40)*, which means viewpoint, an aptly named restaurant nestled in the hills. The view from here is indeed an extraordinary one; on one side, the Baie du Marin, and on the other, the bays of Sainte-Luce and Diamant off in the distance. The menu consists of French and Creole dishes.

At **Lagon Bleu** *(150F; closed Tue; ☎05.96.74.80.10)*, guests are invited to eat on a big, airy terrace whose only decorations are the sea and the boats in the marina. Not surprisingly, given the setting, the restaurant serves mainly fish and seafood dishes: a fisherman's platter, *langouste*, tuna steaks, etc.

Sainte-Anne

In the Village of Sainte-Anne

You can do your grocery shopping on the main street at **Salines Service**. In addition, the **village market** lies a little farther along on the left.

If you're looking for a good, inexpensive meal, **Épi Soleil**, in the centre of the village, is the best place to go. You can choose from a variety of sandwiches and Vienna sausages, and then enjoy your meal on a pleasant terrace overlooking the sea.

Athanor *(100F; ☎05.96.76.72.93)*, just a step away from town hall, is another inexpensive place to eat. On the menu, you'll find coquilles Saint-Jacques; kidneys with port wine, served with French fries; crepes and pizza.

Victim of a fire a few years ago, the **Manoir de Beauregard** *(175F; closed Jun 1 to Nov 30; Chemin des Salines, ☎05.96.76.73.40)* (see p 140) has since been fully restored, to the ultimate delight of gourmets. Remarkable traditional Creole cuisine can be enjoyed here, in the midst of a refined setting. The fillet of conch with green pepper is particularly outstanding.

Creole brunch with live music on Sundays, from 11am to 4pm.

La Dunette *(200F; closed Wed; ☎05.96.76.73.90)* is hard to top, as you'll see once you've tasted the Tahitian fish and the lamb *colombo*, completed with a gorgeous coconut flan. La Dunette is a bargain, though the menu is perhaps a little short. There is a pianist in the evenings.

Les Tamariniers *(200F; closed Tue evening and Wed; ☎05.96.76.75.62)*, located right next to the church, also serves good food, and won't cost you an arm and a leg, even though you might be inclined to pass it by in favour of a restaurant on the main street or alongside the beach. If you do so, however, you'll be missing out on a pleasant meal of *navarin de langouste aux légumes* (rock lobster stew with vegetables) or baked fish with tamarinds.

On the waterfront, in a cozy, modest little house, you'll find what some consider to be one of the best restaurants in Martinique, **Poï et Virginie** *(270F; ☎05.96.76.76.86)*. The giant seafood platter (rock lobster, spider crab, crayfish, clams, oysters, etc.) is something of an attraction all on its own. The menu includes some delicious surprises, such as shrimp tails flambéd with aged rum. On Friday nights, guests are also treated to live music.

On the Beach at Pointe Marin

The area around the public beach in Sainte-Anne is crowded with little restaurants, each more appealing than the last. We especially recommend **Touloulou** *(120F; ☎05.96.76.73.27)*, where lobster is the speciality and set menus are 78F and 120 F, and its little brother right next door, **Ti-Loulou** *(50F)*, a great place to go for fried chicken or pizza.

Yet another pleasant restaurant on the beach, **Saveur Cannelle** *(70F;* ☎*05.96.76.95.47)* serves pizza, merguez sausages and crepes on a pretty terrace surrounded by bamboo.

A few steps away, **Chez Marius** *(70F)* is known for its roast chicken and tasty sandwiches.

Set up in a makeshift bamboo-and-corrugated-iron shack, the **Bar Restaurant La Tribune Beach** *(120F;* ☎*05.96.76.77.74)* is another one of the numerous typical beach eateries in the area. You can stop by for a quick drink, or for a grilled fish dinner.

Also on the beach, but slightly more sophisticated, **Les Filets Bleus** *(250F; closed Sun evening and Mon,* ☎*05.96.76.73.42)* stands out for its blue and white decor centred around several extraordinary white statues. You can dine on the rock lobster of your choice. The place also serves delectable turtle soup. Set menus go for 59F (lunch) and 139F (dinner) and a band plays on Friday evenings.

At the end of the beach, **L'Endroit** *(250 F;* ☎*05.96.76.76.74)*, formerly Le Sunny, still serves delicious stuffed crab, sautéed shrimp and *cassolette de langouste*.

In the same area, near the entrance of the Club Med, **La Tanière** *(300F;* ☎*05.96.76.97.36)* is a find. Start off your meal with the *assiette des jours gras* (rock lobster with mayonnaise, avocado, sea urchin tarts, *crudités* and melon). If you still have some room left, try the *magret de canard à la mangue* (duck cutlet with mango) or the sea urchin *blaff*. A meal here is bound to leave you with fond memories.

Domaine de Belfond

Several restaurants have appeared in Domaine de Belfond, where all sorts of hotels are also springing up (the Anchorage, Séjours Antilles, the Flamboyants de Belfond, etc.). **Frédéric** *(200F; closed Mon; 62 Domaine de Belfond,* ☎*05.96.76.95.84)*, for example, which is located inside a pretty white Creole house with an orange-coloured roof, serves such mouth-watering dishes as fish with coconut milk and curried pork. A 99F menu is also available.

However, if you are looking for a quick snack, go to **Restaurant Glacier Beau Soleil** *(*☎*05.96.76.93.34)*.

Les Salines and the Southeast Beaches

Upon arriving at Grande Anse des Salines, you will pass a series of temporary restaurants on the left, many of whose kitchens are set up inside trailers. If you come across one called **Snack Pizzeria des Salines** *(11:45am to 4:30pm)*, make a beeline for it, because the food is great (offerings from the grill, pizza, salads). The remarkably well-organized team that serves you is a marvel of efficiency, adding to the pleasure of coming here.

At Grande Anse des Salines, at the very tip of the point of the same name, you'll find the area's only restaurant (in the true sense of the word), **Aux Délices de la Mer** *(closed Mon;* ☎*05.96.76.73.71)*. You have the choice of eating a full meal on the restaurant's big terrace, or a quick lunch at the snack bar.

The untouched beaches along the southeast coast, for their part, are served by a few snack bars (on the road to Cap Chevalier) and a handful of well-hidden restaurants. One of these is **Chez Gracieuse** *(180F; closed Mon; ☎05.96.76.93.10)*, located right on a little bay at Cap Chevalier. It serves up good, traditional Creole food in a wooden shack, which is a little rickety, but nonetheless charming. This is where you catch the *Taxi Cap (☎05.96.76.93.10)* to Îlet Chevalier, just opposite.

Finally, in Anse Michel, you can treat yourself to a tasty meal of charcoal grilled rock lobster at **Le Peuplier** *(190F; ☎05.96.76.92.87)*, whose terrace is not only located right by the sea, but is also surrounded by flowers.

Le Vauclin

In the centre of the village, not far from the town hall, you'll find a small **grocery store**. Also worth noting is the **Boucherie Vallée**, near the church, and the **fruit and fish market**, alongside the sea on Boulevard de l'Atlantique.

The best place to eat in the village of Le Vauclin is **Chez Julot** *(180F; closed Sun evenings; ☎05.96.74.40.93)*, a hotel on Rue Gabriel-Péri. There's nothing complicated about the place – a few tables with checkered tablecloths in an air-conditioned room, a lot of plants and good home cooking. You'll find both stuffed crab and turtle stew on the menu.

At Pointe Faula, near the beach, there's a nice restaurant named **Sous les Cocotiers** *(50-180F; 11:30am to 10pm, closed Sun evenings and Mon; ☎05.96.74.35.62)*, where you have the choice of eating in the snack bar (50F per person) or in the more traditional restaurant, which serves delicious oysters, among other things.

The pleasant **Cabana Plage** *(50-180F; ☎05.96.74.32.08)*, also at Pointe Faula, is a similar type of place, serving pizza cooked over a wood fire, tuna kebabs and a variety of grilled dishes. A band livens things up on Saturday nights.

Le François

Between Le Vauclin and Le François

On the N6, between Le Vauclin and Le François is **Les Brisants** *(150 F; closed Mon; ☎05.96.54.40.29)*, a hotel and restaurant set back from the road in a pretty park not far from the ocean. Try the *fricassée de coq, riz et haricots rouges*, or the *langouste mayonnaise*.

In the Village

The following are a few places where you can stock up on groceries: the **Champion supermarket**, at the edge of town, on the way to Le Lamentin; the **market**, just opposite the tourist office; and the **Boulangerie-Pâtisserie Roasanne** *(☎05.96.54.49.03 or 05.96.54.61.66)* bakery, near Place Charles-de-Gaulle. There is also temporary market of sorts, in a run-down building located near the church, where you can buy provisions. Also, behind the bakery, on the left, you will find **La Kreyole** *(☎05.96.54.56.30)*, a little restaurant serving local cuisine.

Near the Harbour

La Riviera *(230F; closed Sun evening; ☎05.96.54.68.54)*, located on the road linking the village to the harbour, is worth a detour. Inside this big, beautiful white house, which is also a hotel (see p 141), you can dine on the extraordinary melon omelette, which is the chef's speciality, or enjoy an omelette flavoured with aged rum, a *blaff de soudons* (clams) or sea urchins, or crayfish with coconut and *lambis*. The 100F and 150F set menus make it all affordable.

  ENTERTAINMENT

The area has several nightclubs, where you can dance wildly or take in a performance by a small band. You might try, for example, **H-Club** (*Tue to Sun from 10pm on*, ☎*05.96.56.00.69*), in Ducos; **Beverly Hills** (*Wed to Sun 9:30pm to 4am*, ☎*05.96.74.91.38*) on Rue Diaka in Le Marin or **Zipp's Club** (*Wed to Sun from 10pm on*, ☎*05.96.54.65.45*), in Le François.

In Sainte-Anne, the **Anse Caritan** hotel has its own discotheque, which organizes evenings featuring folk and live dance music. There are also regular performances by the Grands Ballets de Martinique dance company.

The beach-front restaurant **L'Endroit** (see p 146), also located in Sainte-Anne, hosts live music every night. In the village, jazz musicians liven up dinner on Friday evenings at **Poï et Virginie** (see p 145), while a pianist entertains guests nightly at **La Dunette** (see p 145).

La Corniche (see p 144), in Sainte-Luce, features live piano music on Saturday evenings.

A pleasant spot in which to enjoy a drink in Saint-Luce is the **Casa Pepe** bar-restaurant (☎*05.96.62.28.72*), with a large barroom opening onto the sea that welcomes a young clientele in a lively ambiance. The place also has video screens that play concerts and music videos. You can also treat yourself to a good yet inexpensive meal at the adjacent restaurant (see p 142).

Musicians put on a show every Saturday night at the **Cabana Plage** (see p 147), at Pointe-Faula, near Le Marin.

 SHOPPING

Rivière-Salée

Rivière-Salée is home to a small **art centre** (☎*05.96.68.04.83*), where you can pick up pottery, drawings made with sand and a variety of containers, including bottles, covered with sand.

Sainte-Luce

In the Sainte-Luce area – in Monésie, to be precise – there are two artists who have developed the unique technique of creating extraordinary pictures on wood with about 130 different types of sand from which approximately 230 shades of earth are derived, gathered from all over the island. They don't use any paint or colouring in their work. Their studio, which is called **Art et Nature** (*Mon to Fri 10am to 1pm and 2:30pm to 6pm;* ☎*05.96.62.59.19*), is definitely worth the trip. You'll be able to witness the creative process and choose a one-of-a-kind souvenir from one of the works on display.

Rivière-Pilote

The little shop in the **Écomusée de Martinique**, located on the beach at Anse Figuier, has an interesting selection of local handicrafts. The museum is housed in what was once a distillery, just a step away from the little beach, and it's worth stopping by just to take in the attractive setting.

Le Marin

You can't miss the Supermarché Annette, on your right as you head into the village of Le Marin. The **Librairie du Marin** *(Mon to Sat 9am to 1pm and 3pm to 7pm, Sun 8:30am to 12:30pm)* bookshop is hidden away right next door.

Sainte-Anne

All different sorts of souvenir shops brighten the streets of Sainte-Anne. You'll find a little bit of everything here, from genuine handicrafts to cheap junk. Among the better ones are **Le Santal**, a charming shop near the pier, and the larger **La Malle des Îles**, which is located on the square near the church and sells jewellery and handicrafts. **Folie Caraïbes** is a similar type of place, next to which is a small bookstore named **La Galerie** *(☎05.96.76.92.36)*.

There is also an open-air **craft market**, which is like a miniature version of the one on the Savane in Fort-de-France.

The most beautiful beaches in the south, notably those in Saint-Anne and Salines, are also known for their bathing-suit vendors. Indeed, attractive women parade up and down the beach all day long advertizing full swimsuit collections. Now here's a novel way of shopping! Prices are on par with those in shops; what the merchants save in rent they pay their "top models".

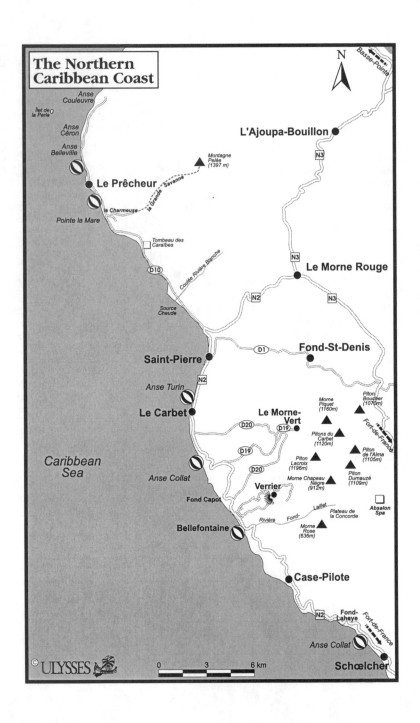

THE NORTHERN CARIBBEAN COAST

U pon visiting Martinique's northern Caribbean coast, you'll discover a landscape entirely different from the idyllic white-sand beaches of the south. The beaches seem wilder, and consist of grey, or even black sand – a reminder of the presence of the notorious volcano, Montagne Pelée, which, at 1,397 metres, is the highest peak on the island. In 1902, this imposing northern giant unleashed its wrath on Martinique with an eruption that claimed 30,000 lives and completely obliterated the city of Saint-Pierre, the "little Paris of the Antilles".

Today, Saint-Pierre, considered a "City of Art and History", is attempting to rise from its ashes. The deeply moving sight of its ruins and monuments is without question the highlight of the tour you'll find outlined in the following pages.

However, the northern Caribbean coast also has much more to offer in terms of culture, beaches, nature and sports. There's Schœlcher, with its casino; Le Carbet, with its long beach; and Anse Turin, where Gauguin spent a brief but significant period of his life as an artist. There are untouched beaches in the north and hiking trails in the forests and mountains alike. In fact, this coast is one of the gateways to the Pitons du Carbet – Piton Lacroix, or Morne Pavillon (1,196 m); Piton de l'Alma (1,105 m); Piton Dumauzé (1,109 m); Piton Boucher (1,070 m) and Morne Piquet (1,160 m).

The northern Caribbean coast is the cradle of Martinique. This is where Columbus landed in 1502, and the era of French colonization started in September of 1635, when the Carib Indians welcomed d'Esnambuc and his companions with open arms. The villages on the northern Caribbean were thus Martinique's first (Case-Pilote, Le Carbet, Saint-Pierre), and boast the oldest buildings and most venerable churches on the "Island of Flowers".

FINDING YOUR WAY AROUND

By car

The *Route Nationale* 2 (N2) runs along the northern Caribbean from Fort-de-France to Sainte-Pierre, where the *Route Départementale 10* (D10), most of which has recently been repaved, takes over. The D10 will take you to Le Prêcheur, and beyond to a few untouched beaches farther north.

From the centre of Fort-de-France, take Rue Ernest-Déproge, which turns into the N2 after the Pont de l'Abattoir.

If you are starting from somewhere in the south (Trois-Îlets, Diamant, Sainte-Anne), take the N5 and then the N1 towards Fort-de-France. Once near the capital, follow the signs for Saint-Pierre, which will enable you to bypass the city and pick up the N2, heading north.

Car Rentals

Schœlcher

Budget: Hôtel La Batelière, ☎05.96.61.66.60.
Europcar: Hôtel Anse Colas, ☎05.96.61.28.18.

Saint-Pierre

Budget: 16 Rue du Gouverneur Ponton, ☎05.96.78.28.38.
Jean-Baptiste: Place du Fort, ☎05.96.78.35.58 or 05.96.78.25.22.

Pop's Car: Rue Victor Hugo, ☎05.96.78.28.78.

Le Carbet

Pop's Car: Hôtel Marouba Club, ☎05.96.78.40.40.
Thrifty Jumbo Car: Carbet de Madimina, ☎05.96.78.08.08.

PRACTICAL INFORMATION

Schœlcher

Tourist office: ☎05.96.61.83.92, ⇥05.96.61.83.93.

Police: ☎05.96.61.15.10

Town hall: ☎05.96.61.25.04, ⇥05.96.61.36.78.

Pharmacies:
Pharmacie Chalono, Centre Commercial La Batelière, ☎05.96.61.32.56.
Pharmacie De Montaigne, Anse Madame, ☎05.96.61.15.28.
Pharmacie du Centre Médical, Route Cluny, ☎05.96.63.79.93.

Case-Pilote

Tourist office: on the main square, ☎05.96.78.74.04 or 05.96.78.75.14, ⇥05.96.78.78.87

Town hall: ☎05.96.78.81.44, ⇥05.96.78.74.72.

Police: ☎05.96.78.81.55

Pharmacy: Calmo Jany, in the centre of the village, ☎05.96.78.85.46

Bellefontaine

Tourist office: ☎05.96.55.00.96, ⇢05.96.55.00.58.

Town hall: ☎05.96.55.00.96, ⇢05.96.55.00.58.

Pharmacy: Roseline Delblon, Bourg, ☎05.96.55.06.76.

Morne-Vert

Tourist office: ☎05.96.55.57.57, ⇢05.96.55.57.60.

Town hall: ☎05.96.55.51.47, ⇢05.96.55.57.27.

Le Carbet

Tourist office: Grande Anse, ☎05.96.78.05.19 or 78.08.20.

Town hall: ☎05.96.78.00.40, ⇢05.96.78.06.54.

Police: ☎05.96.78.05.09.

Bank: Coopérative du Crédit du Nord, Grande Anse, ☎05.96.78.00.84.

Saint-Pierre

Tourist office: Maison de la Bourse, Place Bertim, ☎05.96.78.10.39.

Town hall: ☎05.96.78.10.32, ⇢05.96.78.06.93.

Police: ☎05.96.78.14.13.

Banks: Crédit Agricole, Rue Victor-Hugo, ☎05.96.78.30.29.

Crédit Martiniquais, Rue Victor-Hugo, ☎05.96.78.14.02.

Post office: At the intersection of Rue Victor-Hugo and Rue du Général-de-Gaulle, ☎05.96.78.11.81.

Hospital: ☎05.96.78.18.24 or 05.96.78.14.93.

Pharmacies:
Pharmacie Joë Sainte-Rose, Place Félix-Boisson, ☎05.96.78.17.41.

Le Prêcheur

Tourist office: 35 Lot Aubéry, ☎05.96.52.91.43, ⇢05.96.52.97.73.

Town hall: ☎05.96.52.98.62, ⇢05.96.52.92.02.

Pharmacy:
Pharmacie Anne-Claire Volny, Bourg, ☎05.96.52.95.83.

 EXPLORING

Schœlcher

Schœlcher is in fact a sort of suburb or continuation of Fort-de-France, so much so that you probably won't even be able to determine the exact moment you pass from one town into the next. This is even more surprising when you consider that Schœlcher itself, with almost 20,000 residents, is one of the most heavily populated towns in Martinique.

The town was named after Victor Schœlcher (1804-1893), the illustrious deputy of Martinique and Guadeloupe who fought vehemently against slavery, which was finally abolished on April 27, 1848. The district, however, wasn't named after him until 1888. Until then, it was known as Case Navire, and was part of the district of Case Pilote.

On your way into town, you will see Marie-Thérèse Lung-Fou's superb **statue of Schœlcher**, which shows the great abolitionist breaking a slave's chains, and is inscribed with his famous words, *"Nulle terre française ne peut plus porter d'esclave"* (No French land shall ever more bear slaves). The island's **Centre de Formation aux Métiers du Tourisme** (an occupational training centre for the tourism industry), and the campus of the **Université des Antilles et de la Guyane** are also located in Schœlcher. In addition, a variety of hotels, including in particular the luxurious La Batelière and its **casino ★** (see p 177), have grown up along the lovely **beaches** that stretch as far as the hamlet of **Fond Lahaye**.

Case-Pilote

Heading north, you will soon reach the district of **Case-Pilote**, whose village is one of the oldest on the island; a church was erected here between 1640 and 1645. According to the story, a Carib chief named Pilote, who was especially friendly toward the French, had a hut (*case*) in the area; hence the name Case-Pilote. In 1635, he supposedly agreed to give the French all the property he had in the area in exchange for some land in the southern part of Martinique. Today, the district has about 3,600 inhabitants, who live mainly on vegetable farming, fishing and fish processing.

Above all, make sure to take a look at the baroque **Notre-Dame de L'Assomption ★**, which was built in the 18th century (1776) and is, along with the one in Macouba, the oldest church on the island. Listed as a historic monument in 1979, the church has a remarkable façade. The pediment is decorated with the shell of the pilgrims of Compostela, the emblem of the Dominican order. Inside, there is a 17th century painting of the Holy Family, with an angel holding a crown of thorns over the Virgin Mary's head. You will also find an amazing mosaic depicting Christ's baptism, made with fragments of dishes found after the eruption of Montagne Pelé.

Behind the church, you'll see a cemetery and, right nearby, the **main square ★**, which is surrounded by buildings, notably the pretty town hall and wooden houses, and has a pretty **fountain**. **Parc Orville** and its **war memorial** lie facing of the church, on the exact site of the former slave cemetery.

Bellefontaine

The next village is called Bellefontaine and did not become a parish until 1950. It is a humble but nevertheless charming fishing village with about 1,500 inhabitants. Besides fishing, the residents of Bellefontaine occupy themselves with vegetable farming. Before entering the village, alongside the Rivière Fonds-Laillet, you will see Électricité de France's imposing **power station**, in operation since 1984.

As you enter Bellefontaine watch for the surprising boat-shaped house called **Le Torgiléo**, located on a hillside overlooking the village. A former hotel turned restaurant (see p 174), it was built in 1948. You will then come upon the charming sight of the local fishermen's colourful *gommiers*, fishing boats, resting on the jet-black sand along the shore.

The **church**, tucked away off the main street, is rather unique, with its tall, detached bell tower. Its interior is adorned with metal sculptures by Joseph René Corail.

Visitors might be interested to know that painter Jules Marillac (1888-1950) lived in Bellefontaine from 1933 until the end of his life, and is buried in the local cemetery.

In the heart of the village, there is a small, steep road on the right that climbs five kilometres to the not-to-be-missed **panorama Verrier ★★**, which affords a breathtaking view of the Caribbean, the Pitons du Carbet and Montagne Pelée.

A little farther north, where the N2 intersects with the D20, you will find the **Habitation Fond Capot**, the burial place of the first governor general of the Antilles, Marquis Jean-Charles de Baas, who died in early 1677. The estate was given to the Marquis by Louis XIV.

Morne-Vert

If you turn right on the D19, you will soon end up in Morne-Vert, a pleasant little village perched at an altitude of about 450 metres. By taking this route instead of heading straight for Le Carbet, you'll discover *"petite Suisse"*, or little Switzerland. This is indeed the area's nickname, owing to its lush, mountainous landscape and cool, dry climate. Everywhere you go, you'll come across more and more spectacular views of the Pitons du Carbet and Montagne Pelée.

Le Carbet ★★

After visiting the "Switzerland of the Caribbean", take the D20 to Carbet. The road heads into town close to the beach of Grande Anse. The **Centre de Thalassothérapie du Carbet** *(☎05.96.78.08.79)*, which specializes in sea water therapy, is nearby.

The word "carbet" is of Carib origin, and was used to designate the biggest hut in the village, where all meetings were held. Because there were a lot of Caribs living here, the area became known as "Le Carbet." According to legend, Christopher Columbus "discovered" Martinique when he landed at Le Carbet on June 15, 1502. Belain d'Esnambuc also alighted here in 1635, and Le Carbet became a parish in 1645, making it one of the oldest on the island. Jacques du Parquet, Martinique's first governor, settled here shortly after his arrival. Finally, in 1822, Le Carbet was the scene of a large slave revolt.

Le Carbet's glorious past has helped make it a lively town that attracts a good number of visitors interested as much in Martinique's history and heritage as in the area's beautiful beaches, which stretch nearly three kilometres, from Le Coin to Anse Latouche.

South of the Bourg

Once you have reached the road that runs along the sea, you can turn left if you'd like to take a look at the somewhat dilapidated **Jardin Zoologique Amazona** *(adults 20F, children 10F; every day 9am to 6pm; ☎05.96.78.00.64)*, which houses 60 different species of local and Guyanese animals. From the zoo, there is a road leading inland to the **stadium**, the

Olympic swimming pool *(every day, 8am to 4pm, ☎05.96.78.18.11)* and the **Distillerie Neisson** *(tour and free samples; Mon to Fri 8am to noon and 2pm to 4:30pm, Sat 8am to noon; ☎05.96.78.03.70)*.

After that, head back toward the village. Just before the bridge across the Rivière du Carbet (from which there is a stunning view of the Pitons du Carbet), there is a road on the right, it leads to the **Rhumerie Bally** *(30F; Mon to Sat 8am to 5pm, Sun 9am to noon; ☎05.96.78.08.94)*, located in the **Domaine de Lajus**. The distillery hasn't actually been in operation since 1978, and Bally rums have been produced elsewhere since then. Several vintage aged rums have made the Bally name famous (1982, 1975, 1970, 1966, 1957, 1929).

In the Bourg

Back on the N2, you will finally cross the bridge. The first road on the right leads to the **grounds of Governor du Parquet's plantation**. Then you'll reach the village where within a very limited area, you will see the **church**, the **presbytery**, the **ruins of the Dariste plantation** and even the **supposed site of Christopher Columbus's landing**. In addition, on the pretty square in front of the town hall, with its lovely old fountain, you can visit the **Galerie d'Histoire et de la Mer** *(adults 10F; every day 9am to noon and 3pm to 6pm; ☎05.96.78.03.72)*, set up inside the former market. Here, you can learn a bit more about the history of both the region and the island, as well as Martinique's fishing tradition.

To the right of the church's entrance, against the cemetery wall, there is an amazing tomb dating from 1891, the **Tombeau de la Dame Espagnole ★**, which supposedly houses the remains of a certain Madame Caffiolo and her three children. They died in the hurricane that devastated the area in August 1891, which also claimed the lives of 800 people. These four individuals, whose bodies washed up on the beach of Anse Latouche, are believed to have been passengers aboard the *Nedwhite*, an American steamship that was destroyed in the catastrophe. That is all anyone knows about the origins of this extravagant tomb, so strangely out of place in the little Creole cemetery of Le Carbet. The tomb was registered as a historic monument in 1978.

The Tourist Itinerary

Once you've explored the streets of the village, you can continue your tour in one of two ways. Your first option is to get back on the N2 and drive alongside the lovely grey sand beaches of **Le Four**, **Petite Anse** and the most beautiful of all, **Anse Turin ★★★**. The road then passes through a tunnel known as **Le Trou Caraïbe** (the Caribbean Hole) to the other side of the mountain, where **Anse Latouche** unfolds before you. Before the tunnel was built, it was necessary to make a long detour through the hills of Le Carbet in order to reach Saint-Pierre. The trip between the two cities, which are actually only six kilometres apart as the crow flies, thus proved long and difficult. It is thanks to the determination of Abbé Goux, parish priest of Le Carbet from 1835 to 1861, that this tunnel was bored through the volcanic cliff in 1854. Abbé Goux was an extremely colourful figure who became famous for his enterprising spirit. He is credited, for example, with translating a catechism into Creole, building a bridge, founding a boys' and a girls' school, renovating the church after the earthquake of 1839, and of course, constructing the famous *Trou* that linked his village with Saint-Pierre, the

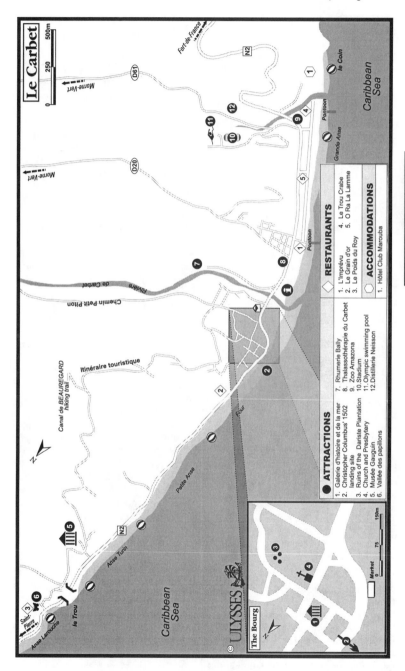

Le Carbet

0 250 500m

Morne-Vert ← D61

Fort-de-France

N2

le Coin

Caribbean Sea

Grande Anse

Pontoon

⑫

⑪ ⑩

⑨ ④

Morne-Vert ← D20

⑤

Pontoon

①

⑧

Rivière de Carbet

Chemin Petit Piton

⑦

Canal de BEAUREGARD hiking trail

Itinéraire touristique

Four

②

N

Petite Anse

N2

Anse Turin

⑤

Saint-Pierre

③ ⑥

le Trou

Anse Latouche

Caribbean Sea

ULYSSES

The Bourg

N

Market

0 75 150m

① ⑤

⑳ ④

②

◆ **RESTAURANTS**

1. L'Imprévu
2. Le Grain d'or
3. Le Poids du Roy
4. Le Trou Crabe
5. O Ra La Lamme

○ **ACCOMMODATIONS**

1. Hôtel Club Marouba

● **ATTRACTIONS**

1. Galerie d'histoire et de la mer
2. Christopher Columbus' 1502 landing site
3. Ruins of the Dariste Plantation
4. Church and Presbytery
5. Musée Gauguin
6. Vallée des papillons
7. Rhumerie Bally
8. Thalassothérapie du Carbet
9. Zoo Amazona
10. Stadium
11. Olympic swimming pool
12. Distillerie Neisson

NORTHERN CARIBBEAN COAST

Paul Gauguin and Martinique

Paul Gauguin was born in Paris in 1848. He travelled extensively throughout his lifetime, spending some of his childhood in Lima (his mother was part Peruvian), and then knocking about in Paris, Panamá, Martinique, Brittany, Tahiti... and the list goes on. He was way off on the Marquesas Islands when he died on May 8, 1903.

With Camille Pissaro as his mentor, Gauguin was originally involved in the Impressionist movement. However, he eventually rejected the technical realism espoused by his contemporaries. Along with others, like Van Gogh and Cézanne, he is now considered one of the fathers of post-Impressionism and a pioneer of modern painting.

On April 10, 1887, Paul Gauguin and his friend, painter Charles Laval, left Paris for Panamá aboard a fishing boat. In search of a more primitive lifestyle, Gauguin abandoned his family. For a while, the two artists lived on Isla Taboga, on the Pacific side of the isthmus. Things went badly for them, and they soon had to join the workforce building the Panamá Canal in order to eke out a living. Stricken by bouts of fever and dysentery, they literally fled, eventually winding up in Saint-Pierre. They settled into a modest little house in Anse Turin, and stayed there from June to November 1887, when they finally had to return to Paris for better medical care.

Some art historians claim that Gauguin's stay in Martinique, albeit brief, played a decisive role in his career as an artist. It was here – before his more well-known Tahiti period – that he painted his first tropical frescoes (about a dozen that we know of). From that point onward, his works began to reveal a bold and original combination of pure colour and shallow perspective. He gradually moved toward sharper contrasts and more schematic shapes.

The following works from Gauguin's "Martinique period" are now scattered all over the world in museums and private collections: *La mare* (Neue Pinakothek, Munich), *Végétation tropicale* (National Gallery of Scotland, Edinburgh), *Bord de mer* (NY Carlberg Glyptotek, Copenhagen), *Conversation tropicale* and *Huttes sous les arbres* (New York), *Martiniquaises dans la campagne* (Paris) *Autour des huttes* (Tokyo), *Au bord de l'étang aux mangos* and *Paysage panoramique* (Rijkmuseum Van Gogh, Amsterdam), *Fruits exotiques et fleurs rouges*, *Dans le village* and *Palmiers* (Geneva).

economic capital of the island at the time.

Your other option is to follow a well-marked tourist itinerary, which starts in the centre of the village of Le Carbet, takes you up into the wilderness and then back to Anse Latouche. The road climbs up to the **Canal de Beauregard** ★, a former irrigation canal built in 1760 on the side of a *morne*. It is also known as the *"canal des esclaves"*, or slaves' canal, there is a hiking trail, see p 169.

The tour then continues downhill, stopping along the way at the **Musée Gauguin ★** *(adults 15F, children 5F; every day 10am to 5:30pm; ☎05.96.78.22.66)*, a small, unpretentious museum where you can learn about Paul Gauguin's 1887 sojourn in Martinique. Unfortunately, the museum displays no original canvases by the artist – only about twenty reproductions covering his "Antilles period". A large part of the museum is devoted to works by local artists and a lovely collection of traditional Creole clothing.

The next stop on the itinerary is the recently built **Vallée des Papillons ★** *(adults 38F; every day 9:30am to 4:15pm; ☎05.96.78.19.19)*, which is worth a visit. Located on the ruins of the 17th-century **Anse Latouche plantation ★★**, it consists of a glass house used for breeding butterflies surrounded by a botanical garden. You'll also find an insectarium and a good restaurant, Le Poids du Roy (see p 175), on the grounds. Anse Latouche, which was founded around 1643, was probably the first plantation in Martinique. It was destroyed during the notorious eruption of Montagne Pelée in 1902. You'll find vestiges of the plantation's golden age, including, most notably, the distillery, a dam dating back to 1716, an aqueduct and a fountain, which used to decorate the formal garden surrounding the main residence. This is a classic example of a Martinican *habitation*, an estate in the Antillean sense of the word, consisting of a plantation, the family mansion, various outbuildings, the gardens, and the slaves' or workers' quarters. A cornerstone of the Antilles' industrial heritage, the Habitation Anse Latouche inspired the model of a typical sugar plantation estate (*habitation-sucrerie*) displayed at the Maison de la Canne in Trois-Îlets (see p 97). Furthermore, the shack where Gauguin and Charles Laval

spent their brief stay in Martinique in 1887 was located on the property grounds.

Saint-Pierre ★★★

The road then reaches the harbour of Saint-Pierre, the "martyred city", where close to the entire population (30,000 people) perished when Montagne Pelée erupted on May 8, 1902. Before this terrible catastrophe, Saint-Pierre, with its theatres, beautiful buildings, imposing residences was the *"petit Paris des Antilles"* (the little Paris of the Antilles) and its bourgeoisie lived a life of luxury.

The city was named by Pierre Bélain d'Esnambuc in honour of his patron saint. When he arrived in Martinique in 1635, d'Esnambuc was warmly welcomed by the Caribs, who authorized him to build Fort Saint-Pierre. Little by little, French colonists settled in the area around the fort and erected first one chapel and then, as the population grew, a second and finally a third. Thus were born the three largest *quartiers*, or quarters in Saint-Pierre, du Fort, du Centre and du Mouillage.

Saint-Pierre's bustling port greatly facilitated the development of commerce and industry, and the city grew accordingly. At the same time, in 1831, a bloody slave revolt broke out in Saint-Pierre, and was brutally suppressed. Another riot, this time on May 22, 1848, helped accelerate the implementation of an order to abolish slavery, which Victor Schœlcher had managed to obtain a month earlier, but which had not been immediately obeyed on the island.

Saint-Pierre's future looked promising as the new century began. When the tragedy occurred, foreshadowed several days earlier (April 25, 1902) by a

NORTHERN CARIBBEAN COAST

shower of ashes, Saint-Pierre was the most important city in Martinique, despite the authorities' decision to move the administration to Fort-Royal (now Fort-de-France) in 1692. Its inhabitants already enjoyed such comforts as electricity, telephones and running water, and its streets were criss-crossed by trolleys and lined with beautiful stone houses. The city boasted three newspapers and several consulates, as well as a world-renowned botanical garden and numerous fountains. All of this was to disappear within a few minutes...

There had been warnings, however, of the impending disaster – the shower of ashes on April 25, as well as rumbling sounds and earthquakes in the days leading up to the eruption. But a municipal election campaign was in full swing at the time, which according to some explains why authorities refused to evacuate the city. Others believe that the type of eruption that occurred, made up of incandescent gas and molten ash, was unknown at the time, and that had there been any flow of lava, an immediate evacuation would have been ordered. Instead, however, a glowing cloud annihilated the city at 8am on May 8, 1902, before anyone had time to react. Volcanologists now refer to this sort of phenomenon as a "Pelean" eruption. Two later eruptions in 1929 and 1932 had no grave consequences, but did force those attempting to reconstruct Saint-Pierre to evacuate the village.

Today, the village has barely 5,000 inhabitants, who live on fishing, tourism, agriculture and livestock breeding. In 1990, Saint-Pierre was proclaimed part of French national heritage, and dubbed the 101st "City of Art and History", which might finally give it a second wind. As far as tourism is concerned, Saint-Pierre, as the true historic capital of Martinique, is of undeniable interest. A visit to the **Musée**

Vulcanologique, discovering the countless ruins of significant monuments and the shipwrecks of the vessels moored in the harbour at the time of the tragic eruption are just a few examples of the rich cultural heritage and tapestry that is commemorated by the residents of Saint-Pierre.

If you're interested in an easy and unusual way to discover Saint-Pierre's many sights, climb aboard the **Cyparis Express** (50F; Mon to Fri 9am to 1:30pm and 2:30pm to 4:30pm; departures from Place des Ruines du Figuier; ☎05.96.55.50.92, ≈05.96.78.18.51), a small train that will take you on a guided tour of the city which lasts approximately one hour.

A description of Saint-Pierre's major monuments follows below.

Quartier du Mouillage

Arriving in Saint-Pierre from Le Carbet, you will pass through the Quartier du Mouillage and end up on the city's main street, Rue Victor-Hugo.

The quarter is near the area of the harbour where boats used to drop anchor, hence the name du Mouillage (mouillage means "anchorage"). In 1902, all but one of the ships moored off the coast of Saint-Pierre were sent to the bottom when the eruption triggered a tidal wave. The sole survivor, which was anchored farther away than the others, was an English boat, the Roddam. Today, those who know how to scuba dive can easily explore about a dozen of these boats, which lie between 15 and 50 metres below surface, only 150 metres from the shore. Jacques Cousteau helped make this site famous when he came here to film the wrecks, which had been inventoried by Michel Métery beforehand.

Alpinia, one of the numerous plant species
found on the "Island of Flowers". - *Lorette Pierson*

Fort-de-France's old city hall is now the Théâtre Municipal.
- *Claude Morneau*

Saint-Pierre

NORTHERN CARIBBEAN COAST

ACCOMMODATIONS

1. La Nouvelle-Vague

RESTAURANTS

1. La Factorerie
2. Le Cargo Bleu
3. Le Fromager
4. Le Plateau du Théâtre
5. Relais du Musée

ATTRACTIONS

1. Monument Franck A. Perret
2. Maison du Sénégal
3. Ruins of the Chapel of the Asile de Bethléem
4. Tomb of Abbé Gosse
5. Ruins of Lycée Colonial
6. Cemetery and Ossuary
7. Presbytery
8. Chapelle de l'Évêché
9. Notre-Dame de L'Assomption
10. Market
11. Place Bertin
12. Hospital Ruins
13. Musée Historique
14. Musée Vulcanologique Frank-Perret
15. Theatre Ruins
16. Cachot de Cyparis
17. Compagnie de la Baie de Saint-Pierre
18. Ruins of Le Figuier
19. Former Stadium
20. Pont de la Roxelane
21. Place d'Esnambuc
22. Rue Monte-au-Ciel
23. Rue Levassor
24. Ruins of the Maison Coloniale de Santé
25. Bureau du Génie
26. Ruins of the Église du Fort
27. Tomb of Mère Onésime
28. Château Depaz
29. Old Fort Cemetery
30. Château Perrinelle

Rade de Saint-Pierre

Wrecks	Depth
A. Italian *Yacht*	40m
B. Sailboat	50m
C. *Gabrielle*	30m
D. *Dalhia*	30m
E. *Diamant*	30m
F. *Barge*	30m
G. *Roraima*	50m
H. Sailboat	35m
I. Large Sailboat	30m
J. *Teresa De Lo Vigo*	de 35 à 40m
K. *Raisinier*	15m
L. *Tamaya*	85m

0　250　500m

© ULYSSES

The *Mobilis* Saga

In the early nineties, officials decided to have a submarine built that would take tourists to explore the ships at the bottom of the Saint-Pierre harbour that were sunken by the volcanic eruption of 1902.

A German-made submarine was delivered to Martinique in 1993. It was then discovered, however, that its construction did not conform to all French standards. Its launching was therefore delayed until 1995. But the troubles of the *Mobilis* (as was named the 50-passenger tourist submarine) were not yet over. After only a few years' of operation it was forced to stop its expensive trips down to Martinique's tragic wrecks.

Since this spectacular Disney-like attraction sadly no longer exists, scuba-diving is the only way to explore the offshore shipwrecks, including those of the *Tamaya*, a three-masted ship that lies 85 metres beneath the surface, and the *Roraima*, a liner somewhat still-intact despite being submerged 50 metres below the sea for close to a century.

The first notable sight you'll come across as you enter the city is a monument erected in memory of the American volcanologist **Franck A. Perret**, which is located in the square of the same name. Perret was one of the first individuals to take an interest in the tragic eruption of Montagne Pelée, and founded the city's volcanological museum (see p 163). The monument was created by Martinican sculptor Henri Marie-Rose.

Opposite the monument, on Rue Gabriel-Péri, stands the **Maison du Sénégal**, one of the oldest buildings in the city. It originally served as a warehouse for a company authorized to deal in slaves. Slave-ships could legally unload their cargo here up until 1817, when slave trading was officially banned. Supposedly, however, the practice continued illegally up until the abolition of slavery in 1848.

If you turn right on Rue de la Raffinerie, you will head towards the **ruins of the chapel of the Asile de Bethléem**, a former nursing home. The arches of the chapel are still standing, and you'll see them between Rue Dorange and Rue de la Raffinerie. In the ruins of the chapel's choir stands the **tomb of Abbé Gosse**, who was the area's parish priest from 1863 to 1875. It was he who founded the Asile de Bethléem in 1875, and he valiantly looked after the establishment until he died of tuberculosis in 1887. Fifteen years later, all of the residents of the home and the nuns who cared for them perished when Montagne Pelée erupted.

A little further north, you will see the **ruins of the Lycée Colonial**. This building, which dates from around 1738, was initially an orphanage, and then housed the *Maison Royale d'Éducation des Jeunes Filles* (a girls' school). The government finally took possession of it in 1883 and turned it into a high school, the Lycée de Saint-Pierre.

Next, take Rue Sainte-Rose to the **cemetery and ossuary**. The latter houses the remains of the victims of the eruption of 1902. A commemorative monument was erected in their honor in

1922. Right nearby, you'll see the **presbytery**, which is surrounded by a beautiful park, and was rebuilt on the same grounds as the former **chapelle de l'Évêché**, or diocesan chapel, whose ruins are still visible.

Back on Rue Victor-Hugo, you can't miss the magnificent **Cathedral of Notre-Dame de L'Assomption ★**, which was rebuilt in 1924 thanks to Victor Depaz, who was studying in Europe when tragedy struck Saint-Pierre in 1902. He never saw a single member of his family again, as they all perished in the disaster. Upon returning to Martinique, he took charge of the family plantation, which he reconstructed, and was among those who set to work rebuilding Saint-Pierre.

On the waterfront, slightly farther north, you will see the metal structure that houses the **market**. It faces **Place Bertin**, where you'll find the **Fontaine Agnès**, a survivor of the 1902 eruption, as well as the **Maison de la Bourse**, faithfully restored in 1992 according to the plans for the original edifice dating back to 1855. This beautiful house now harbours the **Office de Tourisme de Saint-Pierre** *(everyday 9am to 5pm, ☎05.96.78.10.39)*, formerly set up opposite the theatre ruins, and the **Bureau du Patrimoine**, the city's heritage centre.

Quartier du Centre

If you head north on Rue Victor-Hugo, and then turn right on Rue du Gouverneur Ponton, you will reach the **ruins of the hospital**.

Further along, on the right side of Rue Victor-Hugo, you will see one of Saint-Pierre's two museums, the **Musée Historique** *(12F; Mon to Sat 9:30am to 5:30pm, Sun 9:30 to 1pm; ☎05.96.79.74.32)*. As its name sug-

gests, the museum tells the history of the city, devoting the entire first floor to what Saint-Pierre was like before 1902. The building itself served as the town hall from 1923 to 1984, when the municipal government moved to its present offices on Rue Caylus.

Further along, this time on the left, is the **Musée Vulcanologique Franck-Perret ★★** *(10F; every day 9am to 5pm; ☎05.96.78.15.16)*, founded by an American by the name of Franck A. Perret in 1932. Inside a unique room, there are magnificent photographs of Saint-Pierre both before and after the eruption, enabling the viewer to envision the scale of the disaster. The display also includes a lot of bent and partially destroyed everyday objects. The most fascinating piece in the museum, however, is the *bourdon*, or great bell, from the cathedral, which was bent out of shape by the heat, despite the considerable thickness of the metal. At the back of the museum, there is a sort of viewing area perfect for admiring the harbour. The museum is also the starting point for city tours led by certified guides from the Ministère de la Culture. These tours last two hours and include a visit to the museum *(35F)*, or one hour without the museum tour *(25F)*. Morning departures between 9:30am and 10am; afternoon departures between 2:30pm and 3pm.

Make sure to take a look at the **ruins of the theatre ★★★**, which lie on the other side of the street, almost directly across from the museum. Built in the 19th century, the theatre was modelled on the Grand Théâtre in Bordeaux and seated 800. Today, its imposing staircase, the foyer and the stage are still recognizable. At the very top of the staircase, you will see a famous statue, *Saint Pierre renaissant de ses cendres ★* (Saint-Pierre Rising from Its

NORTHERN CARIBBEAN COAST

Ashes), which was sculpted by Madeleine de Jouvray, and unveiled in 1928.

Right next to the theatre lies the famous **cachot de Cyparis ★**, or dungeon of Cyparis. Cyparis, whose first name was "Louis" according to some historians, and "August" according to others, was supposedly the sole survivor of the catastrophe of 1902. On the eve of the disaster, he was arrested in a drunken state for disturbing the peace. According to legend, he survived the eruption nearly unharmed, protected by the 50 centimetre-thick walls of his cell, which he came out of three days later. After being spared, he joined the Barnum and Bailey Circus and showed off his burns and scars to thousands of thrill-hungry spectators.

You are sure to notice the beautiful, freshly repainted building occupied by the **Compagnie de la Baie de Saint-Pierre**, also on Rue Victor-Hugo, near the theatre.

Below the Musée Vulcanologique, on Rue Isambert, which runs along the waterfront, you will find the **Ruins of Le Figuier**, a group of small, single-story houses used as stores and warehouses back in the port's heyday. The *Cyparis Express* (see p 160) sets off from here.

Back on Rue Victor-Hugo, continue heading north, and you will come across the **former stadium** before crossing the **Pont de la Roxelane ★**, which links the Quartier du Centre to the Quartier du Fort. The stone bridge, which is also known as Pont Roche, was built in 1766, and was one of the only structures in the city to withstand the eruption of 1902. Designed by Brother Cléophas, it is made up of a single 10-metre arch and spans the Rivière Roxelane, otherwise known as the Rivière des Blanchisseuses (the Laundresses River).

Quartier du Fort

On your left, just after the stone bridge, you'll see **Place d'Esnambuc**, with its monument commemorating Bélain d'Esnambuc's arrival on the island. If you turn right on Rue Peyniep, which runs along the Rivière Roxelane, you'll soon find **Rue Mont-au-Ciel**, which was recently cleared by archeological digs (1991). The gutter running down the centre was designed to drain off the water from the street. This sloping alleyway, which merits its poetic name (*Monte-au-Ciel* literally means "rises to the heavens"), intersects with **Rue Levassor**, where the ash, up to three metres deep in some spots, has been systematically removed, bringing the street back down to its pre-1902 level. Several of the houses on Rue Levassor, built after the eruption and before the ash was removed, are noticeably higher than the street – so much so that staircases had to be added to them.

At the end of Rue Levassor, you will find the **ruins of the Maison Coloniale de Santé**, which was built in 1839 and once sheltered between 120 and 150 mentally ill individuals, who were cared for by the nuns of Saint-Paul. Inside, you can still see the chairs used to restrain agitated patients.

The **Bureau du Génie** stands on the other side of Rue Levassor, immediately opposite the Maison Coloniale de Santé. Excavations begun in 1987, and still being carried out today, have cleared access to the main house, the reservoirs and the annexes of what was once the quarters of the colony's military engineer corps.

After retracing your steps back to Rue des Chiens, you can examine the spectacular **ruins of the Église du Fort ★★**, the oldest church in Martinique, and apparently, one of the first French churches to be built in the New World. The original wooden church, erected in 1640, was reconstructed in stone in 1660, then restored in 1895. When disaster struck on May 8, 1902, many churchgoers were gathered here for the Ascension mass. Today, its ruins form a majestic pile of stones and statues.

Just after the ruins of the church, turn onto Rue Schœlcher, which later becomes Allée Pécoul. On the right, you will see the **Tombe de Mère Onésime**, the tomb of a woman who administered the education of young Martinican girls for nearly half a century. A magnificent white marble monument, it was given to the congregation of the Sœurs de Saint-Joseph de Cluny by grateful families in 1898. In 1875, Mère Onésime had become the first woman in the Antilles, and the fifteenth in the world, to become a member of the Legion of Honour.

Allée Pécoul then leads directly to the **Château Depaz** *(free tour and rum-tasting; Mon to Fri 9am to 5pm, Sat 9am to 1pm; ☎05.96.78.13.14)*, also known as the Habitation Pécoul La Montagne. After his family was wiped out in 1902, Victor Depaz returned from Europe, where he had been studying, and began to rebuild the family estate. The present "château" dates from 1922. Jacques du Parquet, d'Esnambuc's nephew, founded one of the first plantations in Martinique in 1635, and sold it to the Pécoul family in the late 17th century. It was purchased by Victor's father, Raoul Depaz, at the end of the last century.

Farther on, a superb **waterfall** marks the location of the botanical garden, which was founded in 1803 and, until 1902, was the pride of Saint-Pierre. The garden contained many different varieties of plants and trees imported from a number of tropical countries, and its prestige extended well past national boundaries.

Back on Rue des Chiens, heading north, you will soon come to the **Château Perrinelle**, just after the **former Cimetière du Fort**. In late 1992, excavations partially uncovered the former home of the Jesuits, also believed to be the first stone building erected in Saint-Pierre. In the 19th century, Adolphe Perrinelle owned the estate. Supposedly, his former classmate Victor Schœlcher stayed here in 1840 while carrying out the inquiry that would lead to the abolition of slavery – an endeavour his powerful host could hardly have viewed favourably. Victor Depaz used the main house, destroyed in 1902, as his model when he reconstructed the Habitation Pécoul. His father Raoul had managed the Habitation Perrinelle for many years before purchasing the estate he left his son.

North of Saint-Pierre

Some four kilometres north of Saint-Pierre, there is a trail that climbs the **Rivière Blanche**, today an enormous flow of lava, all the way up to the **Sources Chaudes**, or Hot Springs, which testify eloquently to the dramatic history of the region (hiking trail; see p 169).

One kilometre further, brings you to the **Tombeau des Caraïbes** (Carib Tomb), also known as the **Coffre à Morts** (Case of the Dead). According to legend, the last of the Carib Indians, who were being hunted down by the French colonists, took refuge here before throwing themselves off the cliff.

A short distance beyond, near the D10, there is a monument marking the site of the village of **Sainte-Philomène**, where the rich of Saint-Pierre used to build vacation homes. The village was wiped off the map on May 8, 1902.

Le Prêcheur

Soon, you will enter the village of Le Prêcheur (The Preacher), named after a rock formation shaped like a preacher, which disappeared when Montagne Pelée erupted.

The village is one of the oldest on the island. Colonists started to settle here in 1635, and in 1644, Le Prêcheur became a parish. Its first parish priest was Father Jean-Baptiste Dutertre, who became the first person to write a history of the Antilles, and left behind a richly detailed series of writings grouped together under the title *Histoire Générale des Antilles* (1654). Françoise d'Aubigné, later Madame de Maintenon, Louis XIV's second wife, lived here as a child in the 17th century.

Today, Le Prêcheur has just over 2,000 inhabitants. It is the last village on the northwest coast and is only linked to Grand'Rivière, which is even farther north, by a footpath (see p 169).

In the Village

The most interesting monument in the village is the **church's bell tower**, which dates back to the end of the 17th century, and survived the deadly eruption of 1902. Louis XIV sent a great bell for Le Prêcheur's tower as a gift to Martinique for having provided him with his second wife, Françoise d'Aubigné. Today, the **"royal" bell** is displayed in front of the church.

The **war memorial**, near the town hall, is another curiosity. It actually shows a soldier dead on the battlefield – something highly unusual in this type of monument.

North of Le Prêcheur

After the village, the road heads into thicker and thicker vegetation, and leads to several charming, untouched black sand beaches, namely, **Anse Belleville**, **Anse Céron ★★** and **Anse Couleuvre ★★** (see p 167).

At Anse Céron, there is a dirt road leading to **Habitation Céron ★** *(35F; every day 9:20am to 5pm; ☎05.96.52.94.53 or 52.97.03)*, which is an interesting stop to learn more about what life was like during the island's pro-slavery era. On the grounds of the former plantation, where sugar cane, coffee, cacao, cassava and bananas were cultivated, you can still see the miserable wooden shacks that were once crowded with slaves. The main path, with a big pond on either side, leads to the family mansion, which is relatively small. There is now a restaurant here where you can savour delicious freshwater crayfish (see p 177).

  PARKS AND BEACHES

Schœlcher

The Schœlcher area has several beaches, which are slowly helping to further the development of its tourist industry. Unfortunately, the quality of the water at the beaches varies greatly.

The Beach at La Batelière Hotel (B)

This is the best beach in the area. Theoretically, however, it is only for guests of this prestigious hotel.

Facilities: Diving club; water-skiing.

Anse Madame (A)

You'll find the Schœlcher nautical club and the CRESSMA diving club here.

Plage Lido (B)

A lovely and increasingly popular beach.

Plage Madiana (A)

A recetnly laid-out black-sand beach.

Facilities: children's playground.

Le Carbet

There is a long, almost unbroken stretch of beach in the Carbet area. South of the town it is named **Le Coin**, then, heading north, **Grande Anse**, **Le Four**, **Petite Anse**, **Anse Turin** and **Anse Latouche**.

Plage du Coin (A)

This relatively deserted grey-sand beach is near the Marouba Club (see p 172).

Facilities: bathrooms; lots of restaurants.

Anse Turin ★★★ (A)

The part of the beach at Le Carbet that wins the prize, however, is Anse Turin, which, it is said, captured the imagination of Gauguin. It is a long strip of grey sand, and is very popular among Martinican families.

Facilities: cantines

Le Prêcheur

Anse Céron ★★ (A)

North of the Le Prêcheur village, the road leads to a few idyllic black-sand beaches, which are still wild and somewhat secluded by a row of coconut palms, though some are becoming increasingly frequented. Anse Céron, which faces the Rocher de la Perle, is the first of these beaches and the most easily accessible. Swimming here is both safe and pleasant.

Facilities: showers and bathrooms; picnic tables, snack bar.

Anse Couleuvre ★★ (A)

Beyond Anse Céron, the road enters the forest and becomes extremely narrow, bumpy and tortuous. It is worth tackling, however, for it leads to the magnificent Anse Couleuvre. Once you have reached the parking lot that marks the end of the road, you will have to take a short path to reach this black-sand beach. The sea here, however, is somewhat choppy, so swimming can be dangerous. This formerly secluded beach is quickly growing in popularity, so much so that it is best to go during the week for greater peace and quiet.

Facilities: showers and bathrooms; restaurants.

Anse Lévrier ★★ and Anse à Voile

From the Anse Couleuvre parking lot, a hiking trail leads to Grand'Rivière (see p 169). You can also take this trail part-way for about one kilometre on

NORTHERN CARIBBEAN COAST

foot to other black-sand beaches that remain relatively unspoilt. First get off the main trail and take another on the left, which slopes down toward Anse Lévrier. Then skirt the first beach before finally getting back on the trail leading to Anse à Voile, five minutes away, whence you can take in the lovely view of neighbouring Dominica. Both are outstanding sites where a delightful mystical ambiance holds sway. Swimming in either place is dangerous, however.

 OUTDOOR ACTIVITIES

 Hiking

In **Saint-Pierre**, if you wish to take part in a hiking trip organized by professional guides (members of the Syndicat National des Accompagnateurs en Montagne), contact the Bureau de la Randonnée *(everyday 9am to 5pm; Rue Victor-Hugo, opposite the theatre ruins,* ☎*05.96.78.30.77)*. They lead excursions all over the island. Canyoning expeditions and sea excursions are also available.

The Verrier-Absalon Trail

As you leave the village of Bellefontaine, a short distance after the church, turn right, then left 500 metres farther in order to reach the road that leads up to the Verrier observatory. Once you have passed the observatory, 500 metres farther, take the first left at the crossroads, then turn left again two kilometres later and continue until you reach a place called Chapeau Nègre. The Verrier-Absalon trail, which is six kilometres long and can be hiked in four hours (one way), begins here. It will take you up Morne Chapeau Nègre (912 m) and then all the way to the

Absalon spa. On your way, you'll be able to take in views of Morne Pavillon (1,196 m) to the north and the Baie des Flamands to the south, and examine a variety of landscapes.

The trail is considered difficult, as there are several narrow sections along the crest of the hill, and the climb up requires considerable effort.

Morne Rose-Savane Saint-Cyr

You can pick up this trail from the Verrier-Absalon trail, near the Savane Saint-Cyr. The other end of it can be reached from the sharply curved concrete road on your right as you leave Case-Pilote.

This is a pleasant two-kilometre, one-hour walk (one way) of average difficulty, which will lead you through a dry forest, a cloud forest, and finally a tropical rainforest.

Plateau Concorde

This is another trail that can either be picked up from, or lead to, the Verrier-Absalon trail. In the latter instance, you'll find the beginning of the trail at the end of a small road heading off to your right as you leave the hamlet of Fond Lahaye. The two trails meet midway between the Savane Saint-Cyr and the Absalon spa.

The trail, which is four kilometres long (2 hours and 30 min one way), is easy, and gives you an opportunity to see various different types of trees, including the gum tree, the black laurel and the mountain laurel.

Montjoly-Caplet Via Piton Lacroix

On this trail, you'll tackle the Pitons du Carbet from the west. Heading away from Bellefontaine, you can reach the Montjoly area by means of a country road that intersects the D20 near Morne-Vert. The trail takes you over Piton Lacroix, or Morne Pavillon (1,196 m), as well as Morne Piquet (1,160 m), then back down towards Morne Modeste (545 m). The reward for your constant effort is a series of spectacular views of the Caribbean coast.

The trail, which is five kilometres long and requires five hours of walking (one way), is one of the most difficult on the island. The slopes are very steep, while the terrain is often muddy and sometimes cluttered with slippery rocks.

The Canal de Beauregard

The *"itinéraire touristique"*, or tourist itinerary, which is very well-marked, starts from the centre of the village of Le Carbet (between the service station and the cemetery), and leads to the canal de Beauregard. The trail itself begins between two small stone structures at a place called Bout du Canal, and leads you on a unique walk along a former irrigation canal.

The trail, which is 3.5 kilometres long (90 min one way), may be considered easy, even though the path is only 30 centimetres-wide alongside cliffs ranging from 50 to 150 metres-high. Given the risk of falling, you should avoid this trail if you suffer from vertigo or a fear of heights.

The Hot Springs (Les Sources Chaudes)

This incredible trail starts about three or four kilometres north of Saint-Pierre, at the entrance to a private quarry. After a fairly long walk through the quarry, you'll find yourself climbing up a steady slope towards the side of Montagne Pelée. At a certain point, you'll head down along the bed of the Rivière Blanche, which was filled with ash during the eruptions of 1902 and 1929. Then, you'll reach the famous Sources Chaudes, which provide irrefutable proof that the volcano is still active. The temperature of the springs can reach up to 50°C.

The trail is an easy four-kilometre, three-hour hike. A large part of it is unshaded, however, so make sure to bring along a hat, sunblock and water on hot or sunny days. Furthermore, please note that the Hot Springs trail is closed on Tuesdays, Wednesdays and Fridays, when the surrounding area is used for shooting practice.

Montagne Pelée Via Grande Savane

This is the only trail leading from the Caribbean coast to the top of Montagne Pelée. To get to it, take the first road on the right, in front of the bus stop, as you enter the village of Le Prêcheur *(Route Communale de la Charmeuse)*. The trail affords some extraordinary views of Saint-Pierre and the entire Caribbean coast. You'll be climbing steadily, up to an altitude of about 1,100 metres.

The trail, which is of average difficulty, stretches 3.5 kilometres and takes about two hours. Make sure to bring plenty of water along, as there is very little shade and the heat can be intense.

From Le Prêcheur to Grand'Rivière

This is one of Martinique's classic hiking trails. It starts at the end of the D10, in the parking lot at Anse Couleuvre. Unless you go by boat, this 20-kilometre trail is the only way to cover the distance between Le Prêcheur and the northernmost tip of the island. It passes through the forest reserve managed by the *Conservatoire de l'Espace Littoral et des Rivages Lacustres* (an organization dedicated the conservation of coastal and lakeside areas), enabling you to discover various different types of forests, from dry to tropical, several untouched beaches (Anse Lévrier, Anse à Voile, Anses des Galets) and the beautiful waterfalls at the foot of Montagne Pelée. It might interest you to know that oxcarts were driven along this trail up until the beginning of the century. You'll see remnants of that era (stone bridges, tunnels, etc.) all along the way.

The trail, though very long (20 km; 6 hours one way), is easy.

 Scuba Diving

There are a large number of diving sites along the northern Caribbean coast, each more spectacular than the last. Take, for example, **Cap Enragé**, a little to the north of Case-Pilote, where you'll find a pretty little coral garden teeming with colourful marine animals. Right nearby, you can examine the coral on the sandy sea-bottom at **Fond Boucher**, about 6 metres below the surface.

There is an interesting coral plateau about 2,500 metres off the coast of **Bellefontaine**, and another off the coast of **Le Prêcheur**. In addition, the area around **Rocher de la Perle**, facing Anse Céron, is swarming with both coral fish and larger fish, such as barracudas, horse-mackerels, parrot-fish, etc.

Nevertheless, top billing still goes to Saint-Pierre's harbour, where you can examine the wreckage of a dozen or so boats that sank when Montagne Pelée erupted in 1902. The *Roraima* (50 m) and the *Raisinier* (15 m) are the most interesting.

There are a number of diving clubs in the region, including two in **Schœlcher**, CRESSMA *(☎05.96.61.34.36)* in Anse Madame, and Tropicasub at the Hôtel La Batelière *(☎05.96.61.49.49)*.

In **Case-Pilote**, you'll find the Club Subaquatique de Case Pilote *(☎05.96.61.03.88)*.

Le Carbet is particulary good for diving, with club Submaroubase *(☎05.96.78.40.04)* at the Marouba Club.

Saint-Pierre, for its part, is not to be outdone. An excellent diving network has developed around the spectacular shipwrecks in the harbour. The local Bulles Passion *(at the Ruins of Le Figuier, Rue Bouillé, ☎05.96.78.26.22)* takes divers out every day at 9:30am and 2:30pm. Tropicasub *(☎05.96.78.38.03)*, near the restaurant La Guinguette (see p 176) also offers daily excursions. Another noteworthy outfit is the Centre U.C.P.A. *(☎05.96.78.21.03)*.

 Pleasure Boating

A few places to practise jet-skiing, water skiing and sailboarding: Loisirs Plaisirs *(☎05.96.78.43.00)* at **Anse Latouche**, and Loca Sport *(☎05.96.78.01.48)* at the Marouba Club in **Le Carbet**.

Small glass-bottomed boats able to seat up to four passengers may be rented in **Saint-Pierre**. Known as "Aquavision", they look something like pedalboats, but are motorized. They are available at

Bequi Boat *(200F per hour, ☎05.96.78.16.42)*, near the restaurant La Guinguette (see p 176). No license required.

Swimming

Though the island boasts numerous beaches that are a pleasure to swim at, the village of **Le Carbet** also boasts a beautiful olympic-size swimming pool *(everyday 8am to 4pm; ☎05.96.78.18.11)*.

Mountain Biking

Mountain bikes can be rented from Loca Sport *(☎05.96.78.01.48)*, at the Marouba Club in **Le Carbet**.

ACCOMMODATIONS

Schœlcher

There are several *gîtes ruraux*, country houses, in the area, despite its proximity to Fort-de-France. One, for example, belongs to **M. Charles Arcade (no. 011,** ¦¦¦) *(1,765F per week; below the owner's residence; Fond-Rousseau, Terreville - 97223 Schœlcher)*, and another to **M. Lin Gazon (no. 043,** ¦¦) *(1,190F per week; below the owner's residence; 12 Rue Roland-Janvier, Enclos - 97223 Schœlcher)*.

For hotels, the recently built **Anse Colas** *(770F; ≋, tv, pb, ℜ; Route du Petit Tamarin - 97223 Schœlcher, ☎05.96.61.28.18, ↝05.96.61.04.78)*, located in a residential area, is a good choice. The design of the hotel's buildings combines traditional Creole style with modern comfort, and the rooms have been decorated with the same

idea in mind. Outside you'll find a lagoon-style swimming pool surrounded by a beautiful exotic garden.

La Batelière *(950-1,500 F; tv, ≋, pb, ≈, ℜ; 20 Rue des Alizés - 97233 Schœlcher, ☎05.96.61.49.49, ↝05.96.61.70.57)*, the first luxury hotel ever built in Martinique, has something of a mythical aura about it. This legendary place houses one of the island's two casinos, an extremely popular discotheque, a fitness centre, two restaurants, three bars, a variety of boutiques, etc. It looks out on the sea, and has a beautiful beach with facilities for every kind of water sport imaginable.

Morne-Vert

Those wishing to stay in the "Switzerland of the Antilles" have the choice between the **Bel Air Village** *(320-380F; tv, pb, ≈, K; on the D20 Quartier Bout Barrière - 97226 Morne-Vert, ☎05.96.55.52.94, ↝05.96.55.52.97)* and the **Miellerie** *(1,200F per week; pb, K; ☎05.96.55.57.58, ↝05.96.55.57.43)*. Both offer fully equipped studios and apartments (by the week at the Miellerie).

There is also a noteworthy *gîte* in the area. It belongs to **M. Eucher Gatien (no. 19,** ¦¦¦) *(2,095 per week; next to the owner's residence; Quartier Bois Lézard - 97226 Morne-Vert)*.

Le Carbet

For those looking for a peaceful setting, we recommend the *gîtes* belonging to **M. and Mme Benoît Maizeroi (nos. 054-056)** *(1,635-2,185F per week; near the owners' residence; Quartier Bout-Bois - 97221 Carbet)*, which are located in the hills of Anse Turin.

Ulysses' Favourites

For luxury:
La Batelière (Schœlcher, p 171)

For families:
Marouba Club (Le Carbet, p 172)

For businesspeople:
La Batelière (Schœlcher, p 171)

For water sports enthusiasts:
La Batelière (Schœlcher, p 171)
Marouba Club (Le Carbet, p 172)

If you're looking for a reasonably priced, nice little hotel in the popular Le Carbet area, try **Christophe Colomb** *(250-300F; pb, K; rue Principale in Grande Anse - 97221 Carbet; ☎05.96.78.05.38, ⊷05.96.78.06.42)*. The place is very small (10 rooms in all) and very modest, but the beach is right nearby, and the prices are hard to beat.

The **Carbets de Madinina** *(440F-520F, ≡, pb, ≈, K; Quartier Le Fromager - 97221 Carbet, ☎05.96.78.08.08, ⊷05.96.78.06.92)*, located on a hillside a few kilometres from Le Carbet, is a cluster of villas containing a total of 24 rooms. Removed from the bustle of town, you can enjoy a relaxing stay in a verdant setting.

🛥 Just before reaching Le Carbet from the south, you're bound to see the **Marouba Club** *(1,040-1,240F ½b, 1,260-1,460 fb; ≡, pb, ≈, ℜ; 97221 Carbet, ☎05.96.78.00.21, ⊷05.96.78.05.65)*, a bungalow village with 125 rooms in all. The place is geared towards families, and even has a "mini-club" for children between the ages of 3 and 12.

Saint-Pierre

Despite its obvious cultural and historical attractions, Saint-Pierre has a surprising lack of decent accommodations. Hopefully, all the plans surrounding Saint-Pierre's nomination as a "City of Art and History" will encourage some hotel-owners to invest in the area in the near future. Fortunately, though, there are a few *gîtes* around Saint-Pierre. One of these belongs to **Mme Pierrette Couloute (no. 052, ▐▐)** *(1,625F per week; below the owner's residence; Jardin des Plantes, 97250 Saint-Pierre)*, and three others to **M. and Mme Bruno Jubert (nos. 135-137)** *(1,390F per week; units adjoining the owners' residence; Quartier Trois-Ponts, 97250 Saint-Pierre)*.

You can also fall back on **La Nouvelle Vague** *(250F; ℜ; 97250 Saint-Pierre, ☎05.96.78.14.34)*, a tiny hotel with five no-frills rooms, located by the water on Place Bertin. Although there is nothing luxurious about this place, it is worth keeping in mind for its low rates and convenient location. What's more, it has a good restaurant (see p 175).

Another option is the **Résidence Surcouf** *(350F; pb, ≈, K; Quartier du Fort - 97250 Saint-Pierre, ☎05.96.78.32.73, ☞05.96.78.13.82)*, which provides furnished tourist accommodations 1.5 kilometres from the village of Saint-Pierre, on Allée Pécoul in the Quartier du Fort. These are fully equipped bungalow units surrounded by a park, which stretches over an area of three hectares.

Le Prêcheur

This is another peaceful spot with little to offer in the way of accommodations, except, once again, for a couple of *gîtes*. You can contact **M. Armand Clovis (no. 150, ⫾)** *(1,790F per week; second-floor apartment; La Charmeuse, le Prêcheur - 97250 Saint-Pierre)*, or **Mme Eliette N'Guela (no. 063, ⫾)** *(1,645F per week; independent unit; 11 Cité Poihé, Le Prêcheur - 97250 Saint-Pierre)*.

 RESTAURANTS

Schœlcher

Le Sunset *(180F; closed Sun; ☎05.96.61.22.36 or 05.96.61.11.82)* is tucked away in a gorgeous tropical garden in Anse Madame. To get there, take the "Schœlcher Nord" exit from the N2, and then, after passing under the highway, take your second right. The rib steak *à la crème de passion* alone is worth the trip. The restaurant is located in the same building as a small hotel, a bar and a discotheque.

The Anse Colas hotel (see p 171), located on Route du Petit Tamarin, has a nice little restaurant, the **Pomme-Cannelle** *(250F; open daily; ☎05.96.61.28.18)*, with an attractive terrace overlooking a lagoon-shaped pool. The menu is made up of French and Caribbean specialities, most notably, chicken stuffed with *lambis*, duck with ginger and red snapper with vanilla.

Why not treat yourself to the luxury of a good meal at **Bleu Marine** *(300F; open daily; ☎05.96.61.49.49)*, located in the prestigious La Batelière hotel (see p 171). Here, too, the terrace is near the pool, commanding a beautiful view of the sea on the horizon. The *Ballets Martiniquais* dance company performs here in the evenings occasionally, to the delight of guests still savouring their salmon *cigares* or yam *arlequins*.

Le Foulard *(300F; closed Sun; ☎05.96.61.15.72)*, a seaside restaurant located right in town (take the "Schœlcher Centre" exit from the N2), has a great reputation. The daily specials are reportedly always better than the dishes offered on the regular menu, which are pretty mouth-watering themselves (*escargots* with morel mushrooms, rock lobster crêpes, a Grand Marnier soufflé...)

Case-Pilote

If you want to avoid spending your money on restaurants, there is a **8 à Huit** grocery store near the small market town's main square.

There's no denying the charm of **Céleste's Village** *(open daily; ☎05.96.78.72.78)* located right on the main square in Case-Pilote. This spruce café-restaurant serves simple French and Creole cuisine at reasonable prices.

You might have a little trouble finding **Le Maniba** *(200F; closed Sun and Mon; ☎05.96.78.73.89)*, which is hidden in

Ulysses' Favourites

For the finest dining:
      Bleu Marine (Schœlcher, p 173)
      Le Poids du Roy (Le Carbet, p 175)

For authentic Creole cuisine:
      Le Poids du Roy (Le Carbet, p 175)
      L'Habitation Céron (Le Prêcheur, p 177)

For the romantic ambiance:
      Le Trou Crabe (Le Carbet, p 175)

For wine lovers:
      Le Trou Crabe (Le Carbet, p 175)

For the view:
      Le Fromager (Saint-Pierre, p 176)

the Maniba residential complex. The complex, just a stone's throw away from the historic village of Case-Pilote, has received some harsh criticism for its audacious style. Be that as it may, the chef of this French and Creole restaurant prepares very good food, such as curried crayfish brochettes and, as an appetizer, *feuilletés de lambis au gratin*.

Bellefontaine

In Bellefontaine, you have only to look up to spot the incredible ship-shaped silhouette of **Torgiléo** *(150F; closed Sun night and Mon; ☎05.96.55.02.92)*. The restaurant has been concocting delicious traditional Creole cooking for a short while now. This unique place is reached via a narrow and extremely steep road, abreast of the pier.

Le Carbet

Among the many waterfront restaurants in Le Carbet, one is a real bargain.

It's called **La Paillotte** *(85F, ☎05.96.78.03.79)*, and it serves decent Creole food at affordable prices

La Datcha *(125F; closed Sun night; ☎05.96.78.04.45)* is one of the many restaurants at the Plage du Coin, at the south entrance of Le Carbet. Here you can sample grilled or curried fish right by the ocean. The place also boasts a fish tank from which you can choose a lobster (200F/kg). Live music Saturday nights until 2am.

At Grande Anse, not far from the Centre de Thalassothérapie, you'll find a large, colourful terrace looking right out onto the beach. This is **L'Imprévu** *(125F; closed Sun and Mon evenings; ☎05.96.78.01.02)*, which serves the usual shark *touffé*, fricassees and chicken stuffed with *lambis*, but also has delicious desserts, such as pineapple *Imprévu* and Tête Douet ice cream. The Friday night "grill party" with live music has become a tradition at L'Imprévu, and is always a lot of fun.

On the beach at Le Coin, you'll find **O Ra La Lanme** *(125F; open daily;*

☎05.96.78.08.48), which is a bargain. The terrace is decorated with lots of tropical plants and dark wood, and the tables are covered with checkered cloths. Take a seat and enjoy the delicious *coq au vin* or barbecue platter (chicken, lamb and porkchops). There is also a "brochette party" every Saturday night.

🦀 Set up inside one of the buildings of the former Habitation Anse Latouche, which is slowly being brought back to life (see p 159), **Le Poids du Roy** *(180F; every day lunch and supper with reservation, for parties of 10 or more;* ☎05.96.78.18.07) boasts an absolutely remarkable setting. The name (The King's Weight) was used to designate all inspection offices for weights and mesures in France's dependencies starting in 1690. Martinique's office was located here, at the Habitation Anse Latouche. In a setting that will take you back to the 17th century, you can savour Creole ham with onion preserves, filet of red snapper with cream of avocado or an exotic fruit omelette. You are sure to look back on the experience with fond memories.

🦀 **Le Trou Crabe** *(200F; closed Sun pm;* ☎05.96.78.04.34) is a pleasant little restaurant with a romantic charm about it. It is located alongside the beach at Le Coin, just a step away from the Amazona zoo, and serves good Lyonnaise and Creole cooking. Try the pike quenelle with Nantua sauce, the *fleur de l'îles* (a baked filet of beef served with pineapple and bananas au gratin) and to top it all off, the pineapple flan. Le Trou Crabe also has a well-stocked wine cellar, something that is unfortunately hard to find in Martinique. Dinner and dancing on Saturday evenings.

Back on the waterfront, another excellent option is **Le Grain d'Or** *(215F,* ☎05.96.78.06.19), which serves delicious seafood to guests seated either inside, in a large dining room, or out, around an attractive swimming pool.

Saint-Pierre

NORTHERN CARIBBEAN COAST

You can stock up on fruits and vegetables every morning at the **Marché de Saint-Pierre**, on Place Félix-Boisson. Moreover, on Fridays and Saturdays, from dawn to 1am, the market stocks just about everything you could hope to find in a colourful and festive ambiance.

In the martyred city of Saint-Pierre, there are two places that are perfect for lunch. If you're craving roast chicken, head to **Au Plateau du Théâtre**, which occupies a charming white house opposite the ruins of the former theatre. Right nearby, in the same building as the Compagnie de la Baie de Saint-Pierre, you will find **Le Cargo Bleu** *(closed Mon; 75 Rue Victor-Hugo,* ☎05.96.78.26.60), which offers a complete lunch menu for 85F.

On Place Bertin, you can enjoy a good, fairly inexpensive meal at the hotel **La Nouvelle Vague** *(80F; closed Mon;* ☎05.96.78.14.34). The menu lists seafood and French and Antillean specialties, all served in a simple, unpretentious manner.

If you're looking for an inexpensive meal, head to the **Relais du Musée** *(80F; closed Wed and Sun;* ☎05.96.78.31.13), which is across from the Musée Historique. There are only a few wooden tables with black chairs in the charming air-conditioned dining room at the back, but the pale green walls and tablecloths add just the right amount of colour to transform this modest restaurant into a great meeting place. There are also a few tables in front, near the oven. You can choose from a variety of pizzas baked in a wood-burning stove, or order a sandwich to take out.

La Guinguette *(90F; closed Mon night; ☎05.96.78.15.02)*, located right on the beach in the Quartier du Mouillage, is another modest, friendly restaurant. Decorated with fishing nets, fruit and exotic plants, this place is exceptionally appealing. The food may be entirely traditional (barbecued crayfish, shark *touffé*, coconut blancmange), but the atmosphere is unique.

La Factorerie *(100F; 11:30am to 2:30pm, closed Sat; ☎05.96.78.12.53)*, located in the Quartier du Fort, has built itself a good reputation. Make sure to try their chicken *colombo* or chicken with crayfish (the restaurant raises its own chickens).

Can you think of anything more exotic than eating delicious Chinese food in the heart of the French Antilles? Here's your chance to do just that, at **Royal Belle-Ville** *(150F; closed Wed noon and Sun pm; ☎05.96.78.10.69)*, located on Rue Victor-Hugo, right in the middle of Saint-Pierre. Served on cast-iron plates, seafood is an element in both Asian and Caribbean cuisine.

🦞 **Le Fromager** *(180F; every day noon to 3pm; ☎05.96.78.19.07)*, located on the road to Fond-Saint-Denis in the hills overlooking the Quartier du Centre, is worth the trip, if only to take in the spectacular view of Saint-Pierre and its harbour. The menu's not bad, either; the avocado *féroce*, Tahitian-style *chatrou*, and mangoes flambé make a good combination. On Friday nights only, the restaurants opens at 7:30 for its *"soirée grillades"*, highlighting offerings from the grill.

For good fresh fish, head to **Cyparis Station** *(230F; open daily; ☎05.96.78.36.73)*, which you'll find on your way out of Saint-Pierre as you head towards Le Prêcheur. The owner, a fisherman himself, will offer you fish eggs cooked with papaya, sea-urchin *blaff* and breaded fish filets. You can even ask him to take you out on his boat, which he'll probably agree to do with a smile.

Le Prêcheur

In the Village of Le Prêcheur

🦞 On the main road, in the Abymes du Prêcheur area, you will find a pleasant restaurant named **Chez Ginette** *(180F; noon to 3:30pm, closed Thu; ☎05.96.52.90.28)*. All the walls are adorned with brightly coloured naive art depicting scenes from the history of Le Prêcheur and Martinique. In a relaxed atmosphere, you can enjoy fish grilled over a wood fire. The chef's specialty, *boudin de langouste*, has earned all sorts of praise.

On your way into the village from Saint-Pierre, you can stop at **La Belle Créole** *(400F; closed Wed and Sun for lunch; ☎05.96.52.96.23)*. The decor may be somewhat sparse, but the servings are generous. The shark pâté, filet of fish poached in coconut milk and *croquettes de légumes pays* are just a few of the chef's creations. The terrace looks right out on the sea.

At the north edge of town, on the left, you will see **Le Mélodie** *(200F, closed Tue and Sun evenings; ☎05.96.52.90.31)*, a delightful place where eating *accras* has become an art form. The rock lobster, sea bream with pineapple and shark *colombo* are also delicious. Guests can dine on a large, shady terrace facing the sea, or right on the beach.

North of Le Prêcheur

Between the parking lot at the end of the D10 and the stunning Anse Couleuvre black-sand beach lurks **Restaurant Moana** *(140F; open for lunch only, closed Tue; ☎05.96.52.97.74)*, set up under some sort of large *carbet*. Seafood, grilled chicken or fish, *assiète antillaise*. Utterly laid-back ambiance, slightly anarchic even (poster of Che on the wall).

A delightful crayfish restaurant by a river constitutes a new and very interesting addition to the **Habitation Céron** *(140F; Anse Céron, ☎05.96.52.96.03)*, which has been experiencing a revival over the last few years (see p 166). The fixed-price menu (140F) also includes a tour of the whole plantation.

  ENTERTAINMENT

Nightlife on the northern Caribbean coast centres around La Batelière Hotel, in Schœlcher. Its **casino** *(free admission to slot machines, 69F for game room; dress code; noon to 3am for slot machines, 10pm to 3am for game room; ☎05.96.61.73.23)*, is what attracts most visitors. However, the hotel also has a discotheque called **Queen's** *(10pm until dawn, closed Mon, ☎05.96.61.49.49)*, decorated like a big ship, where you can dance until the wee hours of the morning.

Another spot likely to attract night owls is **Le Sunset** *(7pm to 1am, closed Sun)*, at Anse Mitan, where you'll find a

restaurant, a piano bar and a hotel all under one roof.

Saint-Pierre

In Saint-Pierre, the pub-like **Snack Bar Caraïbe** *(everyday 9am to 1am; ☎05.96.78.30.59)* has a some 30 different kinds of beer to choose from as well as live music.

Finally, there is a movie theatre in Saint-Pierre, the **Élysée** *(☎05.96.77.18.46)*, on Rue Lucy.

Le Carbet

In Le Carbet, people get together at the discotheque at the **Marouba Club** holiday resort. Live entertainment. On Thursdays, a big night featuring cockfighting, ballet and zouk is organized.

Musicians liven up Saturday evenings at the **La Datcha** restaurant, and Friday nights at **L'Imprévu**. **Le Trou Crabe**, for its part, organizes Saturday-night dinner dances.

 SHOPPING

Saint-Pierre

You can go bargain-hunting near the Musée Vulcanologique at the **craft stalls**, an improvised market where you can find T-shirts, madras fabrics and jewellery at negotiable prices.

Look Caraïbe *(every day 8:30am-6pm; ☎05.96.78.33.69)*, located on Place Bertin, in front of the market, is the place to go for a wide range of souvenirs-pottery, jewellery, paintings, postcards, etc.

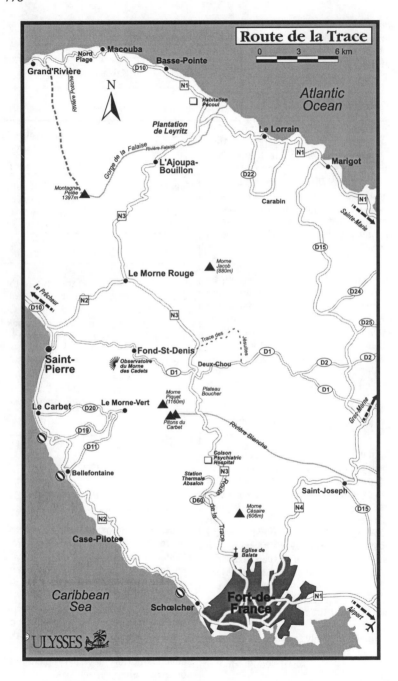

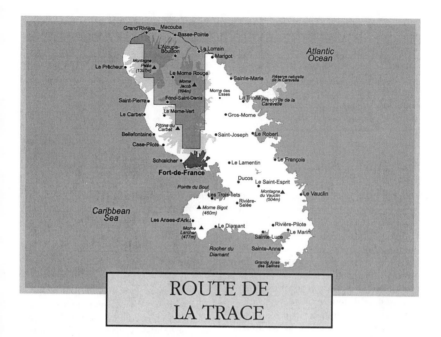

ROUTE DE
LA TRACE

This tour is an essential part of any trip to Martinique; you can't claim to know the island if you haven't taken the famous Route de la Trace through the spectacular, luxuriant vegetation of the tropical rainforest, where the only sounds to break the silence are the singing of the birds, the gentle splashing of the waterfalls and the rushing of the streams.

Our suggested tour covers the "*trace*" (french for trail), which was opened in the 18th century as a means of bypassing the Pitons du Carbet and is now something of a tourist attraction. The Parc Régional de la Martinique does however ensure that the area is developed in complete harmony with the environment, and in this spirit an extensive network of hiking trails was created, enabling visitors to explore the dense jungle.

Farther along on the tour, you'll pass through such picturesque villages as Fond-Saint-Denis and Ajoupa-Bouillon, virtually overflowing with flowers. There, enchanted by the dazzling colours and heady fragrances of the blossoms, you'll truly understand why Martinique's first inhabitants referred to it as the "Island of Flowers".

This tour also skirts around Montagne Pelée. Though the most direct route to the deadly volcano is by way of Morne Rouge, some visitors might prefer tackling its north face, via Grand'Rivière, where the road stops and you feel as if you've reached the end of the world.

Montagne Pelée, which is at least 400,000 years old, stands at 1,397 metres. Since the French first arrived on the island, there have been four eruptions. The first, a small one, was in 1792 and the second in 1851. Then, between 1902 and 1904, fiery clouds wiped out Saint-Pierre and then Morne Rouge, killing 30,000 people. The volcano's last rumblings were recorded between 1929 and 1932, but had no disastrous consequences. These two big eruptions were a new phenomenon to observers, involving the expulsion of clouds of incandescent ash and the formation of viscous domes in the volcano's crater. They have since been termed "Pelean." Today, there are hiking trails leading to the volcanic cones created by the 1902 and 1929 eruptions.

Our tour will end on the northern Atlantic coast, a historic region steeped in agricultural tradition. In the past, the area was dotted with rival sugar plantations. Today, though, bananas and pineapples are the main crops. You'll continue along through the gorgeous, but somewhat forbidding landscape, of this coast. Indeed, the beaches here are altogether different from those in the south. Constantly pounded by a heavy surf, they are unsuitable for swimming, so much so that it certainly won't be the beaches that draw you to this northernmost part of the island, past the far reaches of Basse-Pointe, the birthplace of Aimé Césaire, to a tiny fishing village named Grand'Rivière.

FINDING YOUR WAY AROUND

By Car

From Fort-de-France, head north (follow the signs for "Morne Rouge, Route de Balata") on Route de Balata, which starts as Boulevard Allègre, and later turns into the N3, better known as Route de la Trace. After passing through the tropical forest, you will reach the coast, and can then take the N1 to Le Lorrain and, if you wish, on to Basse-Pointe. From there, you can take the *Route Départementale* 10 (D10) all the way to Grand'Rivière.

From the southern part of the island (Trois-Îlets, Diamant, Sainte-Anne), take the N5 and then the N1 to the outskirts of Fort-de-France, then follow the signs for Balata.

Car Rentals

CH-Ozier La Fontaine: Hôtel de la Plantation de Leyritz, Basse-Pointe, ☎05.96.78.53.92.

Véro Locations: Centre Commercial Nordis Fond Brulé, Le Lorrain, ☎05.96.53.74.01.

By Boat

You can also reach Grand'Rivière by boat, which is an interesting alternative to driving. To do so, you'll have to negotiate a fee with one of the fishermen in the village of Le Prêcheur, on the northern Caribbean coast.

A well-known hiking trail also links the villages of Grand'Rivière and Le Prêcheur (see p 169).

PRACTICAL INFORMATION

Fond-Saint-Denis

Tourist office: in the town hall, ☎05.96.55.80.34.

Town hall: ☎05.96.55.88.88 or 05.96.55.89.89, ⇌05.96.55.89.91.

Morne Rouge

Tourist office: Immeuble Magalon (Magalon Building), ☎05.96.52.45.98.

Police: ☎05.96.55.34.33.

Town hall: ☎05.96.52.30.23.

Bank: Crédit Agricole, 9 Rue Schœlcher, ☎05.96.52.32.82.

Pharmacy: Pharmacie Osman Duquesnay, Rue Principale, ☎05.96.52.33.08.

Gas Stations:
Texaco, on the right before entering the town
Esso, after the stadium, on the way out of town, towards Ajoupa-Bouillon.

Laundry: Pressing La Capress, near the town hall.

Ajoupa-Bouillon

Tourist office: Immeuble Boulon (Boulon Building), Quartier Racine, ☎05.96.53.32.87.

Town hall: ☎05.96.53.32.22, ⌐05.96.53.35.20.

Gas station: In the centre of town, near Snack Universium.

Le Lorrain

Tourist office: Rue Schœlcher, ☎05.96.53.47.19.

Police: ☎05.96.53.45.08.

Town hall: ☎05.96.53.44.22, ⌐05.96.53.40.42.

Hospital: Hôpital Principal, ☎05.96.53.48.07.

Pharmacy: Pharmacie Renard, 22 Rue Schœlcher, ☎05.96.53.44.23.

Gas station: Shell, on the way into town from the north.

Banks:
BNP, Rue Principale, ☎05.96.53.45.05
Crédit Agricole, 6 Rue Schœlcher, ☎05.96.53.41.93;
Crédit Martiniquais, 20 Rue Schœlcher, ☎05.96.53.42.60.

Basse-Pointe

Tourist office: Tapis Vert, ☎05.96.78.99.01.

Police: ☎05.96.78.52.85.

Hospital: ☎05.96.78.50.76.

Town hall: ☎05.96.78.50.44, ⌐05.96.78.97.16.

Pharmacy: Pharmacie Onier Flor Hackaert, ☎05.96.78.50.62.

Bank: Crédit Agricole, ☎05.96.78.50.58.

Grand'Rivière

Tourist office: town hall, ☎05.96.55.72.74.

Town hall: ☎05.96.55.77.77, ⌐05.96.55.72.62.

 EXPLORING

Balata ★

Before you've even left Balata, one of Fort-de-France's comfortable suburbs, the road already seems to be heading into the forest.

ROUTE DE LA TRACE

Église de Balata

From a distance, towering over the tropical vegetation, you'll spot the stunning silhouettte of the **Église de Balata** ★ *(☎05.96.64.34.18)*, a small but faithful reproduction of Paris's Sacré-Cœur church inaugurated in 1926. To get there, follow the directions on the little sign reading "église" to the left of the road. From the parking lot, you can take in a lovely view of Fort-de-France and its surrounding area.

Farther on, a **Halte Panoramique** *(30F, drink included; everyday 8:30am to 4:30pm; ☎05.96.64.64.90)* has just been set up on the grounds of the Habitation La Liot, where cocoa, cinnamon, Indian wood and vanilla were cultivated in the mid-19th century. The 400-metre viewpoint affords stunning vistas over the Caribbean, the Atlantic Ocean and the Pitons du Carbet alike.

Afterwards, make sure to stop at the **Jardin de Balata** ★★★ *(adults 35F, children 15F; every day 9am to 5pm; ☎05.96.64.48.73)*, a beautifully arranged botanical garden which is worth at least an hour of your time (see p 186).

Farther on, you'll cross Rivière Blanche (where there are picnic tables and souvenir stands) by means of the **Pont de l'Alma** and soon afterwards arrive at a place called Deux-Choux. Take a left on the D 1, which will take you to Fond-Saint-Denis.

Fond-Saint-Denis ★

A visit to Fond-Saint-Denis requires a 12-kilometre detour, but is well worth it. Stop for a few minutes to admire the **Cascade Saut de Gendarme**, on the way. A rest area has recently been laid out next to the waterfall. Then, as you near Fond-Saint-Denis, you will be greeted by the delightful vision of vivid flowers lining the road; there is an even greater profusion of them in the village itself. The **church**, surrounded by blossoms, and the little **town hall** overlooking the road are positively charming.

Apparently, there is a fierce competition between Fond-Saint-Denis and Ajoupa-Bouillon for Martinique's "town-with-the-most-flowers" title, and you'll thank heaven for this rivalry as you drink in the enchanting scenes that have resulted from it.

The **Observatoire du Morne des Cadets**, built in 1932 to make it easier to study Montagne Pelée, is also located in Fond-Saint-Denis. An ultramodern seismograph is used to monitor the volcano's slightest activity. A network of about twenty geophysics stations are involved in this process, continually transmitting data to the observatory, where the information is then processed by computer.

From the observatory, there is a breathtaking view not only of the famous volcano, but also of the Pitons du Carbet and Habitation Pécoul (see p 185).

In front of the church, there is another attraction that intrigues many visitors: the **war memorial**, which, as in almost every other French *commune*, was erected in honour of local citizens who participated the First World War. This one has a large base, but the statue itself, a bronze soldier, stands barely 30 centimetres high! It is actually only a model of the monument. Apparently, the residents of the village, who had to pay for the memorial themselves, decided that the proposed project was beyond their means, and that the model would do just fine.

With barely 1,000 inhabitants, Fond-Saint-Denis, which only dates back to 1835, is the island's least populated district. Most *Denisiens* live on river fishing and livestock breeding.

Retrace your steps back to Route de la Trace (N3) and continue on to Morne Rouge.

Morne Rouge ★

Many visitors use Morne Rouge as a starting point for exploring Montagne Pelée (see p 188). In fact, the mountain is so close that the district's 5,000 or so inhabitants are known as *Péléens*.

Up until the beginning of this century, the area now occupied by Morne Rouge was studded with beautiful residences belonging to wealthy inhabitants of Saint-Pierre.

Established as a *commune* (district) in 1888, Morne Rouge ceased to exist (administratively speaking) between 1902 and 1908, following Montagne Pelée's eruption on August 30, 1902, which took the lives of 1,500 people. It was wiped from the island's administrative map once again from October 1929 to May 1930, when threats of another eruption forced its inhabitants to evacuate the area.

The district, which is located at an altitude of 450 metres, is aptly named, as *morne* is an Antillean synonym for "hill" and the area's fertile volcanic soil is indeed red (*rouge*).

Morne Rouge is an important pilgrimage site in Martinique. Every year on August 30th, large numbers of believers flock to the **church**, which houses a magnificent **statue of Notre Dame de la Délivrande**, sculpted in Normandy. They then move on to the **Calvaire de la Délivrande**, listed as an historic monument since 1991. In this way, they pay homage to the Virgin, while dramatically evoking the memory of the catastrophe of August 30, 1902.

Trivia buffs will be interested to learn that Morne Rouge's town hall houses a bust believed to be the first **black Mar-**

ROUTE DE LA TRACE

ianne (the symbol of the French Republic).

While you're in the Morne Rouge area, pop over to the **Jardin MacIntosh** (see p 187) and the **Maison du Volcan** *(15F; Tue to Thu 9am to noon and 2pm to 4pm, Fri to Sun 9am to noon; ☎05.96.52.45.45)*, a small museum located in the centre of the village near the stadium.

Finally, it is worth noting that Chanflor mineral water, available all over the island, is bottled in the *commune* of Morne Rouge.

Ajoupa-Bouillon ★

The next stop is the other candidate for the "town-with-the-most-flowers" title, Ajoupa-Bouillon, which was supposedly named after one of the first colonists to settle in the area, a man named Bouillon, who built a makeshift shack here (in the language of the Arawaks, *ajoupa* meant a hut made out of branches).

The district is the island's largest in terms of territory (11,114 ha), but has one of the smallest populations. Its 1,700 inhabitants live on farming and, more importantly, raising river crayfish, a local speciality.

Make sure to take a look at the village's small baroque **church**, built in 1846. Originally nothing more than a simple chapel, it was later enlarged and improved upon — so well that it managed to survive both the hurricane of 1891 and the eruption of Montange Pelé in 1902. Its former bell-tower was replaced by the present one in the 1960s.

There are two remarkable natural sites in the area. The first, **Gorges de la Falaise ★**, lies on your left as you enter the village. After climbing over a few rocks, you'll discover a lovely waterfall. Secondly, you can head off on the **Les Ombrages floral and botanical trail ★**, which leads across the bottom and sides of a ravine with streams running through it. For more information, see "Parks and Beaches", p 187.

On the way out of the village, you can't miss **La Maison de l'Ananas** *(50F; ☎05.96.53.39.18 or 05.96.53.30.02)*. Indeed, within seven kilometres of this new attraction, you will notice signposts advertizing it every tenth of a kilometre. Guided tours of pineapple and banana fields in a four-wheel-drive vehicle are offered here. The one-day package includes a swim in the river, an introduction to fishing and a Creole meal for 450F per person.

Le Lorrain

After Ajoupa-Bouillon and its abudance of flowers, you'll reach the junction of the N3 and the N1. At this point, you can either turn left and continue on to the northernmost part of the island, or head right, towards Le Lorrain, less than five kilometres away.

Banana blossom

Le Lorrain, which is located at the end of a rough bay, was known in the past as Grande Anse. In 1680, a parish was established here, and in 1837, Le Lorrain was officially named a *commune*, or district. This is the heart of "banana country", and a large number of the district's 8,000 inhabitants rely on this fruit for their living.

Le Lorrain was the birthplace of Raphaël Confiant, author of numerous novels, including several written in Creole, and a number of important essays (*Éloge de la Créolité*, with Patrick Chamoiseau and Jean Barnabé). In 1994, his novel *L'allée des soupirs* was short-listed for the prestigious *Prix Goncourt*.

Behind the church, your eye will surely be drawn to the arresting **war memorial**, showing a French soldier from the First World War striking a casual pose. The work of an anonymous sculptor, this statue has a naive quality about it that gives it a great deal of charm. In 1993, however, its appearance was altered considerably; the pink-faced soldier standing so proudly alongside his guardian angel (symbolizing France) originally had black skin.

The **church**, for its part, houses a wooden bas-relief depicting Saint-Hyacinthe, the patron saint of the parish, as well as an amazing fountain once used as a baptismal font.

The town hall keeps a jealous watch over the **Marianne** in its courtyard. The statue was given to the *commune* by France in 1889, to mark the centennial of the French Revolution.

Heading back northwards, you'll pass the **ruins of three plantations** : Viré, on the left; Capot, on the right, where you can still make out the shape of the jail in which recalcitrant slaves were confined; and Chalvet, farther along on the left.

Basse-Pointe

A short distance before Basse-Pointe, there are two other noteworthy plantations. The first is **Habitation Pécoul**, which was built in the 18th century. The superb main residence is listed as an historic monument. The estate, however, is still privately owned and is therefore off-limits to tourists.

You'll have better luck farther on if you take the small road on the left to the **Plantation de Leyritz ★★**, which once belonged to Michel Leyritz (1681-1764). In the early 1970s, the former colonial plantation and its eight-hectare park were transformed into a top-notch tourist resort, including a hotel, a restaurant and a museum. In 1976, the plantation was the scene of an important summit meeting between American President Gerald Ford, British Prime Minister James Callaghan, West-German Chancellor Helmut Schmidt and French President Valéry Giscard d'Estaing.

On your tour of the estate, you'll see several remarkable examples of 18th century plantation architecture, such as the rum distillery, the cane mill with its paddle wheel, and the masters' quarters, which is decorated with superb mahogany furniture. Make sure not to miss the magnificent gardens, laid out in part by writer Joseph Zobel, author of *La Rue Cases-Nègres*, and an amateur of floral design.

Leyritz Plantation is also home to the one-of-a-kind **Musée des Poupées Végétales ★★** *(adults 15F, children 5F; every day 8am to 6:30pm; ☎05.96.78.53.92)*, literally a museum of plant dolls, where artist Will Fenton

ROUTE DE LA TRACE

displays his extraordinary dolls, made out of dried leaves and flowers and clothed in traditional or modern dress.

Past the plantation, you'll enter the village of Basse-Pointe, where the legendary Aimé Césaire, writer, poet and Deputy and Mayor of Fort-de-France since 1945, was born on June 21, 1913. Pineapple and banana crops support most of the district's 4,400 inhabitants, a large percentage of whom are of East Indian origin, descendants of the workers brought in to replace the blacks in the fields after slavery was abolished in 1848.

On your left as you leave the village lies the **Rhumerie JM** *(free visit and samples; Mon to Sat 7am to noon and 1pm to 4pm;* ☎*05.96.78.92.55)*, which produces a prestigious aged rum. Beyond the distillery, take the D10 north to Macouba.

Macouba

It won't take you long to reach the modest village of Macouba, which has 1,400 inhabitants. In the language of the Caribs, *macouba* designated a type of fish which was once common in the area. This little fishing village could hardly have a more appropriate name.

In 1694, the famous Père Labat, another legendary Martinican, became Macouba's parish priest.

The road soon becomes very narrow and plunges into the tropical forest. Crossing the **metal bridge** ★★ over the Rivière Potiche is bound to make you dizzy. You'll eventually reach what seems like the end of the line in Grand'Rivière.

Grand'Rivière ★★

This isolated village is unquestionably worth the trip. This is where the road stops, at the northernmost tip of the island, and where the fishermen's houses cling to cliffs plunging down into the choppy sea.

Other than the "end of the world" feeling, the reigning sense of peacefulness and the sight of fishermen braving the forbidding sea, Grand'Rivière has no tourist attractions as such, unless you count the lively and colourful **fish market**. Nevertheless, you won't regret a visit to this village and a chance to soak up some of its unique atmosphere.

  PARKS AND BEACHES

Balata

Jardin de Balata ★★★

A visit to the **Jardin de Balata** *(adults 35F, children 15F; every day 9am to 5pm;* ☎*05.96.64.48.73)*, a botanical garden in the hills of Fort-de-France, is an absolute must. Jean-Philippe Thoze spent 20 years landscaping the grounds of his grandmother's house. When this exotic garden was opened to the public in 1986, its first visitors were delighted to discover over 195 species of plants, trees and flowers. The grounds have been laid out in such a way as to afford spectacular views of the Pitons du Carbet, Ravine Didier and Fort-de-France. It will take you about an hour to explore the entire garden and the pretty Creole house nestled in its midst, which contains some lovely antique furniture.

Morne Rouge

Jardin MacIntosh

Jardin MacIntosh *(25F; Mon to Fri 9am to 4:30pm;* ☎*05.96.52.34.21)* is in fact an anthurium plantation, which was created in 1978 on the grounds of the Habitation Longchamps.

Anthurium

Ajoupa-Bouillon

Gorges de la Falaise ★

Gorges de la Falaise *(adults 20F, children 15F, guided tour 35F;* ☎*05.96.52.52.42 or 05.96.53.37.56)* is a park with essentially one hiking trail leading to a beautiful waterfall. Visitors are supplied with waterproof boxes for their camera equipment and can also rent non-slip shoes. As the trail passes through water of variable depth, it is only appropriate for those who know how to swim — and haven't forgotten their bathing suits.

Sentier Botanique et Floral Les Ombrages ★

On the **Sentier Botanique et Floral Les Ombrages** *(adults 15F, children 5F; every day 9am to 5pm;* ☎*05.96.53.31.90 or 05.96.53.32.87)*, which you'll find your way out of the village of Ajoupa-Bouillon, you'll see a wide variety of indigenous and imported trees, bushes and plants. This floral and botanical trail winds across the bottom and sides of a ravine to a superb Creole garden, and finally on to the ruins of a former distillery.

Le Lorrain

Le Lorrain's beach is big and has some attractive viewing areas, but the surf here is so heavy that swimming is almost always dangerous.

Grand'Rivière

Grand'Rivière's beach is pretty, too, dotted with fishermen's boats, but the relentlessly heavy surf also makes it unsafe for swimming.

 OUTDOOR ACTIVITIES

 Hiking

Circuit d'Absalon

The trail starts right after the *Jardin de Balata*, so you have to turn left on Route d'Absalon (D60) to reach the former spa of the same name.

Because it's easy and right near Fort-de-France, this trail is extremely popular. It makes a 4-kilometre loop through

ROUTE DE LA TRACE

the forest, which takes about two hours one way to hike.

Morne Césaire

A little farther north, Route de la Trace (N3), intersects with the Fond l'Étang forest road in a sort of hairpin turn to the right. Take the latter road for about one-kilometre, and you'll reach a parking lot that marks the beginning of the trail.

This is a two-kilometre trail of average difficulty, which should take you approximately two hours to cover (one way). It's a lovely walk through the rainforest, including a newly reforested area.

Trace des Pitons

This superb trail through the Pitons starts at the Colson Psychiatric Hospital, a little further north on the N3. It's a 5.3-kilometre loop, which ends at the firing range near the village of Colson.

This is a difficult trail, which takes at least 5 hours and 30 min to hike. You should not set out on it unless you are in excellent shape, as you'll have to climb all the way to the top of Piton Dumauzé (1,103 m) and then continue on towards Piton de l'Alma. At one point, the trail intersects with another, which leads to Piton Lacroix. As the trail is exhausting, you should set out early in the morning on a clear day and bring along food, water, sturdy shoes and a raincoat.

Plateau Boucher - Morne Piquet

Still farther north on Route de la Trace (N3), you'll reach Plateau Boucher, a grassy plain with houses on it.

This is the start of a difficult three-kilometre climb (one way; 3 hours) to the top of Piton Boucher (1,070 m). The trail affords some great views and a chance to familiarize yourself with the region's mountain vegetation. Set out early in the morning and don't forget to take along food, water, sturdy shoes and a raincoat.

Caplet - Fond-Saint-Denis

You'll find the starting point of this trail on the D1, about one-kilometre before the village of Fond-Saint-Denis on your way from Route de la Trace (N3).

This is a straight, easy path (4 km; 3 hours one way) leading to Caplet, in Morne-Vert. As it can be enjoyed by just about anybody, it's a good choice for a family outing.

Trace des Jésuites

Back on the N3, two kilometres past the Deux-Choux intersection, a small parking lot located immediately after a tunnel marks the starting point of the famous Trace des Jésuites, which ends at the D1, between Deux-Choux and Gros-Morne.

This is an easy five-kilometre (3 hours one way) trail offering all those who so desire, a chance to familiarize themselves with the luxuriant vegetation of the tropical rain forest — lianas, ferns, mosses, white gum trees, magnolias, philodendrons and orchids.

Montagne Pelée

The most direct route up Montagne Pelée is by way of the **Aileron** trail, which starts at the end of the road bearing the same name (D39), near the first shelter. To get there, turn left on

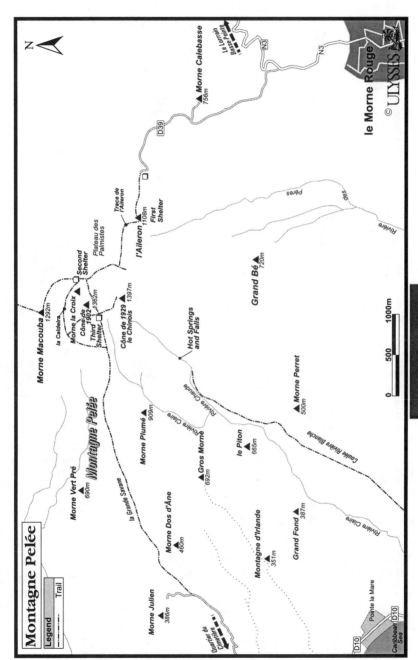

Montagne Pelée

Legend
▬ Trail

N

Morne Macouba
1292m

la Caldeira

Morne la Croix
Côneide 1362m
1902

Second
Shelter

Third
Shelter

Cône de 1929
le Chinois 1397m

Plateau des
Palmistes

Trace de
l'Aileron

l'Aileron
1108m
First
Shelter

Morne Calebasse
756m

D39

Le Lorrain
Basse-Pointe

N3

N3

le Morne Rouge

© ULYSSES

Montagne Pelée

Morne Vert Pré
690m

la Grande Savane

Morne Plumé
909m

Rivière Claire

Rivière Chaude

Hot Springs
and Falls

Grand Bé
720m

Rivière des Pères

Morne Perret
500m

Morne Julien
386m

Quartier du
Cimetière

Morne Dos d'Âne
460m

Gros Morne
692m

Montagne d'Irlande
351m

le Piton
665m

Grand Fond
387m

Coulée Rivière Blanche

Rivière Claire

Pointe la Mare

Caribbean
Sea

D10

D10

0   500   1000m

ROUTE DE LA TRACE

the D39 after the village of Morne Rouge (see p 183).

This is a very popular trail, but is nevertheless fairly challenging and fully deserves its "average difficulty" rating. You can't tackle it in rainy weather, as it's a winding trail and the soil is somewhat loose, but you probably wouldn't want to anyway, as the trail's main interest lies in the breathtaking views it affords.

After 2.5 kilometres (2 hours) of walking, you'll find yourself at an altitude of some 1,250 metres — about 430 metres higher than where you started. You'll reach the second shelter, which marks the starting point of another trail, the **Caldeira**, a difficult 2.5-kilometre hike which takes 2 hours and 30 min. After climbing down to the foot of Morne Lacroix, you'll start heading upwards again for 400 metre, to the top of the volcanic cone produced by the tragic 1902 eruption.

Finally, near the third shelter, there is a 500 metres trail leading to the top of the **Chinois**, another cone, which dates from 1929. The climb, of average difficulty, will take you about 30 minutes one way.

Carabin - Morne Jacob

Near the village of Le Lorrain, there is a trail that leads through a banana plantation, then tackles Morne Jacob (800 m). To reach the starting point, take the D22, on the east side of the village, and then a country road leading to Carabin.

This is a five-kilometre trail of average difficulty which will take you about three hours one way. Its main appeal lies in the striking view it commands of the Atlantic coast.

Savane Anatole via Désiles

This trail starts from the D10, one-kilometre past Macouba, near Nord Plage.

The path, which is easy, leads five-kilometres (2 hours and 30 min one way) across various farm to the Maison du Moine (monk's house), located on the Savane Anatole, where it intersects with the trail leading to Montagne Pelée via Grand'Rivière.

Montagne Pelée via Grand'Rivière

This is the only trail leading up the north face of Montagne Pelée. It is the longest (8 km; 4 hours and 30 min one way), but also the most gradual hike up the mountain. You can reach it from the D10, a short distance before Grand'Rivière.

This trail, which is of average difficulty, ends near the second shelter, where the Caldeira trail begins.

 River Rafting

On the way into **Grand'Rivière**, Carbet Caraïbe (☎*05.96.55.72.88*), which is also a restaurant (see p 194) organizes expeditions down the river with **Basalt**. All sorts of excursions are available, some including mountain biking and even bungee jumping.

 ACCOMMODATIONS

Morne Rouge

Martinique has but one youth hostel, the **Auberge de Jeunesse** (*Avenue Jean-Jaurès, Haut du Bourg - 97260 Morne Rouge, ☎05.96.52.39.81,*

Ulysses' Favourites

Accommodations

Charming hotels:
>   Plantation de Leyritz (Basse-Pointe, p 192)

For luxury:
>   Plantation de Leyritz (Basse-Pointe, p 192)

For history buffs:
>   Plantation de Leyritz (Basse-Pointe, p 192)

Restaurants

For the finest dining:
>   La Fontane (Balata , p 192)
>   Plantation de Leyritz (Basse-Pointe, p 194)
>   Yva Chez Vava (Grand'Rivière, p 194)

For the location:
>   Auberge de la Montagne Pelée (Morne Rouge, p 193)
>   Pointe Nord (Macouba, p 194)

For the romantic ambiance:
>   L'Abri (Ajoupa-Bouillon, p 193)

ROUTE DE LA TRACE

≈05.96.52.39.64), located at the foot of Montagne Pelée, in Morne Rouge. You can choose between rooms with one or two beds *(85F)*, and lodging in a four- to six-bed dormitory *(75F)*. Bedding costs 20F extra.

Ajoupa-Bouillon

In the flower-filled district of Ajoupa-Bouillon, you'll find a charming hotel, **L'Abri Auberge Verte** *(425 F; pb, ≈, ℜ; 97216 Ajoupa-Bouillon, ☎05.96.53.33.94, ≈05.96.53.32.13)*. A family-run establishment, it has a dozen rooms and is located at the heart of a lush estate. You can relax alongside the swimming pool, in the midst of an orchard, drinking in the stunning

setting and inhaling the heady fragrance of the flowers. The owners also organize horseback riding excursions on the grounds of their estate, to give visitors a chance to see their farmland and the facilities for the breeding of fighting cocks. On the down side, the cocks wake up early, so bring earplugs if you want to sleep in. Also, the welcome is not always the warmest.

Le Lorrain

South of town, **La Sikri** *(150 F-210 F, ℜ; 97214 Le Lorrain, ☎05.96.53.81.00, ≈05.96.53.78.73)*, a *relais créole*, is a modern house with a few rooms on its second floor. It lies in the heart of the Martinican countryside, in a region covered with banana plantations. Somewhat out of the way, in the Quartier Étoile, this place is most notable for its tranquil atmosphere.

Basse-Pointe

🏨 If you're looking for luxury, head to the **Plantation de Leyritz** *(380-430 F; tv, ≡, pb, ≈, ℜ; 97218 Basse-Pointe, ☎05.96.78.53.92, ⌐05.96.78.92.44)*. In 1970, the former plantation, which had belonged to Michel Leyritz, was converted into a prestigious tourist centre. Today, the complex includes a 50-room hotel, a restaurant and a museum. The grounds also contain the ruins of the plantation itself. About 20 of the hotel's rooms are in bungalows; the loveliest are in the larger buildings, however, and each is decorated with mahogany furniture, complete with a large canopy bed. To get to the Plantation de Leyritz, take the D21 to the left, a little before the village of Basse-Pointe.

Grand'Rivière

There are two noteworthy hotel- restaurants in Grand'Rivière. The first, on your way in, is **Le Chanteur Vacances** *(220F; ℜ; 97216 Grand-Rivière, ☎05.96.55.73.73)*, which is hidden amidst the narrow streets of this charming village, and will make you feel as if you're taking part in the daily life of the 1,000-or-so people who live here. The pleasant rooftop terrace affords a nice view of the sea. The rooms, for their part, are small and modest.

Farther on, take a right immediately after the tourist office (*syndicat d'initiative*), and you'll find yourself at **Tante Arlette** *(200 F; ℜ; ☎05.96.55.75.75)*, a similar, but sim-

pler establishment located in the heart of the village.

 RESTAURANTS

Balata

🏨 **La Fontane** *(250F; closed Sun and Mon; 4 km from Fort-de-France on Route de Balata; ☎05.96.64.28.70 or 05.96.64.65.89)*, a gourmet restaurant located in the hills above Fort-de-France, is worth a trip. In fact, it's almost worth going just to see the colonial setting and old-style furnishings. Try the citrus fruit *méli-mélo* with crab, followed by the lamb with *cèpes* (wild mushrooms) or the duck with fruit. Top it all off with a *giraumon* flan.

Fond-Saint-Denis

In the little village of Fond-Saint-Denis, good restaurants are hard to find. One notable exception is the **Auberge du Mont Béni** *(185F; every day for lunch only; on the D1 between Fond-Saint-Denis and Saint-Pierre, ☎05.96.55.82.42)* where delicious crayfish with coconut and good goat stew are served.

Morne Rouge

If you're planning on doing your own cooking, you might want to stop at the **Champion grocery store**, located on the way into town, on the left.

For a quick bite to eat, head over to **Le Refuge de l'Aileron** *(every day 8am to 6pm, ☎05.96.52.38.08)*, the little snack bar at the beginning of the hiking trail that leads up Montagne Pelée. Other options include **Le Gîte Péléen**, a

Maison du Bagnard with Rocher du Diamant in the distance –
Martinique in a postcard. - *Office du Tourisme de la Martinique*

Domaine de la Pagerie near Trois Îlets, birthplace of Marie-Josèphe Rose Tasher de la Pagerie, who would later become Empress Josephine, wife of Napoleon I.
- *C. Hervé-Bazin*

Round Yawl Regattas, a typically Martinican sport.
- *Ekta First*

snack bar set right in the heart of the village, and **Le Bambou** *(open only for lunch; ☎05.96.52.39.94)*, on the south edge of town.

Another economical choice is **Barbecue du Nord** *(100F; Rue Schœlcher, ☎05.96.52.44.98)*, whose daily menus run between 35F and 100F.

On the road to Saint-Pierre, you will find **L'Amandier** *(100F; closed Sat and Sun evening; on the N2, between Morne Rouge and Saint-Pierre, ☎05.96.52.33.29)*, a pleasant place that serves homestyle Creole cuisine in a pretty little stone house.

The restaurant in the **Auberge de la Montagne Pelée** *(180F; every day for lunch only; Route de l'Aileron, ☎05.96.52.31.40 or 05.96.52.32.09)* is initially appealing because of its spectacular location at an altitude of 800 metres, with the awe-inspiring silhouette of the volcano towering in the background. The food is very good, as well as inexpensive. Two dishes of particular note are the filet of fish with seafood and the *belle Créole* leg of lamb. The place has been undergoing extensive renovations in the last few years, and only the restaurant was open at press time.

Ajoupa-Bouillon

L'Universium *(☎05.96.53.35.71)*, located in the centre of the village is a good place to grab a quick bite to eat before continuing your tour of northern Martinique.

If, on the other hand, you'd like to linger over a good meal in a romantic setting surrounded by flowers, try **L'Abri** *(150F; open for lunch only; in the Sance quarter, in the northeast part of the village, ☎05.96.53.33.94)*, the

Auberge Verte's restaurant (see p 191). The dining room is located inside the former warehouse of a plantation now devoted to market and subsistence gardening and pineapple growing. Remember that the house speciality is crayfish fricassee, and make sure to top off your meal with a coconut dessert.

Le Lorrain

There are two places to purchase what you need to make your own meals, a tiny grocery store opposite the church and a supermarket on the north edge of town.

If you're in the mood for a sandwich, the **Délifrance** chain has a shop *(1321 Rue Joseph-Clerc)* in Le Lorrain.

The best place to eat in Le Lorrain, however, is the **Relais des Isles** *(150F; closed Sun; ☎05.96.53.43.85)*, just north of town. It serves innovative Creole cuisine, including several wonderfully prepared crayfish dishes.

Set in the midst of a banana plantation just south of town, **La Sikri** *(200F; closed Sun; ☎05.96.51.81.00)* is an unpretentious place where you can enjoy delicious Creole cuisine. In keeping with the rural character of this region, the vegetables are grown in greenhouses behind the inn.

Basse-Pointe

You'll find a good little restaurant right in the heart of the village of Basse-Pointe, **Chez Mally** *(80F; open for lunch only; Ruelle Saint-Jean, ☎05.96.78.51.18)*. It would be a shame not to taste the *pâté en pot*, chicken *colombo* or home-made jams.

ROUTE DE LA TRACE

Another noteworthy option is **Le Petit Palais** *(150F; closed Sun evening; Place Félix-Éboué, ☎05.96.78.52.20)*. With dishes like *coquille de crabe, langouste grillée* and *fricassée de lambis*, this is the perfect place for seafood addicts.

🦐 But the big draw for curious visitors in Basse-Pointe is the **Plantation de Leyritz** *(120F; Route D21, ☎05.96.78.53.92)*. You won't be disappointed, because in spite of the impressive setting, the prices are extremely affordable. Start with a banana coquille, then move on to the fish with basil *en papillote* and top it all off with a seasonal fruit charlotte. See also p 192.

Macouba

🦐 About two kilometres past the village of Macouba, on your way to Grand'Rivière, you'll spot **Pointe Nord** *(160F; closed Mon and evenings; Route D10, ☎05.96.78.56.56)*, a gem of a restaurant located in the ruins of an old distillery. Go for lunch, as the place is usually closed in the evening. You can sit on their raised terrace or take a table below, in the Relais Vert, which serves complete meals for 85F.

Grand'Rivière

For something quick and simple, there are two nice little places in Grand'Rivière to choose from. The first is **Le Bout du Bout**, a snack bar, and the second is the counter at **Floup-Floup** *(☎05.96.55.71.60)*. At the latter, which is located near the end of the main street, on the left, a charming woman in traditional dress will offer you delicious coconut ice cream, fresh fruit juice and *accras*.

The beautiful, spacious dining room of the **Chanteur Vacances** *(80F; open for lunch and with reservation in the evening; ☎05.96.55.73.73)*, has a simple beauty, in a hotel-restaurant hidden away in the narrow streets of the village. Top billing on the extremely affordable menu goes to the crayfish.

You can't miss **Le Carbet Caraïbe** *(140F, ☎05.96.55.73.11)*, located just outside the village of Grand'Rivière. The bill of fare includes chicken or grilled fish for 79F, as well as a delectable crayfish fricassee. Guests also get to enjoy a superb view of the sea. As if to cover all the bases, there is even a souvenir shop on the premises.

Turn right after the tourist office to reach **Tante Arlette** *(160F; ☎05.96.55.75.75)*, which also serves crayfish, in a large room with rows of tables draped with pink and white cloths.

🦐 Grand'Rivière's most renowned restaurant, however, is **Yva Chez Vava** *(180F; open for lunch and with reservations for dinner; Avenue du Général-de-Gaulle, ☎05.96.55.72.72 or 05.96.55.72.55)*, which you'll spot easily on your way into the village. The restaurant, owned by Vava and her daughter Yva, has built itself an almost legendary reputation by serving excellent crayfish and rock lobster dishes made according to old recipes handed down by fishermen. In 1992, the owners' efforts to keep Martinique's culinary heritage alive were richly rewarded when Gault Millau (a French high-class culinary guide) awarded their restaurant a gold key, thus classing it among the finest French restaurants in the world.

SHOPPING

It would be almost criminal to leave the region without buying some flowers, be they anthuriums, heliconias, cannas or roses. You can do so at several places, including **Plantation MacIntosh** *(☎05.96.52.34.21)* in Morne Rouge and **Jardins de l'Ajoupa** *(☎05.96.53.32.10)* in Ajoupa-Bouillon.

ROUTE DE LA TRACE

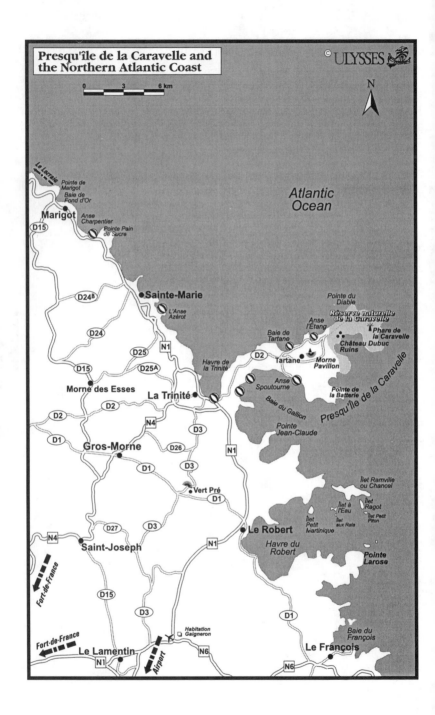

Presqu'île de la Caravelle and the Northern Atlantic Coast

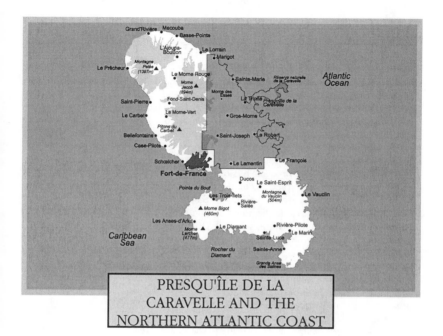

The Presqu'île de la Caravelle, which juts out into the Atlantic like a giant breakwater, stretches so far out from the rest of the island that it has developed a character all its own. In French, "presqu'île" means literally, "almost an island". *"The result is a sober landscape, etched by the wind, aloof as a group of monks living in bitter solitude. Retreating out into the waves, Caravelle has, as it were, cut itself off from the luxuriance of the moist land"*. These are the words Patrick Chamoiseau uses to describe the peninsula, whose landscape, with its sheer cliffs, sparse vegetation and jagged coastline, is unique in Martinique. The following tour will take you to this extraordinary place, which was once a haven for smugglers, and guide you across the peninsula from west to east and back again. You'll crisscross the farmland in the interior of the island, through fields of sugar cane and banana plantations.

Also, in the heart of *"béké* country", you'll discover Le Robert and its magnificent bay, which shelters a string of little islands. You'll then head back up the northern Atlantic coast, all the way to Marigot, passing through bustling villages and drinking in breathtaking views of the sea as it gets rougher and rougher.

This area, formerly known as Cabesterre, bears traces of the last war in which the Carib Indians ever took part. It was around 1660 when the French colonists finally decided to take over this stretch of land along the Atlantic coast. Throughout his term as governor, Jacques du Parquet had taken the utmost care to maintain friendly relations with the Amerindians and thereby avoid bloody confrontations, which he believed would hinder the development of the fledgling French colony. However, shortly after his death in 1658, the tide turned and the colonists planned an invasion, and then a massacre.

The raid on Cabesterre started out from Saint-Pierre. The various missionary orders on the island were engaged in a sort of race to establish parishes, and the Dominicans, moving outward from the interior, were outstripping the Jesuits, whose strategy of gaining territory by way of the sea was not an effective one. There was only one basic rule – first come, first served. Accordingly, the Dominicans managed to occupy the entire northern Atlantic coast, from La Trinité to Grand'Rivière, which they proceeded to develop.

It was at this point that one of the most colourful figures in the history of Martinique, Père Jean-Baptiste Labat, entered onto the scene. An explorer, historian, soldier (he successfully countered English attacks), builder and inventor rolled into one, this missionary marked the history of the northern Atlantic coast. He was parish priest of Macouba in 1694 and founded the parish of Le Robert the same year. Then, between 1696 and 1705, he worked on revitalizing Habitation Fond Saint-Jacques, revolutionizing the way in which rum was produced and thus establishing Sainte-Marie as a shining example for other Dominican territories to follow. Today, you can visit the former plantation, which has been admirably restored.

FINDING YOUR
WAY AROUND

By Car

From Fort-de-France, take the *Route Nationale* 1 (N1) from Boulevard du Général-de-Gaulle, in the direction of Le Lamentin. Continue on the N1, following the signs for Le Robert. This road runs all the way up the northern Atlantic coast, as far as Marigot, our destination, and beyond. The only time you'll have to leave it is to explore the magnificent Presqu'île de la Caravelle by means of the *Route Départementale* 2 (D2). You'll return to Fort-de-France on the D15, which crosses Morne des Esses, and then the N4, which you'll pick up near Gros-Morne.

If you're starting from the southern part of the island (Trois-Îlets, Le Diamant, Sainte-Anne), take the N5 toward Le Lamentin. You'll be able to pick up the D3 on your way around a traffic circle located near the airport. This road leads to the N1, which will take you toward Le Robert.

Car Rentals

The major international car rental companies have counters at Lamentin Airport. Please see p 38 for a complete list.

Here are a few rental agencies located in other districts:

Le Robert
Tropicar: ☎05.96.65.39.65 or 05.96.65.39.66.

Tartane
Caravelle, ☎05.96.58.68.95.
Thrifty: Baie du Galion, ☎05.96.58.02.22.

La Trinité
Discount: ☎05.96.58.51.63.
Tropicar: ☎05.96.58.26.81.

Sainte-Marie
Europcar: Hôtel Primerêve, ☎05.96.69.21.09.

? PRACTICAL INFORMATION

Le Lamentin

Hospital: Hôpital du Lamentin, Boulevard Fernand Guilon, ☎05.96.57.11.11.

Police: ☎05.96.51.16.34.

Town hall: ☎05.96.51.41.59, ✆05.96.51.67.88.

Banks:
BNP, 67 Rue Ernest-André, ☎05.96.51.15.53.
Crédit Agricole, Place d'Armes, ☎05.96.51.13.13.

Pharmacies:
Pharmacie Georges Bonnes, 54 Rue Ernest-André, ☎05.96.51.12.88.
Pharmacie Éliane Monan, 5 Rue Emma-Forbas, ☎05.96.57.10.21.

Le Robert

Tourist office: in the town hall, ☎05.96.65.10.05 or 05.96.65.75.47, ✆05.96.65.47.31.

Police: ☎05.96.65.10.16.

Town hall: ☎05.96.65.10.05, ✆05.96.65.13.10.

Banks
BRED, Masarde Catalogue, ☎05.96.65.17.41.
Crédit Martiniquais, Rue Schœlcher, ☎05.96.65.13.76.

Pharmacies:
Pharmacie Emmanuel Nossin, 24 Rue Courbaril, ☎05.96.65.04.32.
Pharmacie Gina Gaillard, 30 Rue Schœlcher, ☎05.96.65.15.81.

Laundry: Laverie Top Net, ☎05.96.65.17.18.

La Trinité

Tourist office: ☎05.96.58.69.98, ✆05.96.58.70.07.

Police: ☎05.96.58.20.13.

Town hall: ☎05.96.58.20.12, ✆05.96.58.48.46.

Hospital: Centre Hospitalier Général, Louis-Domergue, Route du Stade, ☎05.96.66.46.00.

Pharmacies:
Pharmacie Renée Cirba, 5 Rue Joseph-Lagrosillière, ☎05.96.58.21.51.
Pharmacie Rose-Marie Éloidin, 2 Rue Joseph-Lagrosillière, ☎05.96.58.23.94.

Bank: BNP, ☎05.96.53.21.55.

Sainte-Marie

Tourist office: ☎05.96.69.13.83, ✆05.96.69.40.62.

Police: ☎05.96.69.30.09.

Town hall: ☎05.96.69.30.06, ✆05.96.69.03.05.

Banks:
BNP, Rue Schœlcher, ☎05.96.69.31.62
Crédit Agricole Mutuel, Centre Commercial Lassalle, ☎05.96.69.22.44.
Crédit Martiniquais, Petit Bourg, ☎05.96.69.29.18.

Pharmacy: Pharmacie Claude Édouard, 81 Rue Schœlcher, ☎05.96.69.30.37.

Gas stations: Esso and Totale near the Distillerie Saint-James.

CARAVELLE & NORTHERN ATLANTIC

Marigot

Tourist office: ☎05.96.53.62.07, ≈05.96.53.65.10.

Town hall: ☎05.96.53.50.03 or 05.96.53.50.09, ≈05.96.53.54.83.

Pharmacy: Pharmacie Danièle Venkatapen, ☎05.96.53.51.15.

Morne des Esses

Pharmacy: Pharmacie Germaine Durpes, ☎05.96.69.91.80.

Gros-Morne

Tourist office: ☎05.96.67.60.73, ≈05.96.67.94.87.

Police: ☎05.96.67.53.70

Town hall: ☎05.96.67.50.11, ≈05.96.67.68.64.

Bank: Crédit Agricole Mutuel, 8 Avenue Jules-Ferry, ☎05.96.67.50.35.

Pharmacy: Pharmacie du Marché, 6 Avenue Jules-Ferry, ☎05.96.67.58.63.

Saint-Joseph

Tourist office: Rue Séphora-Louis-Félix, ☎05.96.57.88.95, ≈05.96.57.60.04.

Police: ☎05.96.57.88.95.

Town hall: ☎05.96.57.60.06, ≈05.96.57.60.04.

Bank: Crédit Agricole Mutuel, 2 Rue Ernest-Deproge, ☎05.96.57.66.61.

Pharmacy: Pharmacie Suzette Cadignan, Rue Eugène-Maillard, ☎05.96.57.62.74.

 EXPLORING

Le Lamentin

Like Schœlcher to the west, Le Lamentin is almost a continuation of Fort-de-France. This eastern suburb, however, plays an essentially industrial role. Though most of its enterprises are concentrated in the Lézarde industrial park, the area is also home to a large refinery and an international airport.

Despite all this, one should remember that Le Lamentin, with a population of 30,000, is the second largest city in Martinique. It was named after large sea mammals, manatees, that once inhabited the mouth of its canal. Though the area only became a *commune*, or district, in 1837, there had been a parish alongside the Rivière Lézarde (the longest river on the island at 35 km) since 1688.

Geared as it is toward industry, Le Lamentin has little in the way of tourist attractions. It is something of a crossroad, with routes leading to the northern Caribbean coast via Fort-de-France, to the southern part of the island and to the northern Atlantic coast, the area explored in this chapter. Nevertheless, the **Église Saint-Laurent** is worth a look for its lovely stained glass windows, which are officially part of the national heritage. Apparently, a number of local notables figure in the scenes depicted. Other places of interest include the **Maison de la Culture** *(☎05.96.51.15.33)*, which hosts a variety of exhibitions, the **horse racing track**, and, in the middle of a plain covered with sugar cane, the **Rhumerie**

La Favorite *(free tour and rum-tasting; Mon to Fri 9am to noon and 2pm to 4pm; Lamentin's old road, ☎05.96.50.47.32)*, which markets both white and aged rums, as well as Maman Doudou punches. **La Lorraine**, the Martinican beer advertised all over the island, is also brewed in Le Lamentin.

Right near the racecourse is a brand-new attraction: **La Ferme de Perrine** *(30F; everyday 9am to 5pm; ☎05.96.57.17.16)*, an animal park where you can observe farm animals and a few of their wild counterparts while enjoying a little picnic.

Then, on the road leading to Le Robert, you will soon notice a series of whitewashed buildings on the right. These are the slave huts of the former **Habitation Gaigneron ★**, which line one of the best-preserved black-slave cabin streets in the entire French West Indies. Unfortunately, this site is off-limits to visitors, though you can get a good look at it from the street.

Le Robert ★

After Le Lamentin, the N1 winds through sugar cane and banana plantations, leading you to a spectacular view of the Atlantic Ocean, straight ahead. At this point, you'll head into a large village known as Le Robert on a small street leading right to its lovely **church**, which has a blue bell tower and is flanked by a pretty **cemetery** all in white.

This town of nearly 18,000 inhabitants looks out on one of the most beautiful bays in Martinique, the **Havre du Robert ★★**, which is eight kilometres long and five kilometres wide and seems to have its access guarded by a series of little islands – Îlet Ramville or

Chancel, the largest not only of the group, but perhaps in all of Martinique, aided by Îlet Ragot, Îlet à l'Eau, Petite Martinique, Îlet aux Rats, Petit Piton, Îlet des Chardons and Îlet Larose, also known as Îlet Madame.

The parish was established in 1694, by the illustrious Père Labat. In *Nouveau Voyage aux Îles de l'Amérique*, (New Voyage to the Islands of America) he describes the area as follows: *"This is one of the most beautiful natural harbours imaginable, able to accommodate any size of fleet so comfortably that even the largest vessels can cast anchor in many places..."*

In 1809, Admiral Villaret-Joyeuse was forced to surrender to the English when they succeeded in invading Martinique via Le Robert and stealing across the island all the way to Fort-de-France.

Immediately after the disastrous obliteration of Saint-Pierre in 1902, the qualities of this "natural harbour" became the subject of a detailed study. At the time, there was discussion of building a large eastern port to replace the one that had just been destroyed. These plans, however, were never carried through.

On the waterfront, by the big landing stage, you can take a brief stroll on pleasant, grassy **Place du 22 mai 1848**. From here, you might have a chance to see some *yoleurs* in action.

Also located on the waterfront, where it was moved when the market was renovated, is the charming **Fontaine du Robert**, with its swans, scallop shells and colourful water-lilies.

On the way out of town, you can't miss the unusual round building of the **Collège Paul-Symphor**, on the left.

CARAVELLE &
NORTHERN ATLANTIC

From Le Robert, we strongly recommend that you head over to **Vert-Pré**, less than five kilometres away on the D1. Though this hamlet is at the very most 300 metres above sea level, it offers a stunning view of Presqu'île de la Caravelle and the Baie de Trinité to the north, as well as the entire Plaine du Lamentin to the southwest.

Presqu'île de la Caravelle ★★★

Head north once again on the N1. Just before entering the village of La Trinité, bear right on the D2. Shortly before doing so, you will pass the **Usine du Galion**, the only Martinican sugar refinery still in operation. The D2 leads into the extraordinary world of Presqu'île de la Caravelle, with its breathtaking landscape of peaceful little beaches and sheer cliffs plunging into an emerald sea (see "Parks and Beaches," p 206).

After about four kilometres, a road on the right leads to the beach at **Anse Spoutourne**, on the south side of the peninsula, and **Morne Pavillon**, a small hill which offers a delightful view of the area.

Farther on, the D2 will take you straight to a charming fishing village named **Tartane ★★**, this time on the north side of the peninsula, where you'll find another lovely swimming beach. You can also visit the **Rhumerie Hardy** *(free tour and samples; every day 8:30am to 1pm and 2pm to 7pm; ☎05.96.58.20.82)*, which produces white, pale and aged rums.

The brand new, imposing **Hôtel La Baie du Galion** (see p 210) stands on the hill overlooking the church. It is surprising to find such a large, elegant hotel in an area where up until very recently there were nothing but small establishments. This 150-room giant is a clear indica-

tion of how interested developers are in promoting the tourism industry on Presqu'île de la Caravelle.

Beyond the big point marking the eastern extremity of the Baie de Tartane, the road climbs into the hills, offering a spectacular view of **Anse l'Étang ★★** down below. Then, at your leisure, you can head down to the sea, where you'll discover yet another gorgeous beach. Tartane's Village Vacances Familles resort is nestled right nearby.

Farther along, **Anse Bonneville**, an amazing black sand beach, lies hidden behind the trees.

The D2 comes to an end soon after the entrance of the **Réserve Naturelle de la Caravelle ★★** (see p 206). At this point, you'll have to continue on foot to the **ruins of Château Dubuc ★★** *(15F; Mon to Sat 8:30am to noon and 2:30pm to 5:30pm, Sun 8:30am to noon)*, located in the heart of an enormous estate founded by the Dubuc de Rivery family sometime around 1770. In fact, back in the 18th century, the family owned almost the entire peninsula. In addition to cultivating sugar cane, the Dubucs were involved in various activities that enabled them to put their business skills and isolated location to use, such as smuggling slaves and merchandise in and out of the British West Indies.

According to legend, one of the members of this turbulent family, the pretty Aimée Dubuc, was kidnapped at sea and sold to the Turks. She later became the Sultan of Constantinople's mistress and bore him a son, Mahmud II.

Today, you can wander among the remnants of these bygone days, including the main residence, the jails, some of which were used for slaves, the ox-mill and the lime kiln. There is also a small museum, which houses the various objects found during recent archaeological digs.

One of the many hiking trails that crisscross the nature reserve (see p 206) will take you to the **Phare de la Caravelle**, a lighthouse dating from 1861, which commands a remarkable view of the peninsula's bays.

La Trinité

Back on the main part of the island, you'll enter the bustling village of La Trinité, passing a little **beach** on your way. Later, you can stroll down the elegant promenade, built between 1989 and 1993, that runs along the waterfront. It stretches the entire length of the village and is studded with monuments, handsome lampposts and kiosks, where you can take refuge from the blazing sun.

La Trinité is the island's northern subprefecture. It has 11,000 inhabitants, who live on agriculture (sugar cane, bananas, pineapples and vegetables), fishing and stock-breeding. The village's origins date back to 1678, when the site upon which it stands was established as a parish.

Bring all the patience you've got for the frustrating drive through La Trinité on a narrow, crowded road. Once you've survived this ordeal, head toward Sainte-Marie, the next town on our tour.

Sainte-Marie

Sainte-Marie is another sizeable (20,000 inhab.), dynamic town bustling with activity. It is the largest and most prosperous agricultural centre (producing bananas and other fruits, sugar cane and vegetables) in the northern part of the island. Other sources of income include cattle breeding, food processing and the growing craft industry in the hamlet of **Morne des Esses** (see p 205).

Founded in 1658, Sainte-Marie is the oldest parish on the northern Atlantic coast. Today, a large, graceful blue **church** dominates the village's silhouette. At low tide, you can walk all the way to the cross atop **Îlet Sainte-Marie**, the little island just in front. From there, you can enjoy a charming view of the town and its recently revamped **waterfront**. Be careful, though, because the tide rises very quickly.

As you leave the village, make sure to stop at the **Distillerie Saint-James** ★★ *(free tour and samples; Mon to Fri 9am to 5pm, Sat and Sun 9am to 1pm; ☎05.96.69.30.02)*. Originally founded in the hills of Saint-Pierre, this rum distillery was moved to its present location after the eruption of Montagne Pelée in 1902. Saint-James makes an excellent pale rum and several liqueurs. More importantly, though, you can buy yourself a century-old bottle of aged rum here.

In the distillery's **Musée du Rhum** ★, you can learn about the history of sugar cane cultivation from 1765 to present day. The display, which is set up in a charming Creole house, includes old machinery, etchings, tools and various other objects. Furthermore, The **Espace France-Antilles Magazine** art gallery has just been laid out on the second floor.

The road to the Musée du Rhum also leads to the **Musée de la Banane** *(30F; every day 9am to 5pm; ☎05.96.69.45.52)*, a banana museum attractively set up in the very heart of an authentic banana plantation, the Habitation Le Limbé, which is still in operation. This recently built museum covers every aspect of this other important staple of Martinique's agricultural production. You will learn about both the various stages of banana cultivation and the different varieties of this fruit found on the island. You can also take a pleasant stroll on the grounds, about a four-hectare park surrounding a beautiful Creole house.

Less than two kilometres north, you'll reach the next stop on our tour, **Habitation Fond Saint-Jacques ★★★ *(15F; Mon to Sat 9am to 5pm; ☎05.96.69.10.12)*,** which is located in a remarkable setting. The Dominicans built this plantation sometime around 1660 on land left to them by Marie du Parquet, widow of Governor Jacques du Parquet. It was during this period that the French invaded this region, at the time inhabited by the Caribs and known as Cabesterre. The Caribs were completely wiped out, marking the end of Amerindian civilization in Martinique.

Between 1696 and 1705, Père Jean-Baptiste Labat took control of the *habitation*. In addition to making the estate a not only viable but prosperous enterprise, Père Labat – an engineer, architect, industrialist, historian and scientist – invented a copper still, which improved the distillation process. Under his iron rule, Habitation Fond Saint-Jacques became the most advanced industrial centre in Martinique, a shining example for others to follow.

During the French Revolution, Fond Saint-Jacques became state property, and in 1948, it fell under the jurisdiction of the *Département*. The year 1968 marked the signing of an agreement by which the Université de Montréal, in Québec, Canada, undertook the restoration of the estate, and the plans were subsequently carried through to a successful conclusion. The Conseil Général de la Martinique thus hoped to transform this important part of the island's national heritage into one of northern Atlantic coast's leading centres of activity. Since 1988, extensive archeological digs have been conducted on the property. There is even talk about the discovery of a large slave cemetery. Keep your ears open for more information.

Among the buildings that have been restored, you'll see the **chapel**, erected in 1688 and rebuilt in 1769, the **kitchens** and the **warehouses**. You can also take a leisurely stroll through the **botanical gardens**, laid out between the **ruins** of such structures as the **mill**, the **aqueduct** and the **purgery**, a fine example of ship's-hull construction, another of Père Labat's ideas.

Marigot

Farther on, the N1 runs alongside **Anse Charpentier** and its attractive white sand beach (no swimming allowed), heralded by the **Pain de Sucre** (80 m), (a geological formation similar to the Sugar Loaf in Rio de Janeiro). Immediately after, you'll enter the small but elegant village of Marigot, with its profusion of flowers.

The village, built in the form of an amphitheatre facing the water, offers some lovely, sweeping views of the ocean. For example, from the **town hall**, which is surrounded by flowers and overlooks the sea, you can drink in the spectacular sight of the turbulent waters of the **Baie de Fond d'Or**.

Historians all agree that the present site of the *commune* of Marigot was once the Arawak capital. Later, in 1663, after driving out the Caribs who did the same to the Arawaks beforehand, the French settled here and established the parish of Marigot.

Most of the district's 3,500 inhabitants earn their living by fishing and, more importantly, cultivating eggplants, avocados and bananas, as well as breeding poultry and crayfish.

Morne des Esses

To return to Fort-de-France, get on the D15 on your way out of Marigot. You can then stop at Morne des Esses, a hamlet in the district of Sainte-Marie.

Make sure to stop at the local basket weavers' cooperative, **La Paille Caraïbe** ★★ *(free admission; Mon to Fri 8:30am to 12:30pm and 1:30pm to 5pm, Sat 8:30am to 12:30pm; ☎05.96.69.83.74)*. In the workshop, you can watch skillful artisans making various types of baskets, vases, wastebaskets, and hats out of two different types of straw, *cachibou* and *aroman*, using a Carib weaving technique.

Supposedly, these weaving and dyeing techniques have survived to the present day because the Caribs taught them to runaway black slaves hiding in the area.

Gros-Morne

The N4 intersects with the D15, which leads slightly northeast again, to the village of Gros-Morne ("Big Hill"), located in a large rural district with over 10,000 inhabitants. Its name, as you've probably already guessed, refers to its location atop a hill 240 metres high. Almost exclusively devoted to agriculture (subsistence farming, market gardening and the cultivation of sugar cane, bananas and pineapples), it is the "stronghold of Martinican peasantry."

Despite this impressive title, the inhabitants of Gros-Morne have long been the victims of a stupid, nasty brand of humour. In short, Martinicans make the same kind of tasteless jokes about the Gros-Mornais as Canadians do about "Newfies". This mockery apparently dates back to the French Revolution, when royalist settlers in the south clashed with the merchants of Saint-Pierre, who were fervent republicans. Gros-Morne became a meeting place for members of the royalist resistance. These counter-revolutionaries joined forces with the English in 1794, thus enabling Britain to take over the island again until 1802. According to some, the relentless caricaturing of the Gros-Mornais can be traced back to this bitter feud.

You can visit the village's lovely **church** which houses three altars and a Communion table, all made of marble, and the **Distillerie Saint-Etienne** *(free visit and samples; Mon to Fri 7am to noon and 1pm to 3:30pm; ☎05.96.57.62.68)*, also interesting for the view it offers of the pineapple plantations, which seem to stretch all the way to the ocean.

Saint-Joseph

Retrace your steps until you reach Saint-Joseph, another agricultural district, which has a population of 14,000. Here, too, the main crops are bananas, sugar cane and pineapples, but local inhabitants also cultivate vegetables and what must be a thousand types of flowers (anthuriums, roses, carnations, hibiscuses, bougainvilleas and chrysanthemums).

Less than five kilometres past Saint-Joseph, you'll find yourself back in Fort-de-France.

PARKS AND BEACHES

Presqu'île de la Caravelle

Anse Spoutourne (A)

This beach, lapped by gentle waters, lies on the southern coast of the peninsula. In 1977, the Parc Naturel Régional de la Martinique (PNRM) was established here, with facilities for sailing and tennis.

Plage de Tartane ★★ (A)

This charming beach stretches almost the entire length of the village. The water is sometimes of dubious quality near the hamlet, so you're better off heading to the easternmost part of the beach, known as Hardy La Brêche, where the sea is crystal-clear.

Facilities: Picnic tables; numerous fish restaurants.

Anse l'Étang ★★ (A)

This is another enchanting beach, lined with *raisiniers* and bathed by turquoise waters. This is where Tartane's Village Vacances Familles resort is located.

Facilities: Snack bar; picnic tables; miniature golf.

The Réserve Naturelle de la Caravelle ★★

In 1976, 422 hectares of the easternmost section of the peninsula were set aside as a nature reserve (☎05.96.64.42.59). It is managed by the *Parc Naturel Régional de la Martinique* (PNRM), which is responsi-

ble for both protecting and developing it.

The park has a few hiking trails (see below), which enable you to familiarize yourself with the various plant species in the dry forest and the mangrove swamp. You can catch your breath along the way at Château Dubuc and the Caravelle lighthouse.

La Trinité

The Beach Near the Bourg (B)

As you enter the village from the south, you'll pass a rather lovely little beach. The quality of the water, however, is somewhat variable. As Presqu'île de la Caravelle is so close, it is better to persevere to Anse Spoutourne, Tartane or Anse l'Étang.

Sainte-Marie

Anse Azérot ★★ (C)

This is the last bathing beach on the northern Atlantic coast. Farther north, the sea seems to be perpetually agitated, and the pounding surf makes swimming an altogether foolhardy idea.

Facilities: Pedal boats, windsurfers and jet-skis may be rented at the nearby Primerêve hotel.

OUTDOOR ACTIVITIES

Hiking

La Pointe de la Caravelle

The Office Nationale des Fôrets (O.N.F.) has recently redesigned the hiking trails that wind through the Caravelle nature reserve. Now there are two well-marked and easy-to-find trails.

The first is the **short trail** (follow the white and yellow markers), an easy loop that can be covered in an hour and a half, allowing you to explore the remarkable flora consisting mainly of mangrove swamp trees. Wooden footbridges make this expedition accessible to everyone, and without the risk of getting wet.

The **long trail** (white and blue markers), for its part, first follows the small trail before veering off toward the tip of the peninsula. It runs through the dry forest, the savannah and the mangrove swamp. The trail also offers hikers exceptional views of the surrounding jagged-cliff coast. It takes about 3.5 hours to complete this loop, which can also be rated as easy.

Both these hikes start off at the parking lot, a short distance past the park's entrance, near the Château Dubuc ruins. Make sure you bring plenty of bottled water and a hat, for a good part of the way is devoid of shade.

Morne Bellevue

From Gros-Morne, take the D1 toward Deux-Choux to reach the starting point of this trail, which gives visitors a chance to explore the rain forest and also offers beautiful, sweeping views of the Atlantic coast.

The trail is fairly long (14 km there and back) and requires a total of eight hours of walking. If you are in a group, however, you can avoid the return trip by leaving a second car at the end of the trail, on a forest road leading to Morne des Esses. This is an easy walk; all you have to worry about is protecting yourself from the sun in open areas.

Rabuchon

You can reach this pleasant path by way of Saint-Joseph. To do so, take Route de la Durand (near the stadium), which leads to the forest around Rivière Blanche. The trail lets you explore the rainforest and also affords lovely views of Fort-de-France and the Baie des Flamands.

This is an easy eight-kilometres walk forming a loop, which will take you about three hours. Many people combine this outing with a picnic at the Cœur Bouliki rest area, which has tables, shelters and playing fields.

  Sailing and Scuba Diving

If you'd like to explore the coral reefs and the islets in magnificent **Havre du Robert**, you should contact a company by the name of Passeport pour la Mer (☎05.96.67.55.54, ⇎05.96.67.55.56), which specializes in helping visitors do just that. They arrange catamaran excursions, which leave from the landing stage at Le Robert. In the course of the outing, you'll see a re-enactment of Aimée Dubuc's experiences at Pointe Royale, go scuba diving, explore the islets, learn how to pilot a round yawl and enjoy a *ti-punch*. The excursion lasts from 9am to 4:30pm, and rates run about 400F per person.

You can also set out on an excursion with Escapade Tour (☎05.96.70.58.54 or 05.96.71.58.77) from the landing stage in **Le Robert**. Outings are organized on Tuesdays, Fridays and Saturdays, and include a visit to the islets, the mangrove swamp and the *fonds blancs*. The trip, which lasts the whole day (9am to 4:30pm) and includes one meal, costs 270F per person.

Another option is a long-distance coastal catamaran ride aboard the *De Deux Choses Lune*, which also leaves from the **Le Robert** marina (opposite Biométal). Count on spending 395F per person for the day, which includes exploring the *fonds blancs* (high white-sand bars far out to sea), isles and the mangrove swamp, as well as an aperitif and lunch. Departure at 9:30am every morning. Reservations: ☎05.96.45.54.46 (ask for Véronique).

Another, less elaborate way of exploring the **islets off Le Robert** is to ask the owner of a small boat to take you out and give you a custom tour. If this option appeals to you, try contacting Monsieur Hugues Nomel *(☎05.96.65.16.50)* or Monsieur Jean Baptiste *(☎05.96.65.45.47)*.

If you're in the mood for something different, try renting an "aqua-home", which will provide you with a place to stay where you can enjoy the sea at the same time. These floating houses have four cabins, each able to accommodate two people. Once again, the company to contact, Aqua Location *(☎05.96.65.47.17, ⌐05.96.51.52.69)*, is located in Le Robert.

A place in the vicinity of **Tartane** for scuba-diving enthusiasts: Atlantic Reef, at Anse Spoutourne *(☎05.96.58.08.26)*.

Sea Kayaking

Another way of exploring the magnificent **Le Robert** bay is by sea kayak. If you're interested, contact the Les Kayaks du Robert association *(☎05.96.65.33.89)*.

ACCOMMODATIONS

Le Lamentin

An attractive *gîte* can be found in Lamentin, belonging to **Mme Sonia Billard (no. 136, ¦¦¦)** *(2,285F per week; independent unit, Quartier Bois Rouge - 97232 Le Lamentin)*.

Martinique Cottages *(340-420F; tv, pb, K; 97232 Le Lamentin, ☎05.96.50.16.08 or 05.96.50.16.09, ⌐05.96.50.26.83)* is another good place to stay in the area. Each of the eight bungalows in this miniature vacation village has its own veranda and looks out on either the swimming pool or an attractive garden.

Located half-way between the airport and Fort-de-France, the **Hôtel de la Galleria** *(595F; tv, ≡; 97232 Le Lamentin, ☎05.96.50.94.00, ⌐05.96.50.91.89)* is in the shopping centre of the same name. The hotel boasts 24 sizeable and very comfortable rooms, a few of which are equipped with kitchenettes. Ideal for businesspeople.

Le Robert

Two *gîtes* in Le Robert are worth mentioning; one belonging to **M. Yvon Églantine (no. 064, ¦¦)** *(1,550F per week; below the owner's residence; Mansarde-Catalogne - 97231 Le Robert)*, and the other to **M. Carl Osenat (no. 112, ¦¦¦¦)** *(3,300F per week; independant unit; Quartier Sable Blanc - 97231 Le Robert)*.

On the road leading from Le Robert to Le François (D1), on the left, you'll spot an extremely attractive little hotel with wooden doors. This is the **Hôtel-**

Ulysses' Favourites

Charming hotels:
- Saint-Aubin (La Trinité, p 211)
- Habitation Lagrange (Marigot, p 211)

For the welcome:
- Paradiles (Tartane, p 210)
- Madras Hôtel (Tartane, p 210)

For luxury:
- La Baie du Galion (Tartane, p 210)
- Primerêve (Sainte-Marie, p 211)

For history buffs:
- Habitation Lagrange (Marigot, p 211)

For the tropical garden:
- Le Manguier (Tartane, p 210)
- Habitation Lagrange (Marigot, p 211)

For the view:
- Caravelle Panoramique (Tartane, p 209)
- La Baie du Galion (Tartane, p 210)

For businesspeople:
- Hôtel de la Galleria (Le Lamentin, p 208)

Restaurant Le Miramar *(250F; tv, ≡, pb, ℜ; ☎05.96.65.39.65, ⇌05.96.71.09.20)*, a two-floor hotel with about 20 rooms, some of which even have a terrace with a view of the sea.

The 12 rooms and apartments of the **Hôtel Beauséjour** *(250F; ≡, K; Chemin Bois Désir - 97231 Le Robert, ☎05.96.65.40.62, ⇌05.96.65.47.94)* are located inside two lovely buildings surrounded by greenery.

A short stay on a houseboat can be a lot of fun. **Aqua Location** *(B.P. 113 Parc de la Semair - 97231 Le Robert, ☎05.96.65.46.40, ⇌05.96.51.52.59)* rents out "aqua-homes", a type of catamaran able to accommodate up to eight people. Don't worry if you don't have any sailing experience; a sailor will take a little boat out to meet you and move your aqua-home wherever you like.

Presqu'île de la Caravelle

Overlooking the sea, just after the village of Tartane, lies the aptly-named **Caravelle Panoramique** *(400-490F; pb, K; Tartane, 97220 La Trinité, ☎05.96.58.07.32, ⇌05.96.58.07.90)*, which rents fully equipped studio apartments. You can relax on the hotel's terrace and gaze out at the peninsula's extraordinary landscape long enough to make sure you never forget it.

The **Village Vacances Familles de Tartane** *(330F per night, 2,500F per week; pb, K; ☎05.96.58.03.83)* is in fact located a little farther east, at Anse l'Étang. Not far from the beach, you'll find about 40 modest little houses sprinkled across a hill.

For those who enjoy a pastoral setting, the charming little **Paradiles** *(380-460F; ≡, pb, ≈, K; Tartane - 97220 La Trinité, ☎05.96.58.66.90, ⌐05.96.58.29.67)* stands on a hill overlooking the Hardy distillery. Its new owners have made several changes here since the fall of 1993. It now has 12 studios (2,600F per week for 2 to 6 people) and six rooms located around an attractive swimming pool. Present your *Ulysses Travel Guide Martinique* and receive a 10% discount.

 Around the last bend in the road before reaching the village of Tartane, you will come face to face with the **Madras Hôtel** *(320-390F; tv, ℜ; Tartane - 97220 La Trinité, ☎05.96.58.33.95, ⌐05.96.58.33.63)*, an attractive, all-white building adorned with pretty green and white awnings. Ask for a room facing the sea, since the coast is beautiful here. The hotel has a pleasant restaurant laid out on a terrace overlooking the sea (see p 214), so it is a good idea to opt for the modified American plan (room, breakfast and one other meal for 550F to 650F).

Another appealing spot in Tartane, this time on Morne Pavillon, is **Le Manguier** *(520F; tv, ≈, pb, K, ℜ; Lot Morne Pavillon - 97220 La Trinité, ☎05.96.58.48.95, ⌐05.96.58.27.58)*, whose dazzling white buildings house about twenty studios. To top it all off, there is a small swimming pool surrounded by a garden full of exotic plants.

There are a few "vacation villages" around the beach at Anse l'Étang. Given their proximity to the sea, these places offer families an interesting alternative to the large resorts in the south. Don't be discouraged by their exorbitant daily rates, since you can obtain a substantial discount if you plan on staying a little longer. One such option, located near the Mini-Golf Beach Club snack bar (see p 213), is the **Caribou** *(500F; pb, ≡, K; 97220 La Trinité, ☎05.96.58.09.40, ⌐05.96.58.03.72)*, whose rows of triangular yellow and white bungalows make for a strange sight.

Farther away, but in the same category, the **Village de Tartane** *(700F; pb, ≡, ≈, K, ℜ; Tartane - 97220 La Trinité, ☎05.96.58.06.33, ⌐05.96.58.03.91)* is a series of 59 modern bungalows built around a small swimming pool and a restaurant.

 The brand new beige and white **La Baie du Galion** *(860-940F; pb, tv, ≡, ℜ; Tartane - 97220 La Trinité, ☎05.96.58.65.30, ⌐05.96.58.25.76)* stands on a hill overlooking the village church in Tartane. It is remarkably large and chic for this area, where there were nothing but small establishments up until very recently. With its 150 elegantly laid-out rooms, it stands head and shoulders above the rest of the hotels on Presqu'île de la Caravelle, in the same way it literally dominates the countryside. Its splendid swimming pool, which ends in a waterfall, is a sight not to be missed, along with the lovely restaurant (Le Surcouf) overlooking it. The rooms are decorated with superb mahogany furniture, and some have kitchenettes on the balcony. Tennis courts are also available for guests' enjoyment.

A new hotel was in the works below La Baie du Galion as we were passing

Habitation Lagrange

through (March 1998). **La Goélette**, the establishment in question, is to comprise 40 suites.

La Trinité

There is one noteworthy *gîte* in the area that belongs to **Mme Ginette Vergison (no. 048, ⁉)** *(1,820 per week; in the owner's residence; Brin d'Amour - 97220 La Trinité).*

The extraordinarily romantic and charming **Saint-Aubin** *(480-580F; ≡, pb, ≈; 97220 La Trinité, ☎05.96.69.34.77, ⇆05.96.69.41.14)* is located in a beautiful colonial house with a veranda running all the way around. The stunning view of the Baie de Trinité and Presqu'île de la Caravelle will simply take your breath away. To reach this magnificent pink residence, which appears to be floating on a sea of flowers, you have to head out of the village toward Sainte-Marie, and take the little road on the right.

Sainte-Marie

At Anse Azérot, a little south of the village of Sainte-Marie, you'll find a magnificent new hotel complex called **Primerêve** *(630-1,020F; tv, ≡, pb, ≈, ℜ, K; Anse Azérot - 97230 Sainte-Marie, ☎05.96.69.40.40, ⇆05.96.69.09.37).* With over a hundred rooms in lovely pastel-coloured bungalows, this is a sort of hillside vacation village surrounded by lush tropical vegetation. A staircase leads right down to the beach.

Marigot

Habitation Lagrange *(1,500-2,000F; ≡, pb, ≈, ℜ; 97225 Le Marigot, ☎05.96.53.60.60, ⇆05.96.53.50.58),*

CARAVELLE & NORTHERN ATLANTIC

is one of the most elegant spots on the island. A fabulous exterior, superb period furniture, fresh flowers in all the rooms and suites – the place is absolutely exquisite. The main residence of this former plantation is surrounded by several colonial-style outbuildings. There, in the midst of a magnificent tropical garden, is where you'll find this charming hotel's 18 gorgeous rooms. To reach this idyllic spot, located in the heart of the jungle, you have to drive for about a kilometre along a bumpy road flanked on one side by a little river and on the other by ponds used for breeding crayfish.

Morne des Esses

If you're looking for peace and quiet, try one of Monsieur and Madame Patrick Duchel's *gîtes*, **Les Z'Amandines (nos. 179-182)** *(1,520F per week; four units in two independent buildings; Quartier Saint-Laurent, Morne des Esses - 97230 Sainte-Marie)*, well located on a hillside in a very restful area.

Gros-Morne

There are several *gîtes* in the district of Gros-Morne. The one belonging to **Mme N. Perez de Carvasal (no. 96,** ¦¦¦**)** *(1,805F per week, independent unit; Quartier Croix Girin - 97213 Gros-Morne)* is appealing because of its location alongside a farm.

Saint-Joseph

This pleasant farming village is graced with an absolutely charming *gîte*, which belongs to **M Lucien Bercy (no. 79,** ¦¦¦**)** *(1,860F per week, independent unit; Chapelle, 97212 Saint-Joseph)*.

Habitation Belle Étoile *(350 F; tv, ≡, ≈, ℜ; Route du Stade - 97212 Saint-Joseph,* ☎*05.96.57.62.62,* ⌐*05.96.57.85.57)* is a large, three-story building with about 20 plain but comfortable rooms. You can also look forward to eating well here, as the hotel's restaurant, Aux Fruits de Mer (see p 215), has a long-standing reputation for quality.

RESTAURANTS

Le Lamentin

You can enjoy a relatively inexpensive meal in Le Lamentin at one of the restaurants in the La Galleria shopping centre. You might try the little pizzeria, **Pizza Plus** *(100F; closed Sun;* ☎*05.96.50.40.22)*; or the **Food Circus** *(100F; closed Sun;* ☎*05.96.50.62.50)*, whose owners had the interesting idea of combining a variety of food counters, offering guests a choice of Mexican, Creole and Chinese food, as well as spaghetti, ribs and hamburgers.

La Plantation *(250-350F; closed Sat afternoons and Sun;* ☎*05.96.50.16.08)* is another good restaurant, where Creole *nouvelle cuisine* has been elevated to an art form. In a luxuriant setting, you can savour a yellow banana and foie gras millefeuille, followed by pork tenderloin with green pepper or lamb with garlic cream sauce. Sweet dreams are guaranteed...

Le Robert

There are all sort of places in Le Robert where you can buy your own food, starting with the **market** opposite the town hall. Right nearby, you'll find a **8 à huit**.

Ulysses' Favourites

For the finest dining:
    La Plantation (Le Lamentin, p 212)
    La Madras (Tartane, p 214)
    Le Colibri (Morne des Esses, p 215)
    Habitation Lagrange (Marigot, p 214)

For the lively ambiance:
    Mini-Golf Beach Club (Anse L'Étang, p 215)

For authentic Creole cuisine:
    Le Colibri (Morne des Esses, p 215)
    Aux Fruits de Mer (Saint-Joseph, p 215)

For the terrace:
    Le Don de la Mer (Tartane, p 214)

If you want to grab a quick bite, you can't go wrong with **La Yole Bleue** *(every day 7am to 11pm;* ☎*05.96.65.53.18)*, a beachfront creperie-pizzeria.

Chez Fofor *(250F; closed Sun evening and Mon;* ☎*05.96.65.10.33)*, situated below the village, near the landing stage, is a pleasant place to stop. For 75F per person, you can enjoy a lunch of cod *accras*, grilled ribs or fish court-bouillon. For dinner, the cost is about 250F per person. The restaurant has an attractive second-floor terrace, which is decked with flowers and offers a lovely view of the Baie du Robert.

Finally, for a quick bite to eat on the road between Le François and Le Robert, head to the pizzeria in the **Miramar** *(125F; every day noon to 10pm, closed Sat for lunch and Sun evenings;* ☎*05.96.65.39.65)*, a hotel-restaurant. The restaurant turns into a piano bar every Friday and Saturday evening.

Presqu'île de la Caravelle

Tartane is a fishing village, so there is plenty of fresh fish to be bought on the beach.

You can also enjoy a delicious, inexpensive meal just a few steps away from the lovely beach at Anse l'Étang – just take a seat on the terrace at the **Mini-Golf Beach Club** *(60F; open daily;* ☎*05.96.58.62.90)* and treat yourself to a mouth-watering pizza.

Another economical option is **Ti-Carbet** *(*☎*05.96.58.37.52)*, a snack bar set up inside a hut made of branches, located near the parking lot of the Hardy La Brèche beach (at the east end of the Plage de Tartane).

At the entrance to the village of Tartane, right next to the Madras Hôtel (see p 210) and opposite the basketball court, you can enjoy reasonably priced fare under the awning at **Banga Snack** *(60F)*, where grilled chicken, burgers and sandwiches are served with a smile.

LE & TLANTIC

The village of Tartane also boasts the seaside **Le Dubuc** restaurant *(100F)*. Until just recently, this eatery was tough competition for its neighbour, La Guinguette. Not anymore, however, as the owner of the latter has since packed his bags and set up shop opposite the Hardy La Brêche beach, on the site of the former Hardy rum distillery. His establishment now bears the name **Kalicoucou** *(100F)*, which dishes out grilled meats, pizzas and crepes.

Le Don de la Mer *(120F; closed Fri pm, ☎05.96.58.26.85)*, with its attractive second-floor terrace, is on a slightly higher level – both literally and figuratively. Its menu alone should be enough to convince you: sea urchin *vol-au-vent*, *soudons* in spicy sauce, rock lobster fricassee and flambéed pineapple.

At the entrance to the Caravelle nature reserve, the former Barbacoa has been replaced by **Le Trésor** *(150F)*, a restaurant which features savoury Creole cooking.

Right below the Caravelle Panoramique hotel at Anse l'Étang, you'll find an interesting restaurant by the name of **La Mandarine** *(250F; closed Wed; ☎05.96.58.00.13)*. The shark with sweet cider, just one of the original dishes on the menu, is bound to pique your curiosity.

At the entrance to the village of Tartane, and overlooking the beach, **Le Madras** *(250F; open daily; ☎05.96.58.33.95)*, which is also a 13-room hotel, teams French cuisine with Creole gastronomy. A mere glance at the menu will prove to you what a fruitful alliance this is – sautéed *escargots à la poulette* (a sauce made of butter, egg yolks and a bit of vinegar); rock lobster ravioli and seafood bisque, turtle stew, duck with morel mush-

rooms, iced almond nougat, etc. Barbecue beach parties Fridays and Saturdays. On Sundays, musicians perform on the spot at lunchtime (between 1pm and 3pm).

La Trinité

On the village's main street, facing the sea, you will find a **MATCH supermarket** and, right nearby, the local **market**.

Sainte-Marie

In the Musée du Rhum (see p 203), **Le Saint-James** *(160F; every day lunch and supper with reservation, closed Sun; ☎05.96.69.07.33)* offers guests the option of sitting indoors, in its pretty dining room, or outside on its large terrace. A 60F daily special and a 90F set menu are always available. Among the dishes listed on the menu, the filet of red snapper and crayfish bisque are particularly delicious.

Extremely popular with Martinicans, the aptly named **La Découverte** *(200F; every day for lunch and dinner by reservation; ☎05.96.69.44.04)*, or the discovery, lies hidden in the middle of the forest a few kilometres past the village, on the way to Marigot. It is indeed a lovely surprise. You will savour succulent, classic Creole cuisine; the seafood couscous is a real standout.

The **Habitation Lagrange** *(400F; ☎05.96.53.60.60)* offers diners a gourmet feast in one of the most elegant settings in Martinique. The former *maison de maître* now houses a charming hotel (see p 211) whose French-and-Creole gourmet restaurant is one of the best on the island.

Morne des Esses

 Le Colibri *(250F; closed Mon;* ☎*05.96.69.91.95)* will win your heart with its creative Creole cuisine and gorgeous, sweeping view. *Buisson* of river crayfish in a bush, sucking-pig, sea urchin in scallop shells, *christophine* soufflé and more; the chef's imagination seems limitless.

Saint-Joseph

 Aux Fruits de Mer *(150F; closed Sun pm and Mon;* ☎*05.96.57.62.99)*, the restaurant in the Habitation Belle Étoile, deserves its reputation for quality. The menu lists such dishes as sea urchin with cocktail sauce, turtle steak and rock lobster. You can taste much of what's available by ordering the seafood platter, which includes crayfish, crab, clams, *chatrous* and rock lobster.

 ENTERTAINMENT

In the region covered in this chapter, there are a few discotheques where you can kick up your heels until the wee hours of the morning: **Le Palace** *(*☎*05.96.50.26.90)* in Le Lamentin, **Le Top** *(*☎*05.96.58.61.43)* in La Trinité, and the **Gaoulé Live Club** *(*☎*05.96.69.13.06)*.

Those who'd like to show off their singing talent will be pleased to learn that Le Lamentin has a karaoké bar, the **Karaoke Café** *(*☎*05.96.50.07.71)*.

On Presqu'île de la Caravelle, people often get together on Saturday night at the **Mini-Golf Beach Club** *(*☎*05.96.58.62.90)* in Anse L'Étang, where a *zouk* band sets the beat.

There is a movie theatre in La Trinité: **L'Eden** *(Rue Fernand-Clerc,* ☎*05.96.58.20.35)*.

The **Centre Culturel Départemental de Fonds Saint-Jacques** *(*☎*05.96.69.10.12)*, in Sainte-Marie, also presents concerts, exhibitions and other shows.

 SHOPPING

With 100 stores,. Martinique's largest shopping centre, **La Galleria** *(Mon to Thu 9am to 8:30pm, Fri and Sat 9am to 9pm, closed Sun;* ☎*05.96.50.66.63)*, is in Le Lamentin. Accessible via the N1, between Le Lamentin and Fort-de-France.

Make sure to stop at **Tilo** *(Mon to Sat 8am to 6pm, closed Sun;* ☎*05.96.51.25.25)*, a craft studio located on the N1, between Le Lamentin and Le Robert. Over the years, this place has become somewhat of a Martinican institution, as far as souvenirs are concerned. You'll find t-shirts, skirts, shirts, beach towels, tablecloths, etc., all made of exquisite printed fabrics.

In Le Robert, on the same street as the town hall, to the left of the church and the market, you will find the **Bijouterie-Papeterie-Librairie Omer Legros** *(*☎*05.96.65.23.00)*, an attractive shop, which, as its name indicates, sells jewellery, stationery and books.

The hamlet of Morne des Esses, in the district of Sainte-Marie, owes its reputation to **La Paille Caraïbe** *(free admission; Mon to Fri 8:30am to 12:30pm and 1:30pm to 5pm, Sat 8:30am to noon;* ☎*05.96.69.83.74)*, an extraordinary basket-weaving workshop.

CARAVELLE & NORTHERN ATLANTIC

MARTINICAN GLOSSARY
see also p 52.

Ajoupa	The Arawak term for a hut made of branches.
Anse	A bay, usually with a beach.
Arawaks	A peaceful indigenous people; the island's first inhabitants.
Béké	A white person, usually a landowner, born in the West Indies (a Caucasian Creole).
Biguine	A traditional, suggestive West Indian dance.
Câpre, Câpresse	The offspring of one black parent and one mulatto parent.
Caribs	An warlike, cannibalistic indigenous people, who came to the island after the Arawaks.
Carbet	The Carib term for the largest hut in the village, where meetings were held.
Carême	The dry season (from December to May).
Case	A small, traditional house.
Caye	A reef.
Coolies	Labouers from India, who came to the island after slavery was abolished.
Creole	Anyone, regardless of ancestry, born in the Antilles.
Doudou	A term of endearment, meaning "dear".
Fonds blancs	Large sand bars protected by coral reefs, where the water is barely one-metre deep.
Gommiers	Small fishing boats traditionally made out of gum trees using a Carib technique.
Habitation	A plantation, or agricultural property.
Hivernage	The rainy season (from June to November).
Îlet	A small island.
Madras	A scarf with large checks or stripes; the traditional head-dress of West Indian women.

Mangrove	A coastal swamp containing mangrove trees.
Marrons	The word used to designate black slaves who had escaped from their master's plantation.
Métros	Citizens of metropolitan France working in the Antilles.
Morne	A hill.
Mulâtre	Mulatto; the offspring of one black parent and one white parent.
Négritude	A term invented by Aimé Césaire to designate black culture as a whole, in an effort to give a new meaning to the word *"nègre"* ("Negro").
Pitt	A cockfighting arena.
Quadrille	Traditional dance in which a caller tells participants which moves to make.
Quarteron	A quadroon; the offspring of one white parent and one mulatto parent.
Quartier	A hamlet or neighbourhood.
Quimbois	Superstitions associated with herbal medicine, sorcery and magic.
Raisinier	A Seagrape tree, a small tree with round, waxy leaves, often found along beaches.
Savane	Savanna; a grassy expanse.
Senne	Seine; a large fishing net that requires several boats.
Ti-baume	A kind of bush commonly found on the Caribbean coast.
Ti bo	A kiss.
Trace	A path in the woods or mountains.
Yole	Yawl; a boat used for competitive sailing.
Zombi	Zombie; an evil nocturnal spirit.
Z'oreilles	Derogatory term for the continental French; literally "ears".

ENGLISH-FRENCH GLOSSARY

GREETINGS

Hi (casual)	*Salut*
How are you?	*Comment ça va?*
I'm fine	*Ça va bien*
Hello (during the day)	*Bonjour*
Good evening/night	*Bonsoir*
Goodbye, See you later	*Bonjour, Au revoir, à la prochaine*
Yes	*Oui*
No	*Non*
Maybe	*Peut-être*
Please	*S'il vous plaît*
Thank you	*Merci*
You're welcome	*De rien, Bienvenue*
Excuse me	*Excusez-moi*
I am a tourist.	*Je suis touriste*
I am American (m/f)	*Je suis Américain(e)*
I am Canadian (m/f)	*Je suis Canadien(ne)*
I am British	*Je suis Britannique*
I am German (m/f)	*Je suis Allemand(e)*
I am Italian (male/female)	*Je suis Italien(ne)*
I am Belgian	*Je suis Belge*
I am Swiss	*Je suis Suisse*
I am sorry, I don't speak French	*Je suis désolé(e), je ne parle pas*
Do you speak English?	*français*
What is your name?	*Parlez-vous anglais ?*
My name is...	*Quel est votre nom?*
friend (m/f)	*Je m'appelle...*
single (m/f)	*ami(e)*
married (m/f)	*celibataire*
divorced (m/f)	*marié(e)*
widower/widow	*divorcé(e)/veuf(ve)*

DIRECTIONS

Is there a tourism office near here?	*Est-ce qu'il y a un bureau de tourisme près d'ici?*
Where is...?	*Où est le/la ... ?*
straight ahead	*tout droit*
to the right	*à droite*
to the left	*à gauche*
beside	*à côté de*
near	*près de*
here	*ici*
there, over there	*là, là-bas*
into, inside	*à l'intérieur*
outside	*à l'extérieur*
in front of	*devant*
behind	*derrière*

GETTING AROUND

airport	*aéroport*
on time	*à l'heure*
late	*en retard*
cancelled	*annulé*
plane	*l'avion*
car	*la voiture*
train	*le train*
boat	*le bateau*
bicycle	*la bicyclette, le vélo*
bus	*l'autobus*
train station	*la gare*
bus stop	*un arrêt d'autobus*
corner	*coin*
neighbourhood	*quartier*
square	*place*
tourist office	*bureau de tourisme*
bridge	*pont*
building	*immeuble*
safe	*sécuritaire*
fast	*rapide*
baggage	*bagages*
schedule	*horaire*
one way ticket	*aller simple*
return ticket	*aller retour*
arrival	*arrivée*
return	*retour*
departure	*départ*
north	*nord*
south	*sud*
east	*est*
west	*ouest*

CARS

for rent	*à louer*
a stop	*un arrêt*
highway	*autoroute*
no passing	*défense de doubler*
no parking	*stationnement interdit*
no exit	*impasse*
parking	*stationnement*
pedestrians	*piétons*
gas	*essence*
traffic light	*feu de circulation*
service station	*station-service*
speed limit	*limite de vitesse*

MONEY

bank	*banque*
credit union	*caisse populaire*
exchange	*change*

money	*argent*
I don't have any money	*je n'ai pas d'argent*
credit card	*carte de crédit*
traveller's cheques	*chèques de voyage*
The bill please	*l'addition, s'il vous plaît*
receipt	*reçu*

ACCOMMODATIONS

inn	*auberge*
youth hostel	*auberge de jeunesse*
bed and breakfast	*gîte*
hot water	*eau chaude*
air conditioning	*climatisation*
accommodation	*logement, hébergement*
elevator	*ascenseur*
bathroom	*toilettes, salle de bain*
bed	*lit*
breakfast	*déjeuner*
bedroom	*chambre*
pool	*piscine*
floor (first, second...)	*étage*
high season	*haute saison*
off season	*basse saison*
fan	*ventilateur*

SHOPPING

open	*ouvert(e)*
closed	*fermé(e)*
How much is this?	*C'est combien?*
I need...	*J'ai besoin de...*
a store	*un magasin*
a department store	*un magasin à rayons*
the market	*le marché*
salesperson (m/f)	*vendeur(se)*
the customer (m/f)	*le / la client(e)*
to buy	*acheter*
to sell	*vendre*
t-shirt	*un t-shirt*
skirt	*une jupe*
shirt	*une chemise*
pants	*des pantalons*
jacket	*un blouson*
blouse	*une blouse*
shoes	*des souliers*
sandals	*des sandales*
hat	*un chapeau*
eyeglasses	*des lunettes*
handbag	*un sac*
gifts	*cadeaux*
local crafts	*artisanat local*
sun protection products	*crèmes solaires*

cosmetics and perfumes	*cosmétiques et parfums*
camera	*appareil photo*
film	*pellicule*
records, cassettes	*disques, cassettes*
newspapers	*journaux*
magazines	*revues, magazines*
batteries	*piles*
watches	*montres*
jewellery	*bijouterie*
gold	*or*
silver	*argent*
precious stones	*pierres précieuses*
wool	*laine*
cotton	*coton*
leather	*cuir*

MISCELLANEOUS

big, tall (person)	*grand(e)*
small, short (person)	*petit(e)*
short (length)	*court(e)*
low	*bas(se)*
fat (person)	*gros(se)*
slim, skinny (person)	*mince*
a little	*peu*
a lot	*beaucoup*
something	*quelque chose*
nothing	*rien*
good	*bon*
bad	*mauvais*
more	*plus*
less	*moins*
big	*grand*
small	*petit*
hot	*chaud*
cold	*froid*
I am ill	*je suis malade*
pharmacy, drugstore	*pharmacie*
I am hungry	*j'ai faim*
I am thirsty	*j'ai soif*
What is this?	*Qu'est-ce que c'est?*
Where?	*Où?*

WEATHER

rain	*pluie*
clouds	*nuages*
sun	*soleil*
It is hot out	*Il fait chaud*
It is cold out	*Il fait froid*

ENGLISH-FRENCH GLOSSARY

TIME

When?	*Quand?*
What time is it?	*Quelle heure est-il?*
minute	*minute*
hour	*heure*
day	*jour*
week	*semaine*
month	*mois*
year	*année*
yesterday	*hier*
today	*aujourd'hui*
tomorrow	*demain*
morning	*le matin*
afternoon	*l'après-midi*
evening	*le soir*
night	*la nuit*
now	*maintenant*
never	*jamais*
Sunday	*dimanche*
Monday	*lundi*
Tuesday	*mardi*
Wednesday	*mercredi*
Thursday	*jeudi*
Friday	*vendredi*
Saturday	*samedi*
January	*janvier*
February	*février*
March	*mars*
April	*avril*
May	*mai*
June	*juin*
July	*juillet*
August	*août*
September	*septembre*
October	*octobre*
November	*novembre*
December	*décembre*

COMMUNICATION

post office	*bureau de poste*
air mail	*par avion*
stamps	*timbres*
envelope	*enveloppe*
telephone book	*bottin téléphonique*
long distance call	*appel outre-mer*
collect call	*appel collecte*
fax	*télécopieur, fax*
telegram	*télégramme*

ACTIVITIES

swimming	*la baignade*

beach	*plage*
scuba diving	*la plongée sous-marine*
snorkelling	*la plongée-tuba*
fishing	*la pêche*
sailing	*navigation de plaisance*
windsurfing	*la planche à voile*
bicycling	*faire du vélo*
mountain bike	*vélo tout-terrain (VTT)*
horseback riding	*équitation*
hiking	*la randonnée pédestre*
museum or gallery	*musée*
cultural centre	*centre culturel*
cinema	*cinéma*

TOURING

river	*fleuve, rivière*
waterfalls	*chutes*
viewpoint	*belvédère*
hill	*colline*
garden	*jardin*
wildlife reserve	*réserve faunique*
peninsula	*péninsule, presqu'île*
south/north shore	*côte sud/nord*
town or city hall	*hôtel de ville*
court house	*palais de justice*
church	*église*
house	*maison*
manor	*manoir*
bridge	*pont*
dam	*barrage*
workshop	*atelier*
historic site	*lieu historique*
train station	*gare*
stables	*écuries*
convent	*couvent*
door, archway, gate	*porte*
customs house	*douane*
locks	*écluses*
market	*marché*
canal	*canal*
seaway	*voie maritime*
museum	*musée*
cemetery	*cimitière*
mill	*moulin*
windmill	*moulin à vent*
hospital	*Hôtel Dieu*
lighthouse	*phare*
barn	*grange*
waterfall(s)	*chute(s)*
sandbank	*batture*
neighbourhood, region	*faubourg*

ENGLISH-FRENCH GLOSSARY

NUMBERS

1	*un*
2	*deux*
3	*trois*
4	*quatre*
5	*cinq*
6	*six*
7	*sept*
8	*huit*
9	*neuf*
10	*dix*
11	*onze*
12	*douze*
13	*treize*
14	*quatorze*
15	*quinze*
16	*seize*
17	*dix-sept*
18	*dix-huit*
19	*dix-neuf*
20	*vingt*
21	*vingt-et-un*
22	*vingt-deux*
23	*vingt-trois*
24	*vingt-quatre*
25	*vingt-cinq*
26	*vingt-six*
27	*vingt-sept*
28	*vingt-huit*
29	*vingt-neuf*
30	*trente*
40	*quarante*
50	*cinquante*
60	*soixante*
70	*soixante-dix*
80	*quatre-vingt*
90	*quatre-vingt-dix*
100	*cent*
200	*deux cents*
500	*cinq cents*
1,000	*mille*
10,000	*dix mille*
1,000,000	*un million*

Seine net fishing – a dying tradition. - *C. H.-B.*

A row of palm trees leans over fine white sand and warm,
shallow turquoise waters – the perfect beach of Grande Anse des Salines.
- *Tibor Bognar*

INDEX

INDEX

INDEX

TRAVEL BETTER... TRAVEL THE NET

Visit our web site
to travel better...
to discover, to explore
and to enjoy more.

http://www.ulysses.ca

ULYSSES
TRAVEL PUBLICATIONS

Travel better... enjoy more

CATALOGUE

TALK TO US

HISTORY

ORDER

DISTRIBUTORS

INTERNET TRAVEL

ORDER FORM

■ ULYSSES TRAVEL GUIDES

☐ Affordable B&Bs in Québec $12.95 CAN
$9.95 US
☐ Atlantic Canada .... $24.95 CAN
$17.95 US
☐ Beaches of Maine ...... $12.95 CAN
$9.95 US
☐ Bahamas .... $24.95 CAN
$17.95 US
☐ Belize .... $16.95 CAN
$12.95 US
☐ Calgary .... $17.95 CAN
$12.95 US
☐ Canada .... $29.95 CAN
$21.95 US
☐ Chicago .... $19.95 CAN
$14.95 US
☐ Chile .... $27.95 CAN
$17.95 US
☐ Costa Rica .... $27.95 CAN
$19.95 US
☐ Cuba .... $24.95 CAN
$17.95 US
☐ Dominican Republic ..... $24.95 CAN
$17.95 US
☐ Ecuador Galapagos Islands $24.95 CAN
$17.95 US
☐ El Salvador .... $22.95 CAN
$14.95 US
☐ Guadeloupe .... $24.95 CAN
$17.95 US
☐ Guatemala .... $24.95 CAN
$17.95 US
☐ Honduras .... $24.95 CAN
$17.95 US
☐ Jamaica .... $24.95 CAN
$17.95 US
☐ Lisbon .... $18.95 CAN
$13.95 US
☐ Louisiana .... $29.95 CAN
$21.95 US
☐ Martinique .... $24.95 CAN
$17.95 US
☐ Montréal .... $19.95 CAN
$14.95 US
☐ New Orleans .... $17.95 CAN
$12.95 US
☐ New York City .... $19.95 CAN
$14.95 US

☐ Nicaragua .... $24.95 CAN
$16.95 US
☐ Ontario .... $24.95 CAN
$14.95US
☐ Ottawa .... $17.95 CAN
$12.95 US
☐ Panamá .... $24.95 CAN
$16.95 US
☐ Portugal .... $24.95 CAN
$16.95 US
☐ Provence - Côte d'Azur .. $29.95 CAN
$21.95US
☐ Québec .... $29.95 CAN
$21.95 US
☐ Québec and Ontario
with Via .... $9.95 CAN
$7.95 US
☐ Toronto .... $18.95 CAN
$13.95 US
☐ Vancouver .... $17.95 CAN
$12.95 US
☐ Washington D.C. ...... $18.95 CAN
$13.95 US
☐ Western Canada .... $29.95 CAN
$21.95 US

■ ULYSSES DUE SOUTH

☐ Acapulco .... $14.95 CAN
$9.95 US
☐ Belize .... $16.95 CAN
$12.95 US
☐ Cartagena (Colombia) ... $12.95 CAN
$9.95 US
☐ Cancun Cozumel ...... $17.95 CAN
$12.95 US
☐ Puerto Vallarta .... $14.95 CAN
$9.95 US
☐ St. Martin and St. Barts .. $16.95 CAN
$12.95 US

■ ULYSSES TRAVEL JOURNAL

☐ Ulysses Travel Journal
   (Blue, Red, Green,
   Yellow, Sextant) . . . . $9.95 CAN
                                  $7.95 US

■ ULYSSES GREEN ESCAPES

☐ Cycling in France . . . . . . $22.95 CAN
                                 $16.95 US
☐ Hiking in the
   Northeastern U.S. . . . . . . $19.95 CAN
                                 $13.95 US
☐ Hiking in Québec . . . . . . $19.95 CAN
                                 $13.95 US

QUANTITY	TITLES	PRICE	TOTAL

NAME:_____

ADDRESS:_____

_____

Payment: ☐ Money Order ☐ Visa ☐ MasterCard

Card Number:_____Exp.:_____

Signature:_____

Sub-total	
Postage &	$8.00*
Sub-total	
G.S.T.in Canada	
TOTAL	

ULYSSES TRAVEL PUBLICATIONS
4176 St-Denis,
Montréal, Québec, H2W 2M5
(514) 843-9447 fax (514) 843-9448
www.ulysses.ca
*$15 for overseas orders

U.S. ORDERS: **GLOBE PEQUOT PRESS**
P.O. Box 833, 6 Business Park Road,
Old Saybrook, CT 06475-0833
1-800-243-0495 fax 1-800-820-2329
www.globe-pequot.com